Switzerland

at its best

BY ROBERT S. KANE

The World at Its Best Travel Series
BRITAIN AT ITS BEST
FRANCE AT ITS BEST
GERMANY AT ITS BEST
HAWAII AT ITS BEST
HOLLAND AT ITS BEST
ITALY AT ITS BEST
LONDON AT ITS BEST
NEW YORK AT ITS BEST
PARIS AT ITS BEST
SPAIN AT ITS BEST
SWITZERLAND AT ITS BEST
WASHINGTON, D.C. AT ITS BEST

A to Z World Travel Guides
GRAND TOUR A TO Z: THE CAPITALS OF EUROPE
EASTERN EUROPE A TO Z
SOUTH PACIFIC A TO Z
CANADA A TO Z
ASIA A TO Z
SOUTH AMERICA A TO Z
AFRICA A TO Z

Robert S. Kane

Switzerland
at its best

Printed on recyclable paper

PASSPORT BOOKS
a division of *NTC Publishing Group*
Lincolnwood, Illinois USA

1996 Printing

Published by Passport Books, a division of NTC Publishing Group,
4255 West Touhy Avenue, Lincolnwood (Chicago), Illinois 60646-1975 U.S.A.
©1987 by Robert S. Kane. All rights reserved. No part of
this book may be reproduced, stored in a retrieval system,
or transmitted in any form or by any means, electronic,
mechanical, photocopying, recording or otherwise, without the prior
permission of NTC Publishing Group.
Manufactured in the United States of America.
Library of Congress Catalog Card Number: 86-62725

6 7 8 9 ML 9 8 7 6

For Mary Lou and Joel Sleed

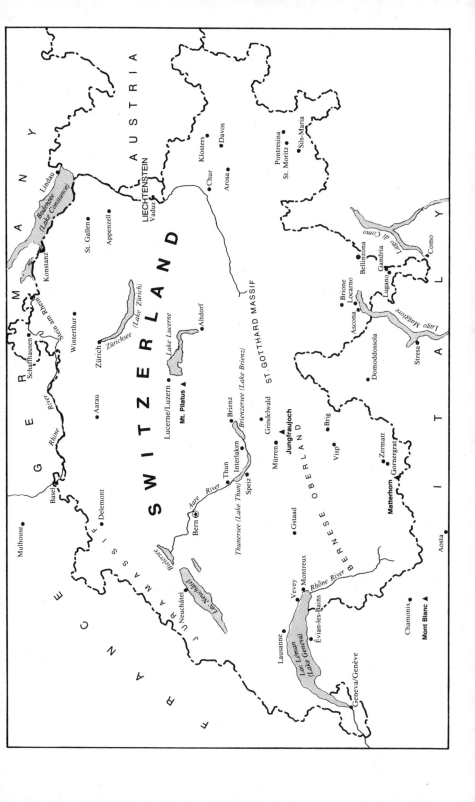

Contents

Foreword

Europe's Alpine Wonderland

The Switzerland of the late twentieth century is a success story that has been overshadowed by the pristine peaks of its snowy mountains. There is, to be sure, no harm in carrying with us, well beyond childhood classrooms, images of a blond-curled Heidi, of solitary cowherds sounding giant carved-wood Alpine horns, or of gaily clad yodelers serenading visitors against a backdrop of pine-walled chalets.

This aspect of Switzerland still is to be experienced. And with pleasure. But it is no more than a dimension of an extraordinarily innovative republic—one of the planet's most advanced—that has been created from landlocked territory wherein staggeringly high terrain substitutes for natural resources, and with a populace speaking not a single unifying language, but rather the tongues of a trio of neighboring powers—ultimately unsuccessful as aggressors, over long centuries.

If ever there was a country whose unofficial battle cry has been "Never Say Die!" surely it is Switzerland. Disillusioned by the tradition-bound veneer of neighboring monarchies, it opted for a democracy so direct that the referendum—a relative rarity across the Atlantic—is a commonplace of political life. Convinced that a solitary national language was not their way, the Swiss successfully placed German, French, and Italian on an equal footing, even to the point of variously naming their confederation *Schweiz*, *Suisse*, and *Svizzera*.

To replace revenue that might be derived in other countries from minerals, oil, or international shipping, the Swiss have achieved wealth (and one of the world's highest standards of living) by means of their own clever devising—as international bankers and financiers, and as high-technology manufacturers of such commodities as pharmaceuticals, machine tools, the cable cars invented to carry nonclimbers to soaring summits, and watches, the creation of which was a peculiarly Swiss craft as long ago as the sixteenth century.

Even relations with the world community bear their own especial imprint. Although it has been militarily neutral since the Congress of Vienna in 1815, Switzerland's humanitarian thrust is international. And ever since mid-nineteenth-century pleasure visitors—mostly from England—followed eighteenth-century geologists and botanists to mountain villages, tourism has been a principal Swiss industry, with not a few of the local tourist offices well into their second century of continuous operation.

The Swiss have been as adept at developing eminently livable, never overlarge cities—even the biggest are happily only medium-size—as at pioneering the concept of the mountain resort that is as appealing in summer as in winter. And Switzerland has size in its favor; its compactness works wonderfully well for the contemporary explorer. French-speaking Geneva in the west is a relative hop and skip from German-speaking Zürich to the northeast. Cosmopolitan Lugano, chief city of the Italian-speaking sector, is a near-neighbor of German-speaking mountain resorts near the frontier with Austria. Both Bern, the charming federal capital, and Zermatt, in the shadow of the Matterhorn—in German-speaking Switzerland— border Suisse Romande, the French-language region.

St. Gallen, in the northeast, is a stone's throw from both Germany and Austria, not to mention the minuscule principality of Liechtenstein. Montreux, on the lovely Lake of Geneva, is a swift and scenic train ride from the ski trails of smart Gstaad. The resourceful Swiss see to it that getting about—their excellent trains ride Europe's most ingeniously engineered rails, and their highways are first-rate—is as effortless as anywhere on the continent. Hotels and, for that matter, restaurants, are mostly family-operated, many by third- or fourth-generation descendants of founders, with standards, by and large, high, and staffs extraordinarily multilingual.

Wherever you go, there are treats in store: Old Masters and paintings by the superlative Swiss master, Hodler, at Geneva's Musée d'Art et d'Histoire, a concert by Zürich's celebrated Tonhalle Orchester, ballet in Bern's opulent Stadttheater, or simply coming upon an unexpected choir rehearsal in Lausanne's sublime Gothic cathedral, are no less diverting than lunch atop Mt. Pilatus over Lucerne, the view of Lake Maggiore from the elevated Church of Madonna del Sasso high above Locarno, a winter sunbath atop Arosa's Mt. Weisshorn, or a summer hike out of Kleine Scheidegg, near Grindelwald, beneath the Jungfrau.

The principal language changes as you move about—German in Chur, French in Neuchâtel, Italian in Bellinzona. Still, whatever the influences—linguistic, cultural, gastronomic—of its bigger neighbors, Switzerland remains distinctively and endearingly Swiss to the core. It is not for nothing that the beautiful national flag—white cross on a red ground, adopted in reverse by the Swiss-founded Red Cross—flies at virtually every turn in this land, and proudly.

ROBERT S. KANE

1

Switzerland
A Mini A to Z

ADDRESSES: Swiss National Tourist Offices are located at 608 Fifth Avenue, New York, NY 10020; 250 Stockton Street, San Francisco, CA 94108; P.O. Box 215, Commerce Court, Toronto, Ontario N5L 1E8; 1 New Coventry Street, London, W1; and 11-bis Rue Scribe, Paris, as well as in other major cities around the world. These offices—whose functions include providing the prospective traveler in Switzerland with gratis information and literature—are part of a worldwide network, whose headquarters—*Schweizerische Verkehrzentrale/Office National Suisse du Tourisme/Ufficio Nazionale del Turismo* (and just plain *SNTO*, for Swiss National Tourist Office, to English speakers)—is at 38 Bellariastrasse in Zürich. In the course of a Swiss journey, the traveler's best friend is the local tourist office—*Verkehrsbüro* or *Verkehrsverein* in German-speaking Switzerland, *Office du Tourisme* in French-speaking Switzerland, *Ente Turistico* in Italian-speaking Switzerland. Addresses of these offices appear in chapters following.

ARMY: It is perhaps worth knowing—you're bound to hear Swiss friends and colleagues saying they are about to serve, or have just served—that every fit Swiss male first serves in the Army at the age of 18—for 17 weeks. But that's only the beginning. Every year thereafter—until he has turned 50—he is obliged to serve for three weeks, the while being paid by his employer. Service is optional for women.

BREAKFAST: Swiss hotels, by and large, attach significance to the first meal of the day. Except in a relative handful of Luxury hotels in bigger cities and the *very* occasional First Class or Moderate category hotel—breakfast (for those who do not order it in their room, invariably an option) is served buffet-style. My honors for the best breakfast buffet of any that I have experienced in Switzerland, is that of the Schweizerhof Hotel in Bern; it includes, besides fresh-squeezed orange and other juices, a choice of cereals, a selection of cheeses, baskets with a variety of just-baked breads and rolls (only Germany's are as delicious); scrambled, sunnyside-up, or soft-boiled eggs, as well as bacon and ham, not to mention assorted jams (including sugar-free), butter, tall pots of coffee, tea, and big pitchers of milk. Arosa's Valsana Sporthotel is runner-up in my breakfast-honor list. Elsewhere, there are variations; most hotels' buffets do not offer eggs, bacon, ham, or fresh-squeezed orange juice except when ordered à la carte. Always, though, there is a choice of cold cereals, bread and cheese, with cold ham and sliced salami often—but not always—a part of the spread. By and large, mountain-resort hotels tend to be more generous than their urban counterparts, but there are exceptions, like the Bern hotel I cite above. Again generally, breakfast is included in the room rate; the same tiny minority of luxury hotels that do not offer buffets are the ones that charge for standard continental breakfasts, supplemented as you wish, with à la carte extras.

CASINOS: They are, to be sure, dotted about the Confederation, as I indicate in a number of chapters following. But there's a *but:* the only permitted game is one called *boule,* and the maximum bet allowable is a very minimal Sfr. 5.

CHEESES: The firm, holey species we know as "Swiss"—and which is imitated albeit not equaled by the cheesemakers of a number of countries, the U.S. among them—is of course *emmentaler;* you'll see it on breakfast buffets, post-lunch/dinner cheese platters, and as the basis (with kirsch, wine, flour, lemon juice, and garlic added) of the hot dunking sauce beloved as *fondue*. Other well-known types are the irresistible (to me, certainly) *Gruyère*, the hard or creamy *tilsit*, the semi-hard *appenzell*, the spreadably soft *tomme; formaggini*—Switzerland's answer to France's *chèvre*, or goat cheese, and *raclette*, which has given its name to a dish. Half a wheel of *raclette* is heated and, as soon as its interior softens, is scraped with a special knife onto a plate, to be served, usually as a first course, in tandem with a boiled potato and a pickle.

CHOCOLATE: Given Swiss chocolate's global celebrity and consistent quality, it should not be surprising that Switzerland leads the world in chocolate consumption: twenty-plus pounds per annum per capita. Not that the Swiss pioneered the chocolate-making business. The Spaniards were eating chocolate in the sixteenth century, and it had become popular in Paris, London, Brussels, Florence, and Berlin before François-Louis Cailler opened the first Swiss factory at Vevey in 1819. Philippe Suchard, Daniel Peter, Henry Nestlé, and Rudolphe and Antoine Lindt were other chocolate pioneers. Tobler and Lindt are today the best-known packaged brands, but every city has a celebrated *chocolatier* or two or three, with its own retail shop(s); Zürich's Sprüngli is perhaps the most celebrated. And it is worth noting that the Migros department-store/supermarket chain makes its own-brand packaged chocolates; they're considerably less expensive than the name brands and certain of them—chocolate truffles especially—are delicious. Other department stores are sources of name-brand chocolates, but bear in mind, if you're making purchases for gifts, prior to a transatlantic departure, that chocolate is sold at the intercontinental airports of Geneva and Zürich at regular—*not* duty-free—prices, from counters with selections limited in contrast to those at bigger in-town stores.

CLIMATE: You are, of course, in a four-season, temperate-zone country, not all that different from the northern American states and southern Canada, but rarely with extremes of heat or cold, relatively low humidity and—with good luck—atmospheric clarity and lack of wind, even up in the cooler mountains, making winter sunbathing not only possible but extremely popular, on ubiquitous Alpine sun-terraces. That said, let me nonetheless urge that you travel with a collapsible umbrella and raincoat at any time of year. The winter sports season runs December through April, but the Alps are beautiful in summer, too. (From anywhere in Switzerland, you may phone 162 for a weather forecast given in the language of the region [German, French, or Italian] in which you call.) Selected average temperatures in Fahrenheit:

	Zürich	Davos	Lugano
Winter (February)	32	22	38
Spring (May)	54	44	60
Summer (July)	63	53	70
Autumn (October)	47	38	54

CLOTHES: You are in a country that is at once wealthy—the standard of living is among the highest in the world—and extremely well dressed. The Swiss, in smaller towns as well as the larger cities, men as well as women, keep up to date on fashion. Be casual during the day for country or urban exploration, dressier for dinners in better restaurants and evenings on the town. Resort-wear—ski duds, boots, and the like—is purchasable in the mountains, but it's as well to have your own—including après-ski changes—with you, allowing for possible replenishment on scene.

CREDIT CARDS: Widely accepted in hotels, most (but not all) restaurants, and most (but not all) shops. American Express and

Visa are the most popular, with Diners Club and MasterCard following.

CURRENCY: The franc (Sfr.), one of the strongest of the world's currencies, is divided into 100 centimes. There are 10-, 20-, 50-, 100-, 500-, and 1,000-franc notes, and 5-, 10-, 20-, and 50-centime, as well as 1-, 2-, and 5-franc coins. Inquire as to rates from bank and currency-exchange firms before departure; you may want to buy some in advance. In Switzerland, best rates are obtained at banks, which have branches at Geneva and Zürich airports, and at change offices in larger railway stations. Hotels—and many shops, in the course of making purchases—will change money, too, but at rates lower than at banks.

CUSTOMS: *Entering Switzerland:* Swiss Customs officers are polite and sensible, assuming that you're entering their country with personal effects for use in the course of your journey. Besides clothing, toilet articles, cameras, film, and sporting equipment, you're allowed a couple of bottles of wine, a bottle of liquor, two cartons of cigarettes (or 100 cigars), and a reasonable quantity of nonmeat gifts. Swiss immigration officers tend *not* to stamp passports, indicating dates of entry into and exit from Switzerland, *unless* you so request.

Returning to the United States: Each person may bring back $400 worth of purchases duty free. That is allowable once every 30 days, provided you've been out of the country at least 48 hours. If you've spent more than $400 you'll be charged a flat 10 percent duty on the next $1,000 worth of purchases. Remember, too, that antiques, duly certified to be at least 100 years old, are admitted duty free and do not count as part of your $400 quota; neither do paintings, sculptures, and other works of art of any date, if certified as original; it's advisable that certification from the seller or other authority as to their authenticity accompany them. Also exempt from duty but as a part of the $400 quota, one quart of liquor. And—this is important—there is no restriction on how much one may bring in beyond the $400 limit, so long as the duty is paid.

DEPARTMENT STORES AND SHOPS: Geneva and Zürich are the Swiss shopping cities of consequence. Major department store chains include *Globus* and *Jelmoli*, with supermarkets (which, in Switzerland, carry wine and spirits—for hotel-room aperitifs). *Migros* and *Co-op* are less expensive department-store/supermarket chains. And there are others. I make specific shopping suggestions in most of the chapters following.

DRIVING: All you need is your home driver's license. If you like, you may import your own car, if it's to be for your own use. The international celebrity of this Alpine country's ingeniously engineered railroads detracts from the also-remarkable highway system. It shouldn't. Swiss roads are, by and large, excellent, and extremely well signposted. Instead of tolls on superhighways, there are fees—the Swiss term them taxes—valid for varying periods, and payable at border crossings. Rental cars, everywhere available in Switzerland, come with the superhighway fee already paid. The *Swiss Automobile Club/Automobil Club der Schweiz* (39 Wasserwerkgasse, Bern) and *Touring Club Suisse* (9 Rue Pierre Fatio, Geneva) assist motorists; the number to phone—Switzerland-wide—in the event of a breakdown is 140. Gas stations traditionally remain open from 8:00 A.M. to 10:00 P.M.; after hours, inquire for the location of a self-service station, where you pump your own, using 10- and 20-franc notes.

ELECTRIC CURRENT: 220 volts AC. Take along a transformer for your shaver or hair dryer and an adapter plug to be attached to prongs of your appliance, so that it will fit into holes of the Swiss outlet. American department stores sell kits containing a transformer and a variety of variously shaped adapters. Alternatively, upon arrival in Switzerland, you may buy a Swiss-made appliance for use during your journey— recommended if your stay will be lengthy.

GEOGRAPHY: Switzerland is a case of big things coming in small packages. With an area of just under 16,000 square miles, it is about the size of a couple of New Jerseys, or if you prefer, a combined Connecticut, Massachusetts, and Rhode Island. But this landlocked, central European, 137-mile-long by 216-mile-wide country—bordered by West Germany to the north, Italy to the south, Austria and Liechtenstein to the east, and France to the west—is magnificently mountainous. A plateau extends from Lac Léman (a.k.a. Lake of Geneva) in the southwest, northeast to Bodensee (a.k.a. Lake Constance) and—with its altitude averaging 1,900 feet—is home to more than two thirds of the populace. But the Alps—at an average altitude of just under 6,000 feet—and the high land bordering them, constitute a whopping 60 percent of Swiss territory. Something like a hundred peaks are in the 13,000-foot range, with a number even higher. These include Dent Blanche (14,294 feet), Matterhorn (14,691 feet), Weisshorn (14,783 feet), Dom (14,911 feet), and—highest of all—Dufourspitze (15,203 feet). Glaciers are mammoth—Gorner (25.8 square miles) and Aletsch (35.5 square miles) to give you an idea. And this is a land of rivers (the Rhine, navigable from Basel to the North Sea, is the principal inland waterway, but the Rhône and Aare are significant, too) and of lovely lakes. Lakes Léman, Constance, and Maggiore are bi- or multinational, but the other biggies—Neuchâtel, Lucerne, and Zürich—are exclusively Swiss. Lastly, there are the fabulous man-made tunnels: a quartet of major highway tunnels (St. Gotthard, 10 miles; Seelisberg, 6 miles; San Bernardino, 4 miles; Great St. Bernard, 3⅔ miles) and four top rail tunnels: Simplon (12¼ miles—the oldest, dating to 1906); Furka (9½ miles); St. Gotthard (9⅓ miles); and Lötschberg (9 miles).

Government: There are some five and a half million Swiss (in addition to nearly a million foreigners) living in a highly democratic land governed by the *Bundesrat,* or Federal Council (each of whose seven members—chosen by Parliament—is president for a year and, as well, the head of a different department of the government), and a two-house Parliament embracing the 46-member *Standesrat* (with two members from each canton) and the 200-member *Nationalrat.* Women have voted in federal elections only since 1971; minimum voting age is 20.

The federal government's functions are limited to foreign affairs and the military, civil and penal law, post office and customs, federal railroads (there are other rail systems as well), and the national coinage. Otherwise, the Confederation of

Helvetia is governed by its 23 cantons (three of which are divided into half-cantons), each with its own capital, governing body, and legislature. Just over half the Swiss are Protestant; about 44 percent are Catholic.

HISTORY: Travel through today's Switzerland—rich and successful, staunchly democratic and physically magnificent, rigorously neutral in the international scheme of things (even to nonmembership in the UN) and smoothly multilingual—and you have the feeling that it all transpired effortlessly, as easily as falling off a log, or to use a more appropriate simile, skiing down an Alp. It wasn't. Not until nineteen and a half centuries after the birth of Christ did Switzerland emerge as the republican confederation—with considerable powers reserved to its score-plus cantons—that we know today.

Rugged terrain notwithstanding, its heart-of-Europe situation lured frequently bothersome outsiders through the mountain passes, as early as the sixth decade before Christ. That was when the resident, Celtic-origin Helvetii (whose Latin name, *Helvetia,* still is used on all Swiss postage stamps and as the basis for the abbreviation "CH" [Confederation Helvetia] on auto license plates) were vanquished by a Roman army commanded by no less a general than Julius Caesar.

The Romans stayed on while their Helvetian subjects thrived over a four-century period. But that central situation again proved more a blessing than a bane in successive invasions by the Germanic Alemanni, the Burgundii from Savoy, and expansionist Francs, only to be split in half by ninth-century Burgundians and Swabians, and ultimately reunited in 1033 by the Holy Roman Emperor. Aggressive Habsburgs were largely responsible, at the end of the thirteenth century, for a historically momentous unity pact—a mutual defense arrangement—agreed to by the cantons of Uri, Unterwalden, and Schwyz (the canton whose name was ultimately adopted by German-speaking Swiss as the name of the confederation), with William Tell—the very same of the bow-and-arrow legend—the hero of that era.

Within a quarter-century, five more cantons joined the initial three, victors in battle against the mighty Habsburgs. By the fifteenth century, the Swiss had become a power of consequence, ever expanding their territory. The early sixteenth century saw 13 allied cantons. There were, to be sure, strains and conflicts in the course of the Reformation (see Chapters 6 and 20), but Switzerland, never neglecting its mercantile and intellectual prowess, thrived as the Middle Ages became the Renaissance, beyond into the Baroque and Rococo centuries, by which time it was attractive to the French. The French-imposed puppet Helvetic Republic was superseded by a restored confederation, thanks to intervention by Napoleon, with restoration—and still additional cantons—a consequence of the Congress of Vienna in 1815, the same year that the Treaty of Paris confirmed the concept of Swiss neutrality—never subsequently violated. A federal constitution was hammered out in 1848. The confederated Switzerland worked so well that the constitution was refined and updated in 1874, the while Switzerland evolved as one of the world's small but superior democracies.

HOLIDAYS: As in every country, they're a pleasure for residents but major ones can be a bother for visitors, who do well to plan around them, noting the possibility of closed museums and other places of interest, certain shops, and some restaurants. Besides Christmas (December 25 and 26) and New Year's (January 1 and 2), take note of Easter Monday, Ascension Day, Whitmonday, as well as Labor Day (May 1) and Independence Day (August 1), observed in many parts of the confederation.

HOTELS: About the hotels in this book: I have either lived in, dined in, drunk in, and/or thoroughly inspected the hotels carefully selected for evaluation in these pages; I disregard the complexities and occasional inconsistencies of the Swiss Hotel Association's star system and have divided hotels (and restaurants) into three price groups: *Luxury, First Class,* and *Moderate.* Bear in mind that I am fussy. In towns of any size and cities I concentrate on *centrally situated* hotels, including country hotels only when they are exceptional and might be of interest to travelers with cars. All hotels in my *Luxury* and virtually all in *First*

Class categories have television and minibars (stocked with liquor, wine, soft drinks, and sometimes snacks—for purchase) in all rooms, as well, of course, as private baths. My *Moderate* category hotels, for the most part, are *better*-Moderate, often with TV and/or minibars and with baths attached to most or all rooms; when all rooms do not have baths, I so indicate. Time was, in the decades after World War II, when—if my informal surveys are correct—an overwhelming proportion of the world's great hotels had Swiss managers. Because standards of West German hotelkeeping peaked in succeeding decades—and because there are so many more West Germans than there are Swiss—I suspect Germans are running many more of the planet's luxury houses today than are Swiss. Still, Switzerland is a land of internationally recognized hotel-training schools (that at Lausanne is the most celebrated, but there are a number of other top-rankers) and the Swiss may well be proud of their hotels. By and large, they set great store by efficient operation, spotless housekeeping, extraordinary staff language skills (I can almost guarantee that with very few exceptions the attendant at the desk of even the simplest hotel will be multilingual—with English one of his or her languages), and—even in full-facility nonluxury houses—not one but a choice of restaurants and bars. (Often it is the restaurants in hotels that are community leaders—not always the case in other countries.) Their enviably high standard of living notwithstanding, the Swiss themselves tend to watch their centimes as hoteliers (see the section, Soap, below) and as travelers. Although globally respected groups like Leading Hotels of the World (with more hotels in Switzerland than any other European country), Relais-et-Châteaux, Hilton International, Inter-Continental, Sheraton, Ramada Renaissance, and Best Western (through its affiliation with Ambassador Swiss) and Swissair's Swissôtels are on scene, the proportion of luxury hotels is not all that high, except in places like Geneva (where the total is 15—staggeringly high for a city with a population well under 200,000), Zürich, and certain of the mountain resorts. By and large, the emphasis is on *First Class* houses, with many *Moderate* options, as well.

LANGUAGES: It breaks down this way: The German-speaking central and eastern parts of the country—by far the largest in area—are No. 1 and are home to 65 percent of the populace whose No. 1 language is German, albeit with a qualification. By that I mean that proper German is the *written* language and the language studied in the schools. The *spoken* language in this part of Switzerland is one or another of the dialects (they vary, city by city, region by region) of Schwyzerdütsch (pronounced, more often than not, *Schweezadootsch*). Be assured, though, that if you speak High German in a hotel, restaurant, or shop—where personnel are accustomed to using the language in its conventional form—the reply will come in High German.

French is the language of the western region termed Suisse Romande, constituting 18 percent of the population. Italian—spoken primarily in but one canton, southeasterly Ticino (and to some extent in neighboring territory) is the mother tongue of some 12 percent of the Swiss people. Still a fourth language, Romansch (with Romance origins) is spoken by less than one percent of the people, mostly in the Grisons canton. (Unlike the Big Three tongues, it is designated a *national,* but not an *official* language.) Most fluent linguists? In my experience, native-Italian speakers win hands down, primarily, I believe, because they constitute the No. 2 minority, and absolutely *must* learn German (to communicate with the dominant language group) as well as English—the principal world language. And because it is a Romance language, with the same Latin roots as their own Italian, they often learn French as well.

Otherwise, it is perhaps worth pointing out, Swiss who do not use languages other than their native tongue as *part of their work,* are not necessarily as fluently multilingual as we foreigners expect them to be. There is no question but that English is the widely spoken No. 1 foreign language, but by no means everyone speaks it.

NEWSPAPERS: There are more than 400 dailies and weeklies, but because of the breakdown by language groups in a country with a relatively small population, circulations are not staggering. The internationally respected *Neue Züricher Zeitung*'s is 130,000 (although the tabloid *Blick* is nearly three times that). *La*

Suisse and *Tribune de Genève* are leading French-language dailies. And the English-language *International Herald Tribune,* jointly published by the *New York Times* and the *Washington Post*—at least those copies of it that circulate in Switzerland—is printed in Zürich.

OPEN HOURS: By and large, sensible and generous. *Banks*—at virtually every turn in every city center—are open from 8:30 A.M. to 4:30 P.M. Monday through Friday, and change offices at the international airports and big-city railway stations are open daily until 10:00 P.M. *Shops* are early birds, open from 8:00 A.M. till 12:15 P.M. and from 1:30 to 6:30 P.M., except Saturday, when they usually shutter at 4:00 P.M. Big-city emporia happily skip lunch-hour closing, although many close Monday mornings. *Office* hours are 8:00 A.M. to noon; 2 P.M. to 6:00 P.M., Monday through Friday. *Post offices* in the big towns are open from 7:30 A.M. through noon, and 1:45 P.M. to 6:30 P.M., but close Saturday at an early 11:00 A.M. Major *museums* in major cities are usually—but not always—open nonstop the day long; most others close for a couple of hours at midday. Monday is the favored closing day but there are many exceptions to this rule. Giveaway "What's On" publications, obtainable from hotel concierges in larger towns and from local tourist offices, have current schedules.

PASSPORTS: Necessary for admittance to Switzerland and to be presented to U.S. Immigration upon your return. Apply at Department of State Passport Offices in a dozen-plus cities (look under U.S. Government in the phone book) or—in smaller towns—at the office of the clerk of a Federal Court and at certain post offices. Allow four weeks, especially for a first passport (valid for 10 years), for which you'll need a pair or two-inch-square photos and birth certificate or other proof of citizenship. There's a $42 fee (subject to change) for first passports; renewals are cheaper. If you're in a hurry when you apply, say so; Uncle Sam will usually try to expedite if you can show documentation indicating imminent departure. Upon receipt of your passport, sign your name where indicated, fill in the address of next of kin, and keep this valuable document with you—*not packed in a* *suitcase*—as you travel. In case of loss, contact local police, nearest U.S. Embassy or Consulate, or Passport Office, Department of State, Washington, D.C. 19524.

PERFORMING ARTS: Highly developed. Even medium-size cities have superb opera houses, concert halls, and theaters. Geneva's *Orchestre de la Suisse Romande* and Zürich's *Tonhalle Orchester* are globally distinguished, as are the *Zürich* and *Basel Ballets,* and other musical groups, from, say, *Orchestre de Chambre de Lausanne* through *Winterthur Philharmonic.* And *festivals*—classical and jazz, film and folk—are splendidly staged, with locales varying, Gstaad to Montreux-Vevey, Bern through Locarno. See *Sound of Music* sections in chapters following.

RATES for selected hotels (where I've stayed or which I've inspected) and restaurants (where I've eaten) are categorized as *Luxury, First Class,* and *Moderate;* these translate pretty much into what they would mean in the U.S.—adjusted, of course, to the purchasing power of the dollar with respect to the Swiss franc at the time of your visit.

RESTAURANTS AND CUISINE: Despite strong gastronomic influences from a pair of bordering countries—France and Italy—whose cuisines are among the world's greatest, Swiss restaurant food in the dominant German-speaking region, is Teutonic accented, albeit with interesting Swiss specialties, Italian dishes (mostly excellently and authentically prepared), and French classics (sometimes delicious, often undistinguished). Suisse Romande—the French-speaking area—is automatically ahead of the game, before one has eaten a mouthful, what with menus printed primarily in the French language. (In what other language does food sound so good?) Standards are generally—but not universally—high in Suisse Romande, with fare essentially if not always successfully French-derived. That leaves Italian-speaking Ticino, No. 3 area in size, but in my experience the most consistently exemplary, with respect to the excellence of its restaurants, all of which, I should make clear, have traditional Italian dishes as their backbone.

Specialties to try? Suisse Romande's *fondue*—a kirsch, wine, and melted-cheese sauce in a bubbling common cauldron, into which diners dip chunks of French bread attached to elongated forks—is perhaps the most celebrated, with one of its variations—*Fondue Bourguignonne* (wherein cubes of meat are cooked in hot oil) is also very popular. *G'schnitzeltes*—chopped veal cooked quickly in a butter sauce (with or without cream) is delicious, and invariably served with the fried-potato cakes called *rösti*—surely the all-time favorite food, as beloved of foreigners as of Swiss. *Rösti* is the usual accompaniment to the No. 1 cooked sausage—*bratwurst*—inexpensive and satisfying as a casual lunch or snack, and everywhere available. *Berner Platte* is a Swiss variation of Alsace's *Choucroute Garnie*—with assorted sausages, smoked pork, and boiled beef, as well as boiled potatoes, heaped upon an enormous bed of sauerkraut. Fresh *fish*—trout from mountain streams, filets of perch, pike variously prepared—is invariably excellent throughout Switzerland. And I save for last the supreme appetizer: *Bündnerfleisch*, sun-dried beef sliced paper thin; it is habit-forming. *Pastries, ice cream,* and *sherbet* are consistently good, as indeed are *breads*—baked in abundant variety and the basis of Switzerland's celebrated buffet breakfasts (see Breakfast, above).

Swiss regulars gravitate toward restaurants' daily specials—*plats du jour* or *tagesplatte,* as you prefer. And most restaurants have prix-fixe multicourse menus (they can be tempting values) as well as à la carte selections. Swiss wines rate a separate section (below) as do Swiss cheese and Swiss chocolate (above). Breakfast service starts in most hotels at 7:00 A.M. (sometimes earlier), usually running through about 9:30 A.M. (often later). Lunch begins at noon and continues through 2:00 or 2:30 P.M., with dinner at 7:00 P.M. generally through 10:00 P.M. and sometimes later in larger cities and posh resorts.

My favorite restaurants? I note, in evaluations that follow in succeeding chapters, eleven restaurants which are, in my experience, based on cuisine, service, and ambience, among the best restaurants in Switzerland. My honor list follows alphabetically:

Agnes Amberg, Zürich
Alex Hotel Grill, Zermatt
Chez Marianne, Lucerne

Eaux Vives, Geneva
Euler Hotel Restaurant, Basel
Girardet, Crissier
Le Wellingtonia, Beau Rivage Hotel, Lausanne
L'Oasis, Grand Hotel Eden, Lugano
Panorama, Dellavalle Hotel, Brione
Rebleuten Hotel Restaurant, Chur
Stadtkeller, St. Gallen.

SOAP: Thrifty Swiss hotel managers provide guests—by and large, at least—with the tiniest slivers of soap to be found in the hotels of any country of which I am aware. Even most luxury-category houses follow this practice, departing from it only in the case of guests occupying suites or, in the case of some, with guests staying three or more days. But there are happy exceptions to the rule, few enough, however, for me to have compiled this little honor list of hotels that, in my experience, provide *every* guest—even those in the less costly rooms—with a decent-sized—not necessarily oversized, but simply decent-sized—bar of soap:
Beau Rivage Hotel, Geneva
De la Paix Hotel, Geneva
Euler Hotel, Basel
Palace Hotel, St. Moritz
Victoria-Jungfrau Hotel, Interlaken.

SWISSAIR would be a remarkable airline even if it were the national carrier of a country with many times the population of little Switzerland. A veritable handful of the world's airlines are in a league with this one—and I speak from experience, having flown most of them. Whatever transpires in the course of planning, undertaking, and completing a Swissair flight—asking for departure times, fares, and the like from Flight Information on the phone; picking up a ticket at a Swissair office; checking in at the airport; waiting in the lounge; making the journey (where meals are an extraordinarily joyful experience); and claiming baggage at its completion—works very well indeed because Swissair brass and Swissair flight crews have carefully, thoughtfully, and skillfully planned it that way.

And Swissair is not all that old. What happened was that, in the years following World War I, a clutch of ex–Air Force officers organized Switzerland's first commercial airlines. By 1930, there were several of them, and rather than compete they amalgamated, uniting in 1931 to form Swissair. The fledgling enterprise started business with a baker's dozen small craft, with a total capacity of 86 passenger seats, a staff consisting of ten pilots, seven radio operators, and eight flight engineers, with flights limited to spring through fall—and then only when the weather was fair. The initial route network was 2,800 miles.

The following year, Swissair became the first European carrier to operate with American-built aircraft, purchased from Lockheed. Shortly thereafter, Swissair went international with service to Munich and Vienna. In 1934, with another American plane seating all of 16 passengers—a heavy load at that time—it hired stewardesses to look after them—the first such in Europe. By 1935, Swissair was flying to London. When it resumed operations—curtailed during World War II—it acquired more American craft. In 1947, the first Swissair plane—a Douglas DC-4—crossed the Atlantic from Geneva to New York. Today, Swissair—70 percent of its shares still in private hands—flies to 99 cities in 67 countries of North and South America, Europe, Africa, Asia, and the Middle East, with its home base at Kloten, the intercontinental airport of Zürich—Europe's ninth largest in volume of traffic.

The North Atlantic sees Swissair linking the two Swiss intercontinental airports, that of Zürich and Geneva's Cointrin, with New York, Anchorage, Atlanta, Boston, and Chicago, as well as Montreal and Toronto in Canada. Food and service? Meals in Economy and Business Class—Swissair's newest category of service, with wide seats, complimentary headsets, cocktails, and wines—are among the tastiest aloft. A Business Class dinner might open with an assorted hors d'oeuvre plate, offer scallops of veal with creamed morels, beef stroganoff, or a filet of fresh fish, as entrées. Cheese is passed in advance of dessert, with coffee following. First class, served with the éclat and style of a meal in a classy Geneva or Zürich restaurant, commences with a platter of hot *amuse-bouches*—savory nibbles—to accompany champagne or cocktails. The meal really begins with caviar, lobster terrine, and Swissair's own *gratin de morilles*—a mushroom triumph—as the spectacular first course. A choice of soups— and then an artfully composed salad—follow. Orange or—more interesting—beer-flavored sorbet is the next course—a palate cleanser. Veal *Cordon Bleu* or Beef Wellington are typical entrées, beautifully garnished. Then comes cheese from a platter and a glass of 20-year-old Port to wash it down. If you're up to it, there's fresh fruit and/or a rich tart for dessert, with cognac, liqueurs, and Swiss chocolates accompanying coffee. On eastbound flights a bacon-and-eggs breakfast precedes landing. And westbound, the so-called prelanding snack might have come from the groaning buffet of a trendy Alpine resort. (Pan Am and TransWorld also link the U.S. and Switzerland.)

TIPPING: Tips are included in restaurant, café, and hotel bills, as well as taxi fares. Tip porters who bring bags to your hotel rooms more or less the equivalent of what you would at home; ditto barbers and hairdressers. And that, happily, is it.

SNOW REPORT: In the United States—between mid-December through early April—call (212) 757-6336 for the Swiss National Tourist Office Snow Report, with information on conditions in major ski areas.

TRAINS/SWISS HOLIDAY CARD: A single expletive— Wow!—is in order for the Swiss train system. It embraces a 3,107-mile network that sees it speed through rolling country-side, climb steep mountains, zoom through tunnels as long as 12 miles (the Simplon), and—inevitably at journey's end, if my not inconsiderable experience is typical—arrive at the destination station *on the minute.* This is a brilliantly engineered, impeccably maintained, efficiently operated system right up there with the other European railroad leaders, the French and the Germans. You may travel virtually everywhere by train. Eastern Switzerland's Rhaetian Railway, for example, is Europe's largest small-rail train network, with 243 miles of track through 118 tunnels and over 498 bridges. The Glacier Express—nicknamed the slowest express train on the planet because its average speed is just 20 miles per hour, connects Zermatt and St. Moritz along a route that includes 291 bridges and 90 tunnels. And you never have to wait more than an hour, often less in the case of frequent intercity runs. Direct trains are less speedy. Regional trains serve smaller destinations; and cog railways cling to the sides of mountains. Without exception, again at least in my experience, there is some sort of food service, even if only an ambulatory vendor-cum-wagon—with coffee, cold drinks, and sandwiches wrapped in waxed paper bags imprinted with the catering department's German-language motto: *Gut Reisen—Gut Speisen* "good traveling, good eating." Additionally, many trains have snack bars and, on major runs, attractive diners. (Do as the Swiss do—travel with chocolate and/or fruit to snack and—as I do—with a collapsible baggage carrier.) Most trains are part of the federal system and their cars are marked with Swiss Federal Railways acronyms in German, French, and Italian: "SBB-CFF-FFS." There are private lines as well, each with its own livery.

If you'll be traveling appreciably within Switzerland, purchase—through Swiss National Tourist Offices in New York, San Francisco, and Toronto (addresses above), your travel agent, at Swiss frontier train stations, or upon arrival at Geneva and Zürich airports—a *Swiss Holiday Card*. It is valid for unlimited travel on the entire Swiss Federal network, most private railroads, lake boats, and all postal motor coaches—the excellent long-distance bus system. You may buy the card for periods of 4 days, 8 days, 15 days, and one month, for either first or second class, with the tabs half price for kids between six and sixteen.

TOURS, TOUR OPERATORS, TRAVEL AGENTS: Agents first: Select one who is affiliated with the *American Society of Travel Agents* (ASTA) and, ideally, who knows Switzerland firsthand. For a first trip, some travelers are happy with a package; tour operators making a specialty of Switzerland include *American Express, Bennett Tours, The Cortell Group, Dial Switzerland, Globus-Gateway, Maupintour, and Olson-Travelworld;* their packages may be purchased through retail travel agents. In studying brochures, note *location* of hotels—in cities you want to be *central*—not out in the boonies; *places actually visited* (not simply passed by on the bus); *free time* at your disposal, especially in cities; and—in case of meals—whether they're prix-fixe or à la carte, and whether lunches and dinners include dessert and coffee. An introductory package behind you, you're ready for return visits on your own—to where *you* want to go, at *your* speed.

WATCHES: The Reformation leader, Jean Calvin (Chapter 6), was indirectly involved in the Swiss watch industry's beginnings for, straightlaced doctrinaire that he was, he forbade the wearing of jewelry in Geneva. And so that city's talented goldsmiths switched to watches, which Calvinist authorities came to regard as separate and distinct from purely decorative jewels. By the end of the sixteenth century, Geneva had acquired a reputation as a center of the watch trade, with a school for watchmakers. As time passed, completely handmade watches were assembled in factories which gave the finished watches their brand names. And so Switzerland's watch industry was born.

More recent years have seen the jeweled movement supplanted by the quartz movement. And Switzerland has had to face stiff competition from newcomers to the scene, Japan especially. Still, the Swiss watch remains the world's prestige watch. You may *say* you're not going to buy a watch in the course of a Swiss trip. But I venture you will. In no other country's cities, towns, even villages, will you pass by so many watch displays. They are everywhere, at every turn, almost as ubiquitous as slot machines in Las Vegas—in hotel lobbies, shop windows, air terminals. Believe me, you miss them as you walk through the business streets of your home city upon your return.

There are some 35 leading makes, Audemars Piguet and Baume & Mercier through Universal-Genève and Vacheron & Constantin; I make suggestions on watch-shopping in chapters following. There is a dearth neither of supremely costly watches in, for example, the Patek Philippe category (experts say that the more a watch model costs the better it sells), nor of moderately priced timepieces; if this latter category interests you, ask to see models with the label of the store in which you're shopping, always checking out details of the warranty before making a purchase.

WINES OF SWITZERLAND: Three caveats at the outset. First is that Swiss wines are expensive, even in the land of production, so much so that it is possible, in restaurants, to order comparable quality wines from neighboring countries—France and Italy, world-class wine-producing countries, both of them—at lower prices. With the consequence that many Swiss restaurant-goers and foreign visitors as well do precisely that.

Second caveat: Forget about Swiss aged wines. Drink the youngest available. And third—especially when you're in the principal wine country—the French-speaking western area north of Lake Geneva and in the Rhône Valley, ask for the local wine. (This is actually valid advice, Switzerland-wide, for vineyards dot the confederation.) White wines tend to be more consistently high quality than red, but get to know both. *Aigle* is perhaps the most celebrated white; *Dôle*, without question, is the premium red. *Vaud* and *Valais* are the top two wine cantons. Look for the above-mentioned *Dôle*, as well as *Fendant* and *Dorin* whites. Vineyards around Lake Neuchâtel produce sound reds and whites, too—with the *Neuchâtel* name. Don't leave Switzerland without getting to know its superb *eaux-de-vie*—aromatic digestifs, or after-dinner drinks, redolent of the fruit from which they have been highly distilled; *Poire William*—pear eau-de-vie—is the most celebrated. Try also such liqueurs as *Marc*, *Kirsch*, and *Pflümli*. *Beer* is popular. And so is mineral water; lightly carbonated *Passuger* is the most popular brand served with meals.

2

Basel

Edging France and Germany

BACKGROUND BRIEFING

The point Basel makes is that despite respectable age, wealth amassed from pharmaceuticals manufacture and as its country's major river port/rail terminus, with Switzerland's oldest university as kingpin of a rich cultural base, a population at the 200,000 mark making it No. 2 in the confederation, and an extraordinary Rhine River situation a stone's throw from France and Germany, it remains a placid provincial town utterly devoid of the zip of Zürich (Chapter 20) or the sparkle of Geneva (Chapter 6)—the two great Swiss cities.

Lack of an Alpine backdrop—Basel is surrounded by lowlands—may have something to do with this lethargic state of affairs. (All of the other principal Swiss cities have picture-postcard locations.) But certainly Basel is not without pedigree. Romans were on scene a couple of millennia back (they named the town *Basilia*). As long ago as the seventh century, it was a seat of Catholic bishops, the while becoming successively controlled by Franks and Burgundians.

In the eleventh century, the Holy Roman Emperors—in whose vast domain it had become a free imperial city—awarded temporal powers to the bishops, who became ruling prince bishops, albeit against the will of the citizenry, which eventually succeeded in curbing their nonspiritual authority.

For two early fifteenth-century decades, Basel hosted prolonged Catholic ecumenical deliberations which came to be known in history books as the Council of Basel. The council brought enough intellectual cachet to the town—the philosopher Erasmus and the painter Holbein the Younger were residents—to have impelled founding of its university under papal patronage in 1460. Basel became linked with the Swiss Confederation in 1501.

By the second quarter of the sixteenth century, Basel had accepted the Reformation. Indeed, it was in Basel that Jean Calvin published his *Institutes of the Christian Religion*. The great Romanesque/Gothic cathedral, after nearly five Catholic centuries, became Protestant in 1529.

ON SCENE
Lay of the Land: The Rhine flows through the city in a northwest-southeast curve, with half a dozen bridges—the most central are *Mittlerebrücke* and *Wettsteinbrücke*—joining Basel proper (the southern and more important section) with northerly *Kleinbasel*, site of the grounds of the every-spring international trade fair on *Messeplatz*, of the *Kongresszentrum* on Riehenstrasse, and of the *Bahnhof* for trains coming from and going to Germany (as distinct from the Swiss and French train stations sharing a building across the Rhine). Central Basel—the core of town where you want to headquarter—is based on the square called *Marktplatz*, just inland from the river via *Eisengasse*, and dominated by the painted red facade of the *Rathaus* (below). The main shopping street, *Freiestrasse*, leads southeasterly from Marktplatz and is paralleled by other important mercantile streets, *Gerbergasse* and *Falknerstrasse*. *Altstadt*, the Old Town, is dominated by the *Münster*, or cathedral (below) on broad *Münsterplatz*, which backs onto a high cliff above the Rhine. Surrounding streets—*Rittergasse*, *Baumleingasse*, and *Augustinergasse*, along with quieter *Heuberg* and *Spalenberg* are Altstadt streets lined by fine old houses, some fourteenth century. *Kunstmuseum* (below), in my view the principal reason for a Basel visit (along with the Münster), is not far from the shops of

Freiestrasse on appropriately named *Picassoplatz*. There are others, to be sure, but the principal concentration of hotels is unfortunately detached from the most interesting part of town; they're in the area of the Swiss/French railroad station around *Zentralbahnplatz*, a ten- to twelve-minute walk along *Elisabethenstrasse* via *Freiestrasse* to *Marktplatz*. A pair of thirteenth-century gates (*Spalentor*, west of the core and *St. Alban Tor*, to its east) more or less frame the city center.

Kunstmuseum (Picassoplatz): It is housed in an intimidating building that is hardly among the outstanding works of the 1930s, publishes no catalogues in the French or English languages, and closes for lunch except between June and September. But this is to carp. Basel's fine-arts museum—reputedly the first such in Europe to have been founded with public funds rather than through private, noble, or royal wealth—is easily the best show in town. I don't know of a museum outside Germany (see *Germany at Its Best*) with finer German Renaissance representation—drawings by the matchless Dürer, a Grünewald *Crucifixion*, Baldung Grien's *Maiden's Death*, Cranach's *Judgment of Paris*. Holbein the Younger is on scene in glorious quantity, with works he created during residence in Basel (a mayor's head, meticulously drawn) and paintings in oil of his wife and two young children, especially. Konrad Witz, often mistakenly thought of as German, was Basel-born in the fifteenth century and the Kunstmuseum does him justice, displaying several dazzlingly detailed altar paintings. Still another altarpiece is by Fra Angelico: *Virgin and Child with Four Angels;* it is a work of especial grace and beauty. Flemish primitives like Hans Memling (*St. Hieronymous*) and Gerard David (*Virgin and Child with Angels*) are memorable. There are Dutchmen like Rembrandt (*David Presenting Goliath's Head to King Saul*) and Van Goyen (*A Village Church*). The elegant eighteenth century takes form with Rigaud portraits and a Hubert Robert landscape. There are later Frenchmen, as well. Start with pre-Impressionists like Ingres, Delacroix, Géricault, and Daumier, the lot of them a prelude for later stars like Degas (*The Cup of Chocolate*), a Pissaro landscape, Tahitians as painted by Gauguin, Van Gogh and Cézanne, Renoir and Monet. The

Swiss? Basel's own Arnold Böcklin (nineteenth century) but more to the point, Paul Klee in quantity, and ever-provocative Ferdinand Hodler. You end on the top floor, with a dazzler of a room full of Picassos (my count is 14), Braque in profusion, along with a dozen-plus Légers, and a gallery of Chagall, along with Matisse, Bonnard, and Rouault. There are, in addition, the German Expressionists—Franz Mark and Oskar Kokoschka, Otto Dix and Lovis Corinth. And contemporary America's New York school—Barnett Newman and Frank Stella, Jasper Johns and Andy Warhol—as frosting on an exceedingly rich cake. Café.

Münster (Münsterplatz): It is as well, in the case of this immense church—a Catholic cathedral for its first five centuries, a Protestant church since the Reformation—to gain perspective by beginning out back—to get an idea of how brilliantly the original architects positioned it on a Rhine-flanking cliff. Return to the front door, noting the pair of twin Gothic steeples overhead, before you step inside—unexpectedly massive, with fine vaults framing a wide central nave, superbly arcaded. Walk to the high altar and choir, the while noticing no-two-alike capitals of the nave's columns. Side chapels brim with sculpted treasures. The fifteenth-century pulpit's curving stairway is a minor masterpiece. The crypt's high points are frescoes surfacing its vaults. And there's a pair of utterly beautiful cloisters.

Historisches Museum (Barfüsserplatz) is housed in a desanctified Franciscan church dating to the fourteenth century, enough of whose Gothic glory remains—immense stained-glass windows and heroic proportions most especially—in what has been a deft conversion embracing both main floor and not-to-be-missed basement. The church's former choir is the showplace, with vast, quite splendid medieval altar triptychs and a clutch of polychrome-sculpted Madonnas of the same era. There are lovely fifteenth-century tapestries, sixteenth-century wood reliefs and—among much else—a series of period rooms dating back several centuries and meticulously furnished.

Kirschgarten (27 Elisabethenstrasse), mostly celebrating Basel's eighteenth century, is a rich merchant's townhouse. The draw is a series of period rooms—Louis XVI primarily. The so-called Blue Salon, with Hubert Robert paintings, is among the handsomer, but the time-frame extends into the nineteenth century with Biedermeier and Art Nouveau periods, as well. And there are collections of porcelain, clocks, and toys.

Antikenmuseum (5 St. Alban-Graben) closed in the mid-eighties for long-term renovations but may have reopened for your visit. It occupies a converted and enlarged early nineteenth-century mansion and brims with classical Greek and Roman art and artifacts. An Attic-origin amphora, or covered vase, with a shield-bearing goddess Athena painted on one of its sides, is perhaps the single loveliest object, but there are as well, to give you an idea, marble busts and statues in bronze, painted plates, and exquisitely wrought gold jewelry.

Rathaus (Marktplatz): The vibrant brick-red facade of the Town Hall will not have escaped you in the course of Marktplatz strolls. Pause to have a look at this originally Renaissance building (with considerable late nineteenth- and twentieth-century additions and an *in toto* restoration, relatively recent). The central section is the oldest—early sixteenth century. Frescoes on the facade add a bit of color to the square. The courtyard, similarly embellished, is noteworthy, too. But the council chamber inside—open only to guided tour groups by prior arrangement—is, alas, anticlimactic.

Museum für Gegenwartskunst (St. Albanweg) occupies a starkly converted ex-factory that's a considerable schlep from the center. Go only if abstract art—mostly by Swiss painters unknown to you—is of especial interest.

Augusta Raurica is a restored Roman town—the oldest on the Rhine—about seven miles east of Basel. If you've a car and a spare half-day you might want to have a look at a hoard of silver—some 70 platters, bowls, and other objects, and an even larger collection of coins, the lot dating to the fourth century, albeit discovered only in 1961. They're displayed in a museum labeled *Silberschatz*. To see as well are an amphitheater—Switzerland's largest Roman remnant—whose original capacity was 8,000, and which is put to contemporary use for concerts and plays; mosaics in the restored Curia of the town's Forum; and other bits and pieces.

Excursions to France and Germany: You're near Mulhouse, Colmar, and Strasbourg in France (see *France at Its Best*) and Germany's Black Forest (see *Germany at Its Best*).

SETTLING IN

Drei Könige Hotel (8 Blumenrain; Phone 25-52-52) is herein awarded pride of place for two reasons. First is location: it's the only hotel flanking the Rhine in Basel proper (there are others [below] across the river in Kleinbasel), a five-minute walk from central Marktplatz. Second is history. It is named for a long-ago meeting of a trio of regional monarchs. There's a showplace suite, antiques-furnished, in which Napoleon is reputed to have overnighted, 86 additional rooms and smaller suites, riverfront terrace-café, bar, and restaurant. Member, Leading Hotels of the World. *First Class.*

Basel Hilton Hotel (31 Aeschengraben; Phone 22-66-22) is an agreeable contemporary house—there are 226 excellently equipped rooms and suites with super U.S.-style baths—that is linked with the Swiss/French train station and Air Terminal by an underground passage. There are three passenger elevators (more than in any other single-building hotel that I know in Switzerland) and each of them is jumbo size by Swiss standards. The Hilton has a pair of restaurants, one very gala (counseled in a later paragraph); the other—Café de la Marine Suisse—irreverently called after the nonexistent Swiss navy, and with authentic U.S.-style hamburgers and steaks as well as Swiss specialties; a really good-size indoor swimming pool, solarium, sauna, and massage room. And smiling Hilton International service. *Luxury.*

Euler Hotel (14 Zentralbahnplatz; Phone 23-45-00) is the prototypical traditional-style hostelry. There are just 65 no-two-alike rooms and suites, with decor based on Louis XVI, and every one I have inspected is a honey. Public spaces—lobby, piano bar, terraced restaurant (about which I write on a later page), snack bar—are a pleasure, too. And service is at once cordial and competent. The Euler (pronounced *Oyler* and named for the family which built it in 1865), like the neighboring Basel Hilton, has a direct underground passage to the Swiss/French Bahnhof and Air Terminal. *Luxury.*

Basel Hotel (12 Münzgasse; Phone 25-24-23) is a contemporary core-of-town house, with 72 quite smart, ever-so-contemporary rooms, based on a theme of brown leather and chrome. There are both a restaurant (evaluated on a later page) and an indoor/outdoor café-brasserie and bar. *First Class.*

Merian am Rhein Hotel (2 Rheingasse; Phone 25-94-66) is "Am Rhein" indeed—directly on the Kleinbasel side, adjacent to Mittlerebrücke. Those of the 40 contemporary rooms that I have inspected are bright as a button, with doubles nice size: be sure to specify river view, for vistas of the cathedral and bridges. The good-value restaurant (about which I write in a subsequent paragraph) moves to an outdoor terrace in summer. *First Class.*

Kraft Hotel (12 Rheingasse; Phone 26-88-77) welcomes with a nineteenth-century lobby-lounge and those of the 35 rooms I have inspected—doubles can be spacious and some facing the river have terraces—are pleasant, although singles are small. The hotel's handsome Schnooggeloch Restaurant moves to a riverfront terrace in summer; I write about it on a later page. *Moderate.*

Victoria Hotel (3 Zentralbahnplatz; Phone 22-55-66) was, to be sure, built while Victoria reigned, but has been spiffily updated. Those of the 115 rooms I have inspected are good-looking, there's a cozy bar, and the restaurant is open nonstop 11:30 A.M. to 11:30 P.M. Opposite the Bahnhof. *First Class.*

Schweizerhof Hotel (1 Zentralbahnplatz; Phone 22-28-33) is an oldie that has been efficiently if not stylishly modernized, with 45 rooms (singles can be small) in the now-outdated style of the 1960s. Small restaurant (breakfast is continental, not buffet) bar-lounge. Chilly. *First Class.*

International Hotel (24 Steinentorstrasse; Phone 22-18-70) is located about midway between the Bahnhof and the core of town. It is of the contemporary-functional school, with 200 rooms, pair of restaurants, bar, pool, and sauna. Ambassador Swiss/Best Western. *First Class.*

Central Garni Hotel (3 Falknerstrasse; Phone 25-44-48) could not be more central. The 25 spotless rooms are equipped with beds that fold down from the wall, with showers (but no tubs) in their baths. Breakfast only. Friendly. *Moderate.*

Jura Hotel (11 Zentralbahnplatz; Phone 23-18-00): Just half of the 80 rooms—all that I have inspected are spotless and reasonably comfortable—have baths. Management serves breakfast only, but there's a restaurant-cum-outdoor café in the building that's independently operated. *Moderate.*

Admiral Hotel (5 Rosentalstrasse; Phone 26-77-77) is brought to your attention only if you're in town for the Swiss Trade Fair and need to be adjacent to Mustermesse, the fairgrounds which are a considerable distance from the center in Kleinbasel. There are 130 neat rooms, restaurant, and bar. Ambassador Swiss/Best Western. *Moderate.*

DAILY BREAD
Euler Hotel Restaurant (14 Zentralbahnplatz; Phone 23-45-00): In an inelegant city that does not emerge, certainly in my experience, as an all-Swiss leader with respect to restaurants, that of the Euler takes on significance. The festive look of the place, to start: crystal chandeliers illuminate a two-level space, whose tables—lighted at dinner by candles in tall silver sticks—are flanked by Louis XV-style chairs upholstered in wine corduroy. The serving staff—maître d'hôtel, captain, waiters,

buspersons—operate with the precision of a smiling symphony. The à la carte is extensive—oysters on the half shell, lobster salad, shrimp cocktail (not often encountered in Switzerland) or an exemplary cream of chicken soup (also rarely offered) among starters; roast lamb, *Châteaubriand*, veal kidneys in a red wine sauce, or a range of fish options among entrées. But the prix-fixe menus are excellent, too. At lunch, for example, you might begin with a bowl of *gazpacho*, continue with leeks and prosciutto in a vinaigrette sauce over a bed of arugula, proceeding to a delicious seafood casserole as entrée. Desserts are offered from a glorious three-tier trolley. And with the check comes a refreshing hot towel, in the style of first-class meal service on the airlines. In my experience, one of the Switzerland's best restaurants. *Luxury.*

Wettstein Grill (Basel Hilton Hotel, 31 Aeschengraben; Phone 22-66-22). The Hilton International people did their homework on this restaurant's name. You learn, in a note on the cover of the menu—in both the German and English languages, with its author a curator of the Historische Museum (above)—that Basel-born Johann Rudolf Wettstein became one of the great Swiss diplomats of the tumultuous Baroque era, and was largely responsible for the Swiss Confederation achieving independence from the Holy Roman Empire. As if that were not accomplishment enough, Wettstein—buried in Basel Münster—was a major mover in the establishment of both the Kunstmuseum and the Historische. But you're hungry. The beautifully designed menu—illustrated with reproductions of prints in the Historische, and with each dish's name published, successively, in French, German, and English—is à la carte, and exemplary. *Carpaccio*—thinly sliced raw beef in a mustard cream sauce—or *foie gras* on a bed of Savoy cabbage—are sensible openers. Hilton International hotels often import U.S. beef so that prime rib and *steak au poivre* are good bets. Fish—sole *meunière* or poached trout—is excellent, as are such other entrées as *médaillons* of veal with wild mushrooms. Ask to have the dessert trolley wheeled over. And conclude with a *digestif* from still another trolley, with a staggering selection of brandies, *eaux de vie*, and liqueurs. *Luxury.*

Schlussel Zunft (25 Freiestrasse; Phone 25-20-26) is a guildhall of yore, with a fabulous eighteenth-century porcelain stove and pewter chandeliers, and a location on the main shopping street. Fare is undistinguished—a meal might open with oddly sauced snails and continued with *paillard de boeuf*, tough and not very tasty, concluding with a conventional dessert. *First Class.*

Safran Zunft (11 Gerberstrasse; Phone 25-19-59) dazzles with its Renaissance facade (it, too, was a guildhall), but the interior is cramped and anticlimactic. The prix-fixe menu at lunch is good value; the à la carte at dinner—perhaps a grilled pork chop garnished with French fries and served with a salad—is *not. First Class.*

Brauner Mutz (10 Barfüsserplatz; Phone 25-19-60), not unlike Safran Zunft, is more elaborate without (its venerable painted facade is striking) than indoors. The main floor is a beerhall, and there's a restaurant—with well-priced prix-fixe menus at lunch—upstairs. *Moderate/First Class.*

Basler Keller (Basel Hotel, 12 Münzgasse; Phone 25-24-23) is atmospheric—a stone-walled *cave* illuminated by rustic chandeliers. There's a fairly priced prix-fixe menu at lunch, but the à la carte at dinner is costly. Still, the level of cooking—a dinner embracing onion soup, *paillards* of veal, *gratin Dauphinois*—is satisfactory, although the staff smiles only tentatively, not quite sure whether to be gracious or faintly hostile. *First Class.*

Schnooggeloch (Kraft Hotel, 12 Rheingasse; Phone 26-88-77). It's worth crossing the Rhine to this Kleinbasel hotel, especially in warm weather when the memorably titled Schnooggeloch— how about that name?—moves outdoors to a terrace on the riverbank, with the cathedral diagonally opposite. The good value prix-fixe menu—soup, an entrée such as veal *cordon bleu*, choice of sweets—is indicated. *First Class.*

Café Spitz (Merian am Rhein Hotel, 2 Rheingasse; Phone 25-94-66) is, not unlike its Kleinbasel neighbor, the Schnooggeloch (above)—brought to your attention because it moves to a terrace-cum-view in summer. There are prix-fixe menus; one such is based on roast beef with *gratin Dauphinois* potatoes. *First Class.*

Fischerstube (45 Rheingasse; Phone 32-66-35) is in Kleinbasel, although it lacks a terrace on the river. Lure is the inexpensive prix-fixe menu—grilled ham steak is a good entrée—served with beer that has been brewed in the little brewery out back; it's glass-walled so that you may have a look. *Moderate.*

Zumstaak (16 Münsterplatz; Phone 25-77-11) occupies quarters in a baroque house and might be just the ticket for lunch (soups, sausages, pasta) or a snack after viewing the neighboring cathedral. There are tables on the square. *Moderate.*

Huguenin (Barfüsserplatz; Phone 23-05-50) is a good-looking, up-a-flight operation in the style of Louis XV—that's indicated for coffee and pastry or the prix-fixe menu (soup or fruit juice, veal steak, ice cream) at lunch or dinner. Central. *Moderate.*

Kunsthalle (7 Steinenberg; Phone 23-42-33) is named for—and in the premises of—a building that houses temporary art exhibitions. The inner of its two rooms is gloomy, but there's a warm-weather terrace. There's no prix-fixe, although lunch of, say *spaghetti Napoletana* with a tomato salad, followed by coffee, makes for a decent meal. Caveat: no credit cards. *First Class.*

Schiesser (Marktplatz), though long established, is more reliable for chocolates and pastries (sold in its ground-floor shop) than for light lunches (open-faced sandwiches are tasty) or coffee in its upstairs café, where service can be slow and erratic. *Moderate.*

L'Escargot (in the basement of the Swiss/French Bahnhof, Centralbahnhofplatz; Phone 22-53-33) is one of a trio of eateries in the main station. It's agreeably French-accented (a rarity in Basel, even though France is just next door), serving France-bound passengers from the French section of the Bahnhof. Build a meal around, say the day's soup or house-made *pâté, entrecôte,* and *frites. First Class.*

Zur Weiten Fahrt (Dreiländer Ecke; Phone 65-46-46). You can't walk to this one; it's a quarter-hour drive from the center to Dreiländer Ecke, which translates as Three Countries Corner— the point where Basel overlooks the Rhine and France (to the left) and Germany (dead ahead). Go for coffee and a snack, or a casual lunch. Closed in winter. *Moderate.*

SOUND OF MUSIC

Stadttheater (Theaterplatz) is a contemporary structure (1975) fronted by a weirdo of an electrically operated mechanical sculpture. Pick up a schedule from its box office or the tourist office (below). Best known tenant is the *Basel Ballet* (with a multinational troupe including not a few Americans, and a repertoire of both contemporary (skippable, in my experience) and traditional ballets that include *Giselle, Petrushka, The Nutcracker, La Fille Mal Gardée,* and *Coppélia,* as well as such Balanchine favorites as *Concerto Barocco* and *Serenade.* Range of opera company presentations extends from Donizetti's *Lucia di Lammermoor* to Benjamin Britten's *Peter Grimes.*

Stadtcasino (Steinenberg 14) is not a gambling hall but rather an auditorium which is home base for the *Basel Symphony;* other concerts as well.

SHOPPER'S BASEL

Do not expect anything like the shopping options of more sophisticated cities, seemingly less frugal, like Geneva and Zürich; you have the feeling that Baselers watch their centimes. *Globus,* a branch of the national department-store chain, fronts on Marktplatz, and has a supermarket/wine shop. *EPA,* another department store, entered on Hutgasse, off Marktplatz, is a reliable source of bargain-priced chocolate. *ABM* and *Pfauen* are moderate-category department stores on Freiestrasse. Other Freiestrasse shops include *Heimatwerk* (very costly Swiss handicrafts); *Schild* (mid-category men's and women's clothing); *Fuglissaler* (porcelain, crystal); branches of both the *Bücherer* and *Gübelin* watch chains; *Franz Carl Weber* (toys); and *Bally* (men's and women's shoes).

INCIDENTAL INTELLIGENCE ══════════════

Basel-Mulhouse Airport is a Franco-Swiss venture, five miles from town in French territory, and is served by buses departing from the Air Terminal in the Swiss/French Bahnhof complex on Zentralbahnhofplatz; customs/immigration formalities are waived for passengers coming from Basel, but *arriving* passengers pass through both French and Swiss customs if they have come from a foreign country. French-speakers in Basel should not expect to find many locals conversant in that language, despite the proximity of France. *Further information:* Verkehrsbüro, Swiss/French Bahnhof, Zentralbahnhofplatz, Basel.

3

Bern

Exploring the Federal Capital

BACKGROUND BRIEFING

There are, to be sure, bigger and grander European capitals; none that I know of, though, is more immediately likable, nor for that matter more effortlessly explored, than Bern. The Bernese have kept pace with the times, expanding their millennium-old city beyond its medieval confines—a finger-like peninsula surrounded on three sides by an engaging loop of the Aare River, in west central Switzerland. But they have retained its charm.

What you realize when you consider Bern is the almost fierce pride that the various towns and cantons of Switzerland maintain. Capital though Bern may be, it is nowhere in Switzerland more apparent that this country is a *confedera-tion*; nothing more centrist would ever do, and Bern is a good example of why that is so. For long a powerful city-state, it controlled considerable territory. It began as little more than a barracks put up by an alliteratively titled noble of German origin—Berchtold V of Bahringen—who was ruling the area on behalf of the Burgundians, themselves clients of the Holy Roman Emperor.

The year was 1191, and the Bernese have researched matters so thoroughly that they know the name of Berchtold's builder (it was Cuno of Bubenberg), that he built at first in wood, using oak trees of the region, later adding a city wall and the still-standing clock tower which formed the town's main gate. Within decades—by which time the town had become a Free City of the empire—the first coat of arms made its appearance with a bear as the focal point. Bernese legend decrees that the name (in local dialect pronounced "Barn") was given the city by Berchtold himself after a hunt in a nearby forest where his first trophy was a bear.

Much of the city, built of wood, was razed in a 1405 fire. The rebuilding on old foundations was of sandstone. The sixteenth and seventeenth centuries saw another major renewal. Indeed, many of the still-used structures in the core of town date from that time. Bern's Golden Age extended from the early sixteenth century until the end of the eighteenth, during which time it amassed a fair chunk of territory along Lake Geneva. The French invasion of 1798 was a near-disaster for Bern; it lost much of its prestige and its territory. In the post-Napoleonic Switzerland that emerged in 1815, a chastened Bern found itself with almost all of the area beyond the city proper, over which it had authority, ceded to two newly formed cantons. In 1848, though, with the creation of the modern Swiss Confederation, Bern was selected as site of the first Federal Parliament. It had become capital of Switzerland.

National eminence notwithstanding, the city's *Altstadt*, or Old Town, has remained intact. Its streets, bordered by what the Bernese call *Lauben* (arcades built into facades of houses on either side) are quite as they have been for centuries; only shops whose entrances they shelter have changed. Indeed, no house may be built or renovated without the arcade being built into its ground floor, and no facade is municipally approved that does not conform to the style of adjacent buildings.

Bern's principal business is the Federal Government. Instead of a strong single executive, prime authority is vested in the seven-member Federal Council. Councilors are elected to four-year terms by members of the Parliament or Federal Assembly. The Assembly not only selects the council; from among the seven serving on it, it elects a council president—which is the closest Switzerland comes to having a chief of state. The position entails relatively little pomp and ceremony; council presidents, to give you an idea, do not make official visits to foreign capitals, as do heads of state and/or government or other other countries.)

The Assembly is bicameral. The *Nationalrat*, or National Council, has two hundred representatives, elected for four-year terms. The *Standesrat*, or Council of States, has forty-six members, two from each canton. Swiss women, it is worth pointing out, have voted in Federal elections only since 1971, when modern-day suffragettes were victorious in breaking a male monopoly that had been in effect since 1291.

ON SCENE
Lay of the Land: What's so nice about this city is that the moment you exit its startlingly contemporary *Bahnhof*, your're in the core of medieval Bern. The station faces *Bahnhofplatz*, diagonally across from tall-spired *Heiliggeistkirche*, the Church of the Holy Ghost, dating to the eighteenth century, with a facade giving onto the city's main street, which goes by a series of names. It begins as *Spitalgasse*; going toward the interior of the fingerlike area delineated by the waters of the Aare River, it runs first into café-lined *Bärenplatz* (which converges into *Bundesplatz*, named for the domed Federal Parliament you can see if you look to the right). Continuing, it becomes *Marktgasse* until it reaches *Theaterplatz* and the Bernese landmark that is *Zeitglockenturm*, the extraordinary clock tower (below) that Bernese shorten to *Zytglogge* in their dialect. At that point Main Street's name changes to *Kramgasse*, for another long block at the end of which you look left to see the *Rathaus*, or Town Hall—with a light, delicate Gothic look that is reminiscent of the *palazzi* of Venice. Continue along what is now called *Gerechtigkeitgasse* for another long block, at the end of which you encounter a pair of bridges spanning the Aare. Cross *Nydeggbrücke* to your right; at its terminus you're high above the municipal *Bärengraben*, Bern's celebrated bear pits (below). Still another bridge, *Kirchenfeldbrücke*, is crossed—it leads from central Theaterplatz—to the modern quarter of the city based on *Helvetiaplatz* around which are clustered the major museums,

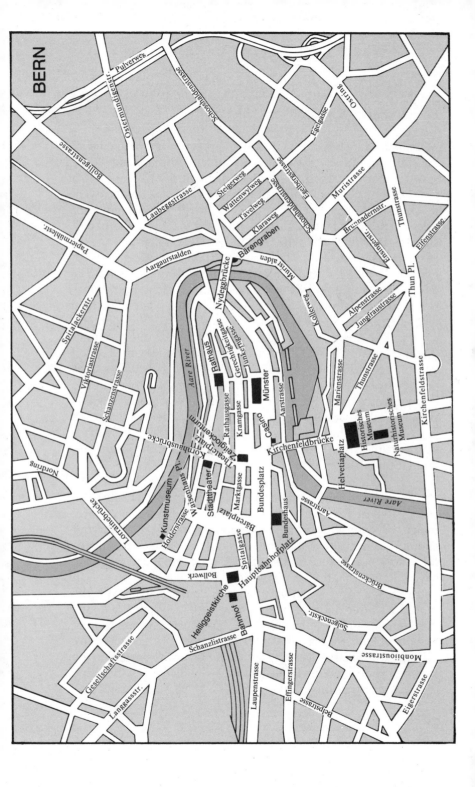

save one (*Kunstmuseum*—the remarkable fine-arts collection, a neighbor of the Bahnhof). Backdrop to all of this: snowy Alps— Eger and Mönch, and as well, the Jungfrau.

Münster (Münsterplatz): Given its supremely intact medieval quarter with nary a skyscraper to spoil the homogeneity, the spire of Bern's cathedral—highest such in Switzerland—is a landmark of especial beauty. Surprisingly, the spire is relatively modern—late nineteenth century—although the remainder of this splendid structure is fifteenth-century Gothic. Perhaps I should say, *almost all* of the remainder. The tympanum, the recessed space over the cathedral's main entrance with an amazingly detailed and quite terrifying interpretation of *The Last Judgment* carved in stone has, in recent years, been transferred to the Historische Museum (below), to protect it from the elements; what you see is a deftly sculpted copy. Take your time and stroll the interior, noting in this originally Catholic church (Protestant since the Reformation) such features as painted vaults over the nave, sixteenth-century choir stalls with scenes of the period—lay as well as spiritual—carved into the seats; painted bosses over the choir—87 all told—each of a religious figure; and perhaps worthy of the most attention, stained glass—some of the best in Switzerland. The trio of windows facing north in the choir, each more than 40 feet high, are late-Gothic masterworks.

Kunstmuseum (Hodlerstrasse 12): Gaining entry is hardly felicitous. A stern-visaged lady in command of the lobby counter looks you over without pleasure, spots a canvas bag on your shoulder, which she motions for and checks, the while demanding a deposit in francs, to be returned only when you claim the bag. Following that, *Meine Dame* requests still more money—an entrance fee. And when you pick up a simple flyer with the museum's three floors of exhibits diagramed, you are asked for a third (albeit minimal) payment. Still, it is all worthwhile. So long as you do not expect a catchall collection—Greek sculpture through the Italian/German/French Renaissance beyond to the Dutch Baroque and the English Rococo—which is not the name of the Kunstmuseum's game. There is, to be sure, a ravishing

Madonna and Child by Fra Angelico. By and large, though, forget Old Masters. Instead take time to become acquainted with Bern-born Ferdinand Hodler (1853–1918). The most prolific of the modern Swiss masters, he is represented in most of the country's important museums (especially that of Geneva—see Chapter 6—where he lived and died). Hodler was as intrigued with the human condition as with the human anatomy—not to mention the natural splendor of his native land. Nudes—ladies in *Le Jour*, men and women both in *La Nuit*—are his trademark Bern works. But there are many others filling a big gallery. Works of Paul Klee—at once mysteriously symbolic and brilliantly decorative—occupy half a dozen smaller basement galleries. (Klee was born near Bern of German parents, and died just before World War II in Locarno, where he had gone from Bern for hospitalization.) Late nineteenth- and early twentieth-century German expressionists are on hand in profusion: Lehmbrück and Marc, Macke and Kirchner. So are Courbet and Delacroix, who preceded the Impressionists in France, themselves brilliantly represented—a Cézanne self-portrait, a woman at her bath by Renoir, a Sisley seashore, a Manet garden, a Degas horse race. This century? The Picassos take your breath away; on scene, as well, are Gris and Braque, Modigliani and Rouault, Bonnard and Vuillard. Linger; there's a cafe.́

Bernisches Historisches Museum (Helvetiaplatz) appears intimidating as you pass through the high wrought-iron gates of the parklike grounds it occupies. Its overscaled proportions, typical of turn-of-century museum design, make a visitor appear very small indeed. But the collection dazzles. I enthuse in an earlier paragraph about the fifteenth-century stone-carved interpretation of *The Last Judgment*, transported for safekeeping from the facade of Bern's Münster. And there's a great deal more, much of it on the same high esthetic level. Consider a series of ravishing Renaissance tapestries, a veritable regiment of mock medieval soldiers—and their horses—in exquisitely wrought armor; weathered maps (including one, somewhat surprisingly, of eighteenth-century London); painted shields and swords; fragments of stained glass; Rococo porcelain, even nineteenth-century bathtubs; and, most amusing exhibits of the lot, cameras and radios from early decades of the present century, in tandem with World War II jukeboxes and movie posters.

Naturhistorisches Museum (Bernestrasse 15, just around the corner from the Historische Museum [above]): All well and good to say you've seen your share of natural history museums at home. I felt that way myself until, in the line of duty, I inspected the extraordinarily lifelike dioramas at Bern's Naturhistorisches. There are a couple of hundred-plus—okapis and tigers through warblers and wolves, with a locally beloved mascot exhibit: the stuffed remains of Barry, a life-saving hero of a St. Bernard. Two neighboring museums—*Schweizerisches Alpines Museum* and *Schweizerisches PTT* [Postal] *Museum* share the building at 4 Helvetiaplatz, and are—unless you're *really* into mountaineering or mail delivery—easily skippable.

Zytglogge (Theaterplatz) is what the Bernese affectionately dub (in dialect) their clock tower. As well they might; its original movement has been working since 1530. The clock sounds four minutes before every hour, 24 hours a day. You want to make it a point to be present for the show. What happens? Well, a rooster crows and spreads its wings, to herald a procession of armed bears. Simultaneously, a jester just above rings a pair of bells preparatory to the turning of an hourglass by still another figure, with the hour struck by a knight radiant in gilded armor. Fun.

Bärengraben (far end of the bridge called Nydeggbrücke): The beloved Bern Bear Pits have been on scene—as a symbol of the animal for which the city is named—for centuries. The legend behind the name relates to Bern's founder, Duke Berchtold V of Bahringen (above) who determined to name the town after an animal he would kill in the course of a hunt in the countryside; his victim, it turned out, was a bear. The current pits date to 1857, and are three in number, and home to a dozen-odd animals who are, not surprisingly, spoiled by the crowds, which supplant a diet of bread, beets, milk, and fruit with virtually limitless quantities of nourishment—biscuits, carrots, nuts,

purchased at stands above the pits—for which the bears (una-
bashed hams) express appreciation by bobbing gratefully on
hind legs. If you're in town around Easter, pop over to see the
season's current crop of cubs; they bear watching.

Rathaus (Rathausplatz) is the Venetian palazzo of a Town Hall
to which I make earlier reference. It's an early fourteenth-
century treasure. Twin Gothic arches of its portico frame front
doors gained by a double stairway from a fountain-centered
square which is one of the prettiest in town. Though it does not
keep regular visitors' hours, ask just inside the entrance if you
may have a peep at the *Grosratssaal*, the restored and refurbished council chamber.

Brunnen, or fountains, represent Middle Ages art at its most enjoyable in cities throughout Switzerland. Nowhere, though, are
they so beautiful as in Bern. And it is to the credit of the Bernese
that they remain undisturbed in original positions—often in the
middle of the street, necessitating driving cars around them.
You'll admire them throughout the Altstadt; look especially,
though, for *Pfeiferbrunnen*, the bagpiper in Spitalgasse;
Kindlifresserbrunnen, a Carnival figure in Kornhausplatz;
Ryfflibrunnen, a crossbow-shooter, in Aargergasse; and
Läuferbrunnen, a courier in Laüferplatz.

Bundeshaus (a.k.a. Parlamentsgebäude, on Bundesplatz): The
Federal Parliament, a ponderous pile designed in the late nineteenth century and opened in the early twentieth, is more
significant politically than architecturally. Withal, you want to
pay your respects, by means of a multilingual guided tour. Given
by guards (they can in their way be as hammy as the overfed
bears in Bärengraben, above), the gratis one-hour expeditions
depart regularly for inspections of the two legislative
chambers—200-member *Nationalrat* and 46-member
Standesrat. Highlights are the Hall of the Dome (with stained-
glass coats of arms of the 22 cantons), and massive murals in
each chamber. The guide explains that Parliament meets four
times a year for a three-week period, and details—it can be more

than you want to hear—procedural matters, including the manner in which the legislature of a democratic country with three "official" languages (and a fourth "national" language) gets its work done.

SETTLING IN

Schweizerhof Hotel (11 Bahnhofplatz; Phone 22-45-01): It is interesting to someone like me who spends a good deal of his waking (and sleeping) hours in hotels, how a house like this one—owned and operated by the third generation of the Gauer family, with the best location in town (as central as it can be, directly opposite the Bahnhof), and with a deserved reputation for good looks, fine food, and warm hospitality—persists in trying harder. By that I mean continuing redecoration of its 110 rooms and suites—some creatively contemporary, some the work of leading Bern artists, the remainder graciously traditional. And maintaining the excellence of its restaurants. The Schweizerhof has a pair. Bigger of the two, Restaurant Français—with an entrance of its own from Bahnhofplatz, the better to serve Bernese regulars—serves what is in my experience the best buffet breakfast in Switzerland (bacon and eggs are always on the menu, along with fresh-squeezed orange juice, cereals, cheeses, sliced cold meats, and a variety of breads and rolls) as well as excellent-value prix-fixe menus at lunch and dinner. The intimate Schultheissenstube is as small as its name is long, and reviewed on another page. There are, as well, a serene bar off the lobby and a disco, Arcady Club, dense and dark into the wee hours. Even corridors of the hotel's five floors are noteworthy; each is a veritable museum of antiques, the range pewter and copper through furniture and sculpture. The staff, reception through room service, is smiling, skilled, and swift. This is one of Switzerland's finest. Member, Leading Hotels of the World. *Luxury.*

Bellevue Palace Hotel (3 Kochergasse; Phone 22-45-81) is imposing enough without—with a splendidly colonnaded Beaux Arts facade—to be mistaken for the Federal Parliament, its near neighbor. The lobby's stained-glass ceiling is supported by Ionic columns. The 160 suites and rooms are a mix—some smart and subdued Louis XV and Louis XV-style; others modern, with plaid accents. The Bellevue Bar, with deep leather chairs, is the best-looking in town, drawing MPs, government biggies, and diplomats as regulars. And I evaluate the restaurants—dressy Grill Room, summer-months Terrassen (with smashing views of Alps and Aare), casual Zur Müng—on a later page. A link of Swissair's Swissôtel chain that's a member of Leading Hotels of the World. *Luxury.*

Bern Hotel (9 Zeughausgasse; Phone 21-10-21) is a long-on-scene, centrally located hostelry that has been agreeably updated. There are a hundred contemporary-decor rooms in soft rust and beige tones, with nice baths, trio of interesting restaurants—one later evaluated—and a lively piano bar. *First Class.*

Metropole Hotel (26 Zeughausgasse; Phone 22-50-21) is core-of-town, with a zippy look to its public spaces—including Vieux Moulin Restaurant, later evaluated, a second restaurant, and a congenial bar. There are 45 rooms in red, white, and blue—twins can be good-sized—and the staff smiles. *First Class.*

Bären and Bristol Hotels (4 and 10 Schauplatzgasse respectively; Phones 22-33-67 and 22-01-01 respectively) are next-door neighbors sharing a management. The 60-room Bristol is somewhat the larger, but Bären houses the sole restaurant—the attractive, bear-motif Bärenstube, about which I write on a later page. Both hotels are attractive and congenial, although rooms I've inspected in the Bären tend to be smaller than those of the Bristol. The Bären is affiliated with Ambassador Swiss/Best Western; both are central and *First Class.*

Savoy Hotel (26 Neuengasse; Phone 22-44-05) boasts half a hundred pastel-hued, Art-Deco–style rooms. Location is central, and management is expert (it's the same Gauer family that owns and operates the Schweizerhof, above) Breakfast only. *First Class.*

City Mövenpick Hotel (Bubenbergplatz; Phone 22-53-77) is contemporary. There are not quite 50 pleasant rooms (management places a chocolate bear on each bed as a good-night gift) and the bonus of an indoor pool. Breakfast only. Central. *First Class.*

Kreuz Hotel (41 Zeughausgasse; Phone 22-11-62) is conveniently situated, neat as a pin, with 75 functional rooms (some with showers, some with tubs) and a cordial management. Breakfast only. Good value. *Moderate.*

Goldener Adler Hotel (7 Gerechtigkeitgasse; Phone 22-17-25) occupies an impressive eighteenth-century building on Bern's main street. There are 15 so-so rooms—clean if hardly beautiful, and most have baths. Restaurant, bar. *Moderate.*

Goldener Schlüssel Hotel (72 Rathausgasse; Phone 12-02-16) is actually better known as a restaurant (below). It is, as well, a 15-bed hotel. Rooms are simple but neat; not all have baths. Central. *Moderate.*

DAILY BREAD

Schultheissenstube (Schweizerhof Hotel, 11 Bahnhofplatz; Phone 22-45-01) is a stellar case of big things coming in small packages. As snug as it is soignée, the Schultheissenstube's serving staff is virtually as large as its limited seating capacity. You are taken very good care of by tuxedoed maître d'hôtel and waiters, ordering from a French-accented à la carte changed daily, in accordance with what tempts the chef in the market. A meal might open with a quail salad or a *crêpe* stuffed with smoked salmon and topped with a dollop of caviar. Soups invariably include lobster bisque. *Mosaïque de poissons* is a mélange of several species of the day's catch, superbly sauced. Filet of rabbit in a basil-flecked sauce, accompanied by made-on-premises noodles, is a delicious entrée. When the *chariot de desserts* is wheeled up, somehow or other you manage to find room for a sweet; they are superb. In my experience, one of Switzerland's best restaurants. *Luxury.*

Ausseren Stand (17 Zeughausgasse; Phone 22-32-05): Setting is a high-ceilinged room, balconied and overhung with giant plants. You're seated on rattan armchairs upholstered in deep green velvet. There are roses at each of the tables, set with pale green linen. Waitresses smile as they bring a meal—the table d'hôte is good value—which might open with chicken salad or vegetable soup, continue with risotto or grilled salmon trout, concluding with light-as-a-feather chocolate mousse or a fruit tart. Everything I have had is utterly delicious. *First Class.*

Zur Muenz (Bellevue Palace Hotel, 3 Kochergasse; Phone 22-45-81) is barrel-vaulted, draws locals, especially for the lunchtime *plat du jour*, and after-theater as well. Not that dinner—embracing, say, a shrimp and mussel ragout or onion soup, chicken fricassee or a grilled *paillard* of veal, and with a masterwork from the Bellevue's pastry chef to conclude—is a bad idea, either. *First Class/Luxury.*

Casino (25 Herrengasse; Phone 22-20-27): To look at it from the outside, the Casino could indeed be a gambling palace or, for that matter, an opera house, what with a pair of imposing towers to the side and a colonnaded facade. Actually, it is a concert hall and series of restaurants, each with its own decor, menu, and, I hasten to add, prices. The middle-level Ratstube—attractive with painted wooden booths and tables set in yellow linen—offers a solid-value prix-fixe menu that might run to cream of asparagus soup, "roastbeef à l'anglaise" (as the menu puts it), a mixed salad, followed by a minimountain of an ice cream sundae. The room called *Le Relais* is pricier and there's a less costly café. The Ratstube is *First Class.*

Ratskeller (81 Gerechtigkeitsgasse; Phone 22-17-71) sounds as though it might be located in the Rathaus or town hall. But it isn't. Nice looking and nicely staffed, it's at its best at lunch when you help yourself to all you like of such daily *plats du jour* as French-origin *gigot d'agneau* (roast lamb) served with *pommes Lyonnaise* and *ratatouille*, filet of sole, ham steak, or chicken—all with accompanying vegetables and/or salads. *First Class.*

La Gondola (21 Bollwerk; Phone 22-33-71) is plain-looking but with corking good Italian cuisine. There's a pair of inexpensive prix-fixe menus at lunch. And the à la carte—with such specialties as a generous antipasto, *ravioli verde di funghi freschi, papardelle,* and *penne*—as well as entrées of meat and fish—is excellent. Alert service. *Moderate.*

Rotisserie (Bern Hotel, 9 Zeughausgasse; Phone 21-10-21): A groaning table—with a side of smoked salmon, other appetizers, and cheeses—faces the entrance of this subdued room, white-walled, maroon-upholstered, with tables nicely spaced, and an attentive staff. Women in each party are presented red roses and the kind of little hot towels popularized by the airlines conclude each meal. The five course *petit menu gastronomique*— cream of chicken soup, vermouth-scented scampi, mango sherbet as a palate-cleanser, the house's beef specialty as an entrée, a choice of desserts—is indeed a winner. *Luxury.*

Vieux Moulin (Metropole Hotel; 26 Zeughausgasse; Phone 22-50-21): The look is red linen-covered tables, wood-beamed ceiling, and ladderback chairs, and the prix-fixe menu is a solid buy, possibly including the day's salad or soup to open, *carbonade de boeuf*—a hearty stew—as entrée; and a tasty dessert. *Moderate.*

Goldener Schlüssel (72 Rathausgasse; Phone 22-02-16): A gilded wrought-iron key hangs over the entrance. This anything-but-ostentatious, two-chamber restaurant is at its best with solid Swiss fare. Go with *Berner Platte,* the capital's version of France's better-known *choucroute garnie.* Like the Gallic counterpart, its base is a giant mound of sauerkraut, topped with ham, sausages of various sorts, and boiled potatoes. Super. *First Class.*

Kornhauskeller (124 Postfach; Phone 22-11-33): You go down a flight to reach this one—where tables are set beneath high vaulted ceilings. This onetime granary/wine cellar (with a still-to-be-seen 36,000-liter vat) has been on scene since 1714. As with the Goldener Schlüssel (above), specialties are rib-sticking local dishes, *Berner Platte* the most reputed. *First Class.*

Bahnhof Buffet (Bahnhof, Bahnhofplatz; Phone 22-34-21): It should go without saying that Bern's ultramod station would be well equipped to provide travelers with sustenance. The *Grill Room* is sleek, with bright linen at the tables and a fast-moving brigade of waiters who produce satisfactory standbys like grilled pork chops, thick beefsteaks, and a choice of veal dishes, the lot properly garnished. In warm weather, the terrace café is a pleasure. Former is *First Class;* latter *Moderate.*

Mövenpick Waisenhaus (28 Waisenhausplatz) is cheerful, welcoming, and like other links of this national chain, with good things to eat. Bratwurst, served not only with *rösti* but, if you prefer, French fries and/or fried onion rings is popular; so are chopped sirloin, and *lasagne verdi. Moderate.*

Tschirren (73 Kramgasse) is the source of what locals term the most delicious chocolates in town. Its café, up a flight, is indicated for pastries, served with morning coffee or afternoon tea. *Moderate.*

Gfeiler (Bärenplatz) is one of a mass of cafés lining Bärenplatz, and packed with gossipy locals at the end of each afternoon. Have wine, beer, or coffee. *Moderate.*

Rosengarten (Rosengarten): Tables fill the terrace of this big café in a rose-filled park, on an eminence above the city. You're a taxi or bus ride away from the center, but the view of town, river, and mountains on a clear day makes the journey worthwhile. *Moderate.*

SOUND OF MUSIC
Stadttheater (Kornhausplatz) is a super setting—mock Baroque with a marvelously elaborate facade and a red plush and gold interior—for such operas as Verdi's *Otello,* such operettas as Strauss's *Die Fledermaus,* such musicals as Cole Porter's *Kiss Me, Kate,* to name a trio of presentations. Ballet, too.

Casino (25 Herrengasse): The graceful *Grosser Saal* of this turn-of-century building (see Daily Bread, above) is the setting for a range of symphonic, chamber, and other concerts. Still other concerts take place in the *Münster*, other churches, and the *Konservatorium*.

SHOPPER'S BERN

Two of the three major department stores—*Globus* (the most impressive, with a basement deli-cum-wines, menswear on Main, women's up a flight) and *Loeb* (with a café on three)—are on Spitalgasse, while *Jelmoli* is on Marktgasse. As you walk along the multinamed main street, variously Spitalgasse, Marktgasse, Kramgasse, and Gerechtigkeitsgasse—you'll come across such stores as *Migros* (a link of a supermarket chain, with an upstairs restaurant), *Schild* (men's and women's clothing), *Franz Karl Weber* (toys), *Feintaller* (men's and women's shoes), *Bücherer* (watches), *Hermès* (pricey French clothes and accessories), *Heimatwerk* (very costly handicrafts), and *Keller* (for a bagful of the best croissants in town). *Gübelin* (a link of a pricey watch chain) is on Schweizerhoflauge. Bern's *open markets* are fun to browse: produce and flowers Tuesday and Saturday on Bundesplatz and Bärenplatz; a multitude of wares at Waisenhausplatz, also Tuesdays and Saturdays; and Thursday evening markets, throughout the core, until 9:00 P.M.

INCIDENTAL INTELLIGENCE ═══════════════

Flughafen Bern-Belp, the city's airport, is five miles to the south; scheduled service to London, Paris, and Lugano. *Further information:* Verkehrsbüro, Bahnhof, Bahnhofplatz, Bern.

4

Chur

And Its Medieval Altstadt

BACKGROUND BRIEFING

Location can be a blessing—but also a bane. Chur, though the only proper city in the easterly Grisons—largest in area of the Swiss cantons—is, withal, overshadowed by such nearby mountain resorts as Arosa, Davos, Klosters (all Chapter 5), and St. Moritz (Chapter 17). The appeal of the slopes and the aura of après-ski in those hotel-packed villages have overtaken urban Chur. Too many travelers know it more for its *Bahnhof*—you often change trains in Chur en route to or from Alpine destinations—than for its background. Not a little of the latter is reflected in the ambience of its *Altstadt*, or Old Town, surpassed by that of no other small city in the Confederation.

Consider the pedigree. Chur credits itself as the city with the oldest history of settlement in Switzerland. As why should it not, given excavations that indicate Stone Age activity as early as two thousand years before Christ? When Romans came as conquerors of the surrounding region of Raetia, no less august an emperor than Diocletian designated *Curia* the chief town of an enormous Roman province that embraced the area of four contemporary cantons, not to mention the principality of Liechtenstein and a fat chunk of Germany.

Chur became an episcopal see as long ago as the fifth century.

Half a millennium later, its bishops had achieved enough power to be ordained *prince* bishops of the Holy Roman Empire, governing temporally as well as spiritually, until townspeople forced them to brake their reins in the mid-fifteenth century. With the Reformation in the sixteenth century, bishops reverted completely to the spiritual fold. And even though the Grisons (a.k.a. Graubünden) of which Chur is capital, became a dominantly Protestant canton, Chur remains the seat of a Catholic bishop (there are but half a dozen such in Switzerland), with its cathedral the centerpiece of its Old Town.

ON SCENE

Lay of the Land: Nicely compact. And well planned, thanks to medieval city fathers whose *Altstadt* remains the core of the city. From the railway station on *Bahnhofplatz, Bahnhofstrasse,* the principal shopping street (with Globus and Vilau department stores) leads south to the busy square called *Postplatz.* There, it changes its name, becoming *Poststrasse,* as it wends its way uphill to neighboring spires of a pair of churches, St. Martinskirche and the cathedral; the latter is located on the square called *Hof.* A Rhine tributary, the *Plessur River,* more or less delineates Chur's southern fringe. *Plessurquai* and *Lindenquai*—flanking each shore—make good strolling territory, as does elevated *Obere Plessurstrasse*—site of Chur's classiest boutiques. Overlooking it all—Chur's splendid natural backdrop—is the peak the city calls its own: *Mt. Calanda.*

Stephenskirche (Cantonschule) makes for an appropriate introduction to this very old city. The church itself is early Christian, dating to the fifth century. Descend to its crypt for a smattering of Roman Chur; still handsome mosaics are embedded in the floor.

Chur Cathedral (Hof): The seat over long centuries of a Roman Catholic diocese which includes the metropolis of Zürich, the principality of Liechtenstein, the vast Grisons canton, and parts, as well, of central Switzerland, Chur Cathedral's principal portal is exquisitely detailed Romanesque—dating to 1206—and its interior is essentially Gothic. Walk beneath the fine vaults of its nave to the high altar—protected by a locked gate when masses are not being said and opened by cathedral staff only upon request—whose treasure is a gilded triptych completed in 1492 by a talented carver-artist named Jakob Ross. A *Virgin and Child*, surrounded by saints, takes up the center panel. They're flanked by religious and lay figures to either side, with angels hovering in the background. Christ carrying the cross is the subject of still another altar, in the cathedral's St. Katherine's Chapel. Capitals of columns in the crypt—no two are alike—are still another cathedral standout. And you do not want to leave before visiting the collection of medieval caskets, reliquaries, vestments, and illuminated manuscripts in the Treasury. The neighboring building—you will be attracted to its Baroque facade—is the Bishop's Palace, not open to the public.

Martinskirche (Museumplatz), not far from the cathedral (above) and with a spire that complements the larger church's, is fifteenth-century Gothic, but you go now to this single-nave Protestant church for the trio of post–Art Nouveau windows designed by Augusto Giacometti, in 1918, each of them a stained-glass treasure.

Rätisches Museum (Hofstrasse), occupying five exhibit-packed floors of a handsomely converted, capaciously proportioned Baroque townhouse just opposite Martinskirche (above), is one of the most important—and enjoyable—historical museums in Switzerland. Chur's Rätisches—you do well to start up top and work your way down—is a marvelous meld of country sleighs and peasant costumes, farmers' tools and their wives' embroideries, engagingly furnished model rooms and displays of glass and silver; musical instruments and ceramics, aged city maps and vivid stained glass. With memorable portraits of local notables at every turn, including that of a formidable seventeenth-century gent named Georg Jenatsch, generous black mustache and wispy goatee foils for his scarlet uniform, set off by lace collar and cuffs and a sword whose sheath is attached to a silk cummerbund.

Bündner Kunstmuseum (Postplatz): Chur's art museum is hardly less significant than its historical museum (above). Bündner Kunstmuseum occupies a delightfully aged house, with its main floor dominated by an imposing glass dome. If you have traveled in England (see *Britain at Its Best*), you'll no doubt recall paintings by the eighteenth-century artist Angelica Kaufmann in museums and country houses. Kaufmann was born in Chur (her birthplace is now a café—see below), and later lived and worked in Rome, as well as north of the Channel. Her hometown museum honors her with an entire gallery of Kaufmann paintings, including a lovely self-portrait. There are, as well, strong samplings of work by two of the Swiss-born Giacomettis—Augusto and Giovanni, a clutch of paintings by the prolific Ferdinand Hodler—surely Switzerland's most popular and most versatile early twentieth-century artist, and an entire room in which are hung color-drenched scenes by Ernst Ludwig Kirchner, the German Expressionist who spent many years in not far distant Davos (Chapter 5), where a small museum is devoted to his work; indeed, one of the Chur Kirchners is a view of Davos and its valley.

SETTLING IN

Stern Hotel (11 Reichgasse; Phone 22-35-55) occupies a core-of-Altstadt house built in the late seventeenth century and deftly converted to hotel use, with decor tastefully rustic—lots of pine paneling with pine furniture to complement it. There are 55 rooms; of those I have inspected, no two are identical and some can be smallish, but they're cozy. The restaurant is worthy of additional comment on a later page, and there are both a bar and roof garden for summer drinks. Friendly. *Moderate.*

Chur Hotel (Welschdörfli; Phone 22-21-61) is eighteenth century without, ultra mod—the motif is sleek Italian Contemporary—inside. There are 35 rooms, a pair of restaurants as well as a disco popular with locals, and a sauna-health club. Heart of town. *Moderate.*

Duc de Rohan Hotel (4 Masanserstrasse; Phone 22-10-22) is offputting to start, with location; just far enough away from the

Altstadt (ten or twelve minutes on foot) as to appear completely detached from it. Its architecture—unappealing shoebox-modern—bears no relationship to Old Chur either, and its reception area and 35 bedrooms are so pedestrian that neither its restaurant (in a detached wing) nor an indoor pool-cum-sauna compensate for the chilliness of the main building. Even breakfast is disappointing. There are, to be sure, a relative handful of really swank hotels in Switzerland where that meal is waitress-served rather than help-yourself-bountiful-buffet. But the Duc de Rohan is the only nonluxury house that I know of in the Confederation where the first meal of the day is conventional Continental rather than all-you-can eat from a groaning board. Ambassador Swiss/Best Western. *Moderate.*

Rebleuten Hotel (Pfisterplatz; Phone 22-17-13) is at least as much restaurant (my evaluation is on a later page) as hotel. The handsomely facaded building goes back to 1483. Its ten neat rooms—some with original beams supporting ceilings—are comfortable and spotless; management is warm and welcoming, and location is central. *Moderate.*

Posthotel (11 Poststrasse; Phone 23-19-45) is worth knowing about, what with its core-of-town location and just over 40 functional rooms. Breakfast only. *Moderate.*

Guarda Val Hotel (in Sporz, five minutes by car above Lenzerheide, a 40-minute drive south of Chur; Phone 34-22-14) embraces a clutch of smartly restored farmhouses of a onetime mountain village, the lot now a year-round hostelry with skiing in winter; golf, tennis, and fishing in summer; and fine views— the altitude is 4,800 feet. There are just under 40 smart rooms and suites. Restaurant, bar-lounge. Member, Relais and Châteaux. *Luxury.*

DAILY BREAD
Rebleuten Hotel Restaurant (Pfisterplatz; Phone 22-17-13): Its bedrooms (above) are, to be sure, plain, but the restaurant of this fifteenth-century house is intricately paneled, illuminated by pewter chandeliers, and moreover, with a kitchen that turns out

unforgettable food. A meal might embrace potato soup rich with ham strips, thick pork chops baked under a bed of plums (the combination is a winner), served with spätzli and an expertly prepared vegetable, and with a rich, made-on-premises sweet to conclude. Owner Ralph Gottiati and his family are invariably on hand to welcome and to make suggestions and small talk. In my experience, one of Switzerland's best restaurants. *First Class.*

Stern Hotel Restaurant (11 Reichsgasse; Phone 22-35-55) hums with happy lunchers and diners. The look is paneled walls, brass lanterns, and waitresses in regional costume. There is an extensive à la carte, featuring local specialties, but the prix-fixe menu—four courses that might run to curried chicken salad, or a seafood ragout, with consommé to follow, an entrée of filet of beef served with buttered noodles and a salad, and dessert—is good value. *First Class.*

Pestalozza (Rabengasse; Phone 22-24-58): Italian restaurants are almost unfailingly—certainly in my experience—reliable in Switzerland. Pestalozza, modishly contemporary (its interior is a foil for the painted facade of the Baroque house in which it is situated) is a prime example of the genre. Open with *antipasto*, the hearty *stracciatella* soup or a pasta, concentrate on a veal entrée, concluding with say, *zuppa Inglese*. Italian wines. *First class.*

Zum Alten Zollhaus (Obertor; Phone 22-33-98) went up as a Customs House several centuries ago. There's a fountain out front, flowers in windowboxes above the entrance, frescoes on the facade. You climb a flight to the dining room, opting for grilled steaks (pork as well as beef), roast turkey, or *bratwurst mit rösti*. Super-gooey ice cream desserts. *Moderate.*

Bahnhofbuffet (Bahnhof, Bahnhofplatz; Phone 22-30-13): Swiss railway station buffets are more often than not commendable. Chur's prix-fixe menu is invariably a sound bet. *Moderate/First Class.*

SOUND OF MUSIC

Stadttheater (Grossratsgebäude) is core of town, at the east end of Grabenstrasse, near a clutch of movie houses. The tourist office (below) will apprise you of what's on—opera, concerts, ballet, other entertainment.

INCIDENTAL INTELLIGENCE ═══════════

Chances are you are en route to or from a mountain resort, so that views from on high, in Chur, will not be of especial interest. Still, there's a cable car to *Dreibündstein*, from whose 6,375-foot summit the panoramas are not to be despised. Chur is a major rail terminus not only for Swiss trains but also for trans-Europe trains linking major capitals. It is, as well, the station at which the narrow-gauge trains of the regional Rhätische Bahn begin runs into the mountain valleys, and from which long-distance Postal buses go south to St. Moritz and other points. *Further information:* Verkehrsverein, Ottostrasse (diagonally opposite the Bahnhof), Chur.

5

Eastern Resorts Trio
Arosa, Davos, and Klosters

BACKGROUND BRIEFING

No question about it. Mountain resort towns, little matter their location, have a certain similarity. Heavy on hotels, restaurants, and places of après-ski diversion, enough shops—especially those with sportswear and sports gear—to coax francs or Deutschmarks or lire or dollars from our pockets, confusing networks of mountaintops variously gained—with the aid of minutely detailed, locally produced maps that can test the mettle of even the most skilled professional geographers—by funicular trains, cable cars, lifts, or a combination thereof; and a relative paucity of cultural diversions.

In the case of Swiss resorts, add another fairly common dimension: rectangular layouts that run the course of excessively elongated valleys, too often necessitating the use of public buses or other motor transport to get about. There can be, as well—as there are in two of the three resort towns of this chapter (Davos and Klosters)—a plethora of railway stations, making it important to determine in advance of arrival, and of departure, the one indicated for you.

Each of our three towns, though with ancient roots, evolved as resorts in the late nineteenth century, after earlier eminence as sites of tuberculosis sanitoriums. They share Chur (Chapter

4) as the nearest city of consequence, constituting a more or less south to north arc—Arosa the most southerly, Davos in the center, northerly Klosters—to Chur's east. And all are as diverting for summer exploration as for athletic winters.

Of the three, Arosa is the most curious and the most interesting because it stubbornly—and commendably—persists in limited access. Anyone you encounter in Arosa is there because he or she made a special point of being there; there are no transients pausing en route to other destinations. By that I mean if you want to pay this town a visit, there is only one way in—and the same way out. The route is through staggeringly beautiful mountains via either road or rail from nearby Chur. There is, in other words, no through traffic, as is the case with bigger Davos and smaller Klosters, each a relative hop and skip from the frontier with Austria, due east.

ON SCENE

Lay of the Land: *Arosa* (at an elevation of 6,000 feet) is delineated at its eastern flank by a pair of lakes—*Obersee*, the more northerly and larger, is edged by the *railway station*, itself adjacent to the funicular station for *Mt. Weisshorn*, the 8,700-foot premier peak, reached after a stop on the intermediate *Mittelstation* and with a restaurant/sundeck at the summit. (*Mt. Hornli*, the lower-altitude alternate peak, is reached by cable car.) The main street, *Poststrasse*, cuts through the center of town to its western edge, with the *Kursaal*, or casino, *Rathaus* (town hall), tourist office, Protestant and Catholic churches, tennis/squash halls (indoor courts), and principal mercantile activity more or less amidships. *Eissporthalle*, a covered ice-skating rink, is northeast of the center, while *Heimat Museum* occupies a fifteenth-century house, chockablock with local lore—antique furniture through antique skis. Its not-far-distant neighbor is an equally aged single-steeple mountain chapel which, though much restored, is charming.

Davos, at an elevation of 5,128 feet, aggressively promotes convention business for its modern *Kongress Zentrum*, but happily does not neglect winter sports or summer hikes. The westerly *Davos Platz* quarter has its own railway station, neighboring Renaissance-era *Rathaus*, or town hall (with eminently visitable *Grosse Stube*, superbly paneled), and *Johanneskirche* (as old as the fifteenth century), with modern Augusto Giacometti stained glass and an exterior the subject of paintings by the gifted German expressionist artist, Ernst Ludwig Kirchner, who moved to Davos in 1917, remaining until he died two decades later. A number of his color-drenched paintings, including some especially lovely ones with Davos subjects, are on display in Davos Platz's *Kirchner Museum*. Two parallel thoroughfares—*Talstrasse* and *Promenade* (with the *Kongress Zentrum-Eisport Halle-Hallenbad* convention center/ice rink/indoor swimming pool complex between them, center of town)—link Davos Platz with the easterly *Davos Dorf* quarter; it has its own train station with *Heimat Museum*—a repository of Davos mementos—documents and weapons, furnishings and paintings—in a nearby historic house. That leaves the mountains. The most celebrated peak is 8,747-foot *Mt. Weissfluhjoch*, reached by the *Parsenn funicular,* whose terminus, *Station Parsenn* is in Davos Dorf, as indeed is the station for the cable car to somewhat less elevated *Mt. Pischa;* both have restaurants-cum-sundecks, as indeed do such other popular peaks as *Jakobshorn, Schatzalp-Strela,* and *Rinerhorn.*

Klosters (at an altitude of 3,917 feet) is near enough to Davos (above) to be linked with the Davos area's *Parsenn* snowfields, by means of a cable car to *Gotschna Grat* (8,400 feet) in the Parsenn region. Still additional cable cars take Klosters visitors to *Mt. Madrisa,* at an elevation of some 7,800 feet. There are actually two Klosters—easterly *Klosters Dorf* and westerly *Klosters Platz* with *Bahnhofstrasse* the unifying shop-lined main street. On it are situated a covered skating rink, giant outdoor swimming pool, main train station, *Küblis* indoor tennis complex, and the delightful *Heimat Museum* of local lore in a venerable house dubbed *Nutli Hüsli.*

SETTLING IN

AROSA

Arosa Kulm Hotel (Phone 31-01-31): The Kulm's history more or less parallels that of Arosa—as a resort. It went up as a frame boarding house in 1882, and as Arosa grew, so did this hotel, with major expansions in 1914, 1929, and most recently in 1975. Current quarters are contemporary, capacious, and comfortable. All of the hundred-plus rooms I have inspected are inviting: a suite in Biedermeier style, a twin that is modified Louis XV, a single with black-and-white-check accents. There are several restaurants (one of which is later evaluated), convivial bar-lounge, konditerei with irresistible pastries to accompany morning coffee or afternoon tea, and glass-walled swimming pool that gives onto Alpine peaks and is adjacent to a fitness center. This is an expertly operated house with a high proportion of repeat guests. *Luxury.*

Savoy Hotel (Phone 31-02-11): You don't expect all that you find inside, given the Savoy's unexceptional modern facade. Ambience deftly mixes the rustic with the contemporary—beamed-ceiling lobby-lounge, more than 100 suites and rooms, several restaurants (see Daily Bread) boîte with dancing, indoor pool with attached sauna and gym, indoor tennis/squash courts, even a bowling alley. *Luxury.*

Tschuggen Hotel (Phone 31-02-21) tops an Arosa hill, its pristine white facade blending with the town's snows in winter. Contemporary fabrics are used to upholster period-style furniture in what are arguably the best-looking public spaces in town. The 100-plus suites and rooms are generous-sized with fine baths. There are three reputed restaurants, a bar with dancing, and an indoor pool/fitness center. *Luxury.*

Valsana Sporthotel (Phone 31-02-75) is a welcoming 86-room, 10-suite house, modern but with warm rustic accents. Bedrooms—their furniture of bleached wood, their baths well equipped—are a pleasure; the lobby is welcoming; there's a bar-lounge with entertainment and dancing; a pair of restaurants, later evaluated; both indoor and outdoor pools; four tennis courts; and a gym-sauna. The staff smiles and the manager, Markus Holdener, is in my experience one of Switzerland's most skilled. Ambassador Swiss/Best Western. *First Class.*

Maran Hof Hotel (Phone 31-01-85) is made to order for golfers; Arosa's nine-hole Alpine course is just opposite. Those of the 55 rooms in the newer of two buildings are the nicer. The lobby is a looker, the restaurant reliable, and there are two special touches: a daily afternoon tea dance and a super rooftop sun terrace. *First Class.*

Eden Hotel (Phone 31-18-77) has an immediately noticeable sense of style, in such public spaces as the mod-look bar/lounge, chandelier-hung restaurant, plant-decorated indoor pool-cum-café. There are 70 nicely fitted rooms (some of the twins are really spacious), and a fitness center. *First Class.*

Merkur Hotel (Phone 31-66-66) is a winner in its class; an easy walk to the center, with a log-walled lobby, pine-paneled restaurant, friendly bar, and 30 rustic-look rooms. *Moderate.*

Panorama Raetia Hotel (Phone 31-02-41) comprises several country-style buildings. There are 40 pleasant rooms, several restaurants, a bar with dancing. *First Class.*

Belri Hotel (Phone 31-12-37): You have to want to be out of the village to book the Belri; it surmounts its own hill. There are just 14 no-two-alike, utterly charming rooms—one with red lacquer poster beds, another with blue-and-white-check twins, a third extravagantly pine-paneled and brass-chandeliered. Pleasant lounge, bar, restaurant. Lovely. *Moderate.*

Alpine Hotel (Phone 31-16-58) is conveniently heart-of-the-village, with 32 functional rooms, reliable restaurant, bar-lounge, sun terrace. Lots of repeaters. *Moderate.*

Central Hotel (Phone 31-15-13) is, to be sure, central, with 15 okay rooms, bar, fitness center, and a restaurant later evaluated. Only so-so. *Moderate.*

DAVOS

Flüela Hotel (Davos Dorf; Phone 6-12-21): Not unlike the

Arosa Kulm (above), which grew along with Arosa, the Flüela is a Davos pioneer. If you ask him, I'm sure genial Andreas Gredig—third generation of his family to own and operate this gracious, delightfully unpretentious hotel—will show you his collection of priceless old brochures of this house, which goes all the way back to 1868. The Flüela has remained small despite rebuilding and refurbishing over the years; there are just 60 suites and rooms, with a staff of 90 to care for a maximum of 130 guests. (If you've stayed at the summer-only Burgenstock Hotels [Chapter 12] and recognize familiar staff faces, it's because the Flüela [which closes in summer] and Burgenstock [shuttered in winter] exchange personnel.) Accommodations are traditional in style, no two alike—and charming. There are a pair of restaurants, one later evaluated; both piano bar and boîte-cum-dancing; a second-floor lounge that's the prototypical grand-hotel public space; and a big indoor pool. The Davos Dorf train station and terminals for principal peaks are near neighbors. *Luxury.*

Central Hotel (Davos Platz; Phone 2-11-81): This 75-room house is modern without, graciously old school in its public spaces, with bedrooms a deft meld of the two, and in many instances generous size. There are two restaurants—paneled dining room and dark-beamed Bündnerstubli (reviewed on a later page); pair of bars (one with dancing); indoor pool; and—last for best—astute management and caring staff. *First Class.*

Belvedere Hotel (Davos Platz; Phone 2-12-81) is the long, white low-slung complex with a domed main building, that is elevated enough to be seen as you walk about, from almost any point in town. It opened as a sanitorium in the last century, but has long been among the finer top-rank hotels of the Eastern resorts. There are 146 rooms and suites, some of them pine-paneled; pair of restaurants; as many bars; swimming pool-fitness center. Operated by the Germany-based Steigenberger chain. *Luxury.*

Derby Hotel (Davos Dorf; Phone 61-166) is a two-building complex in its own broad garden, in which care has been given to the interiors, deft variations on the rustic theme. There are 60 rooms, with the top rankers big, pair of restaurants, posh bar, pool-fitness center. *First Class.*

Europe Hotel (Davos Platz; Phone 5-59-21) is an attractively updated house that opened in 1868 and that, despite frequent refurbishings over the years, retains a period ambience. There are 50 no-two-alike rooms; a pair of restaurants and a pair of bars; as well as a picture-windowed indoor pool-fitness center. *First Class.*

Kongress Hotel (Davos Platz; Phone 6-11-81) is just opposite the Kongress-Zentrum from whose name it borrows. I like the main restaurant and the spiffy main lounge and beamed-ceiling bar. The 80 rooms are in tones of browns and beige, some of them quite spacious. *First Class.*

Terminus Hotel (Davos Platz; Phone 3-77-51)—just opposite the Davos Platz railway station—shelters 45 compact but well-equipped rooms, restaurants, café, and bar. Good value. *Moderate.*

Des Alpes Hotel (Davos Dorf; Phone 6-12-61) has relatively recently redecorated the bulk of its 40 rooms; they're pine-paneled and handsome. The staff is cordial, and there are no less than a trio of restaurants, one later evaluated. Very nice indeed. *Moderate.*

KLOSTERS

Aaba Health Hotel (Phone 4-81-11) started out as a home away from home for vegetarians. I think it's a pity, since it became a hotel for meat-eaters as well, that it hasn't changed its offputting name. But a rose by any . . . This is an attractive modern house. Those of the 47 rooms I have looked at nicely meld nubby textiles, blond wood, and soft upholstery; some have twin-sink baths. The Royal Suite, with a ballroom-size living room, is stunning. There are several restaurants, one later evaluated, bar and bôite-cum-dancing, and—not surprising, given the title of the place—a fabulous fitness center, with a big swimming pool, whirlpool sauna, solarium, gym, even a beauty parlor with all manner of special treatments available. Friendly. *Luxury.*

Walserhof Hotel (Phone 4-42-42) is at least as well known for its Walserstube restaurant (later reviewed) as for its dozen rooms. Still, this is one of the smartest small hotels I know of in Switzerland. The no-two-alike rooms are so good-looking that I asked to see all that were not occupied; each has a super marble bath with twin sinks in the doubles. If you're going to build contemporarily in Switzerland, albeit in rustic regional style, the Walserhof should be your model. This house is a class act and its management is cordial. *First Class.*

Chesa Grischuna Hotel (Phone 4-22-22) is bigger than the Walserhof (above) and without quite the same éclat. Still, those of its 18 rooms that I have inspected are lookers. There are nice touches like afternoon tea served in an inviting lounge. The bar is intimate and the big restaurant is worthy of later evaluation. *First Class.*

Vereina Hotel (Phone 41-161)—with its marvelous octagonal dome and the steeply pitched roof of its nineteenth-century facade—is a Klosters landmark. This is a fine house whose dynamic owner-manager, Stephen Diethelm, is ever on the go, refurbishing, refurnishing, innovating. The 70 rooms are no-two-alike; those I have inspected are attractive. Public spaces—grandly high-ceilinged—include Le Duc Restaurant in the style of Louis XV; the Pub, whose specialty is fondue; a plaid-surfaced Scotch Bar that could be in Inverness; and a glass-walled pool that gives onto a parklike garden, with a pair of tennis courts and—in summer—a sea of chaise longues. The Vereina is fun. *First Class.*

Steinbock Hotel (Phone 4-45-45) is the inviting across-the-street neighbor of the Walserhof (above), chalet style but *smart* chalet style—with a pair of distinctively decorated restaurants;

bar with a fireplace that roars in winter, and 37 rooms; the doubles I have inspected are near king size and many have fireplaces. Charming. *First Class.*

Pardenn Hotel (Phone 4-11-41), away from the center in a parklike garden of its own, is agreeable enough in its subdued way. Public spaces and those of the 65 suites and bedrooms (none with TV) I have inspected are generously proportioned and comfortable without exhibiting any sense of style, not to mention ebullience. Ditto the restaurants and bar-lounge. Swimming pool. *Luxury.*

Surval Hotel (Phone 4-11-21) is small—there are just 14 rooms—but worth knowing about. Accommodations are neat, and there are both restaurant and bar, as well as a small outdoor pool. *Moderate.*

Albeina Hotel (Phone 4-46-56) is relatively recent. There are 50 functional rooms, restaurant, bar, and indoor pool. So-so. *First Class.*

Alpina Hotel (Phone 4-12-33) is a modern 50-room house that is more functional than handsome, with a staff that is civil if not especially cordial. Restaurant, bar, indoor pool. Ambassador Swiss/Best Western. *First Class.*

DAILY BREAD

AROSA

Weisshorn-Gipfel Restaurant (Phone 31-18-70): A hearty lunch-cum-panorama on the summit of Arosa's celebrated Mt. Weisshorn is a requisite Arosa repast. If it's nippy, open with the day's soup, selecting a grilled pork chop or the restaurant's *entrecôte* specialty—served with *frites.* Elaborate ice cream desserts. *First Class.*

Rotisserie zur Schmitte (Savoy Hotel; Phone 31-02-11): Silk-shaded sconces illuminate tables set with red linen in this zippy environment. Open with *hors d'oeuvres variés*, *carpaccio*, or snails, Burgundy style, before tackling a Rotisserie steak, broiled chicken, or grilled scampi. *First Class.*

Grill Room (Arosa Kulm Hotel; Phone 31-01-31): You don't want to leave Arosa without enjoying a meal in a hotel justifiably celebrated for its culinary skills. Open from the à la carte with, say, smoked salmon, or air-dried beef in gossamer slices, and continue with grilled lamb or mixed grill. Skilled, smiling service. *First Class/Luxury.*

Chiesa Valsana (Sporthotel Valsana; Phone 31-02-75)—brick-walled, with framed photos of the Arosa of yore as accents—is the only restaurant in Switzerland that I know of where you'll find porterhouse steak on the menu. It's served with sauce Béarnaise and it satisfies. Trout from mountain streams—*au bleu* or *meunière*—is expertly prepared here, too. And the house pâtissier is so skilled you want to conclude with a baked dessert. Lovely service. *First Class.*

Les Tournedos (Eden Hotel; Phone 31-18-77) is indicated when you hanker after such French classics as hearty beef-based *pot au feu* or a gargantuan *choucroute garnie*—assorted meats, sausages, and boiled potatoes on a bed of sauerkraut. Fun. *First Class.*

Giancarlo (Phone 31-21-15): Make a point of booking dinner on the occasion of a visit to the Kursaal/Casino, where Giancarlo is located. He turns out a tasty selection of pasta and pizza. Spirited service. *First Class.*

Grischuna (Phone 31-17-01) is worth knowing about for its prix-fixe menus, solidly Swiss. Friendly. *Moderate.*

Simmen (Phone 31-12-28): Old Arosa hands invariably advise a sampling of the pastries at Simmen, with coffee, tea, or the excellent hot chocolate. Sound advice. *Moderate.*

Cafeteria Gloor(Phone 31-23-56) is the see-and-be-seen Arosa café. Coffee, a drink, casual lunch, or snack. *Moderate.*

DAVOS

Bündner Stube (Central Hotel, Davos Platz; Phone 2-11-81) is at once smart, lively, and delicious. Ordering from the extensive à la carte, you might compose a meal starting with, say, morille-flecked veal consommé or seafood cocktail, proceeding to a main course of either fish—the grilled filet of sole served with Hollandaise sauce is superior—or a meat entrée like roast rabbit, a house specialty. Super sweets. *First Class.*

Trattoria Toscana (Des Alpes Hotel, Davos Dorf; Phone 6-17-61): A canopy striped in the Italian colors—red, white, and green—hoods the counter of the open kitchen in this restaurant. Why not open with a platter of *antipasto misto*, the Roman-origin soup called *stracciatella*, a plate of *risotto* or of *tagliatelle*. Veal specialties—*scaloppini* in a Marsala sauce of *involitini*—the pride of Livorno—are favored entrées. Very nice indeed. *First Class.*

Rinaldi (Davos Platz; Phone 5-45-55): In a resort whose hotels and restaurants are heavily Italian staffed, you can't—or at least I can't—have too many Italian meals. Rinaldi suggests opening with a well-sauced pasta before tackling his *saltimbocca, piccata,* or *steak alla pizzaiola. First Class.*

Panorama (Davos Platz; Phone 3-55-24) is indicated when you're in or about the Eissporthalle. Lure is well-priced prix-fixe menus, built around such entrées as veal steak or bratwurst. *Moderate.*

Stübli (Flüela Hotel, Davos Dorf; Phone 6-12-21) is a popular gathering place morning through midnight, with the special attraction Swiss specialties; casual lunches and snacks as well. À la carte at dinner. *Moderate/First Class.*

Schneider (Davos Platz; Phone 3-64-41) has long been a beloved Davos institution. Go for morning coffee with pastry, a pleasant lunch, or tea in the afternoon—of course with pastry. And I defy you to leave Davos without having stocked up on a selection of Schneider's melt-in-the-mouth chocolates. *Moderate/First Class* (except for those chocolates, which are *Luxury*).

KLOSTERS

Walserstube (Phone 4-42-42) is at least as well known as the small but lovely Walserhof Hotel (above) of which it is a part. Select either of a pair of paneled rooms, one with red draperies and chair seats, the other nicely accented in blue. There are several tempting prix-fixe menus; the least pricey might embrace five courses—a morilles and asparagus salad, watercress soup, turbot accompanied by *pesto*-sauced noodles, filet of beef or lamb, with cheese and dessert. Special. *Luxury.*

Chesa Grischuna (Phone 4-22-22)—not unlike Walserstube (above) is as much known as a restaurant as it is a hotel. The look is nifty rustic, the à la carte brimming with such delicious options as *foie gras frais,* snails served casserole-style, or onion soup as starters; grilled salmon, a fricassée of scallops, Zürich-style veal with *rösti,* or roast lamb among entrées. Desserts deserve the separate card they are accorded; the Grand Marnier soufflé is a winner. *First Class/Luxury.*

Greenness (Aaba Health Hotel; Phone 4-81-11) stubbornly retains the name with which it was christened when the Aaba was a vegetarian hotel—no longer the case. The environment is handsome, and the à la carte can make for a memorable meal that might begin with truffle-flecked avocado salad, a *gratin* of mushrooms, or snails in puff pastry. Lobster pancakes are a house hit, among entrées, as is roast breast of guinea hen. *Luxury.*

Alte Post (Phone 4-17-16) is Klosters' prototypical rustic restaurant, with one room in red, the other in beige. They share a

Franco-Swiss menu, with a *foie gras terrine* among appetizers, trout *bleu* or *meunière*, and a number of beef entrées, *tournedos* and *entrecôte* among them. *First Class.*

Pizzeria/Trattoria (Vereina Hotel; Phone 4-11-61): Happiness in Klosters is a *pizza Margherita*—one of half a dozen varieties—at the Vereina. Not that pasta is neglected here, either; *agnolotti verdi* is a delicious example. And there are other Italian favorites, *bollito misto* among them. Convivial. *First Class.*

Höwald (Phone 4-30-45) is unpretentious and reliable, with walls paneled, linen placemats on candlelit dinner tables, and fare an apt Italo-Swiss meld. A meal might run to ravioli as an opener, grilled ham steak following, and *apfelkuchen* smothered with raspberry sauce to conclude. *First Class.*

Wynegg Hotel (Phone 4-13-40), though a small, simple hostelry, has become popular as a restaurant; the fact that its paneled ground-floor eatery is favored by Britain's Prince Charles may have something to do with its popularity. Still, soups (the barley especially) are bracing, fish (like trout) expertly prepared, veal entrées satisfactory. *First Class.*

A Porta: Easiest way to check out the day's arrivals is to pop into A Porta for coffee and pastry, a snack, or casual lunch. *Moderate.*

SOUND OF MUSIC
Concerts, recitals, folklore evenings, and other special events are scheduled from time to time in Arosa, Davos, and Klosters; tourist offices (below) publish event schedules regularly.

SHOPPER'S DAVOS
Biggest of our three resorts, Davos offers the most extensive shopping options. Stores are mostly on Promenade, one of the two thoroughfares that link Davos Platz with Davos Dorf. *Jelimoli*, a good-sized link of a department-store chain, is at the Davos Platz end of Promenade. Other shops on that street include *Blaser* (trendy men's and women's clothing); *Peter Ettinger* (sporting goods and duds, both men's and women's); *Cinema*

(sweaters and other sportswear; men's as well as women's); *René Schad* (watches and jewelry); outlets of both *Ralph Lauren* and *Benneton* apparel chains; and branches, as well, of *Migros* and *Co-Op* supermarket networks.

INCIDENTAL INTELLIGENCE

Further information: Verkehrsbüro, Poststrasse, Arosa; Verkehrsbüro, Promenade, Davos Platz; Verkehrsbüro, Bahnhofstrasse, Klosters.

6

Geneva/Genève
Elegance on the Lakeshore

BACKGROUND BRIEFING
Write about travel for a living, as I do, and you learn early on
to be more grudging in the employment of one adjective—
elegant—than any other.

Still, in the case of the premier city of Suisse Romande—
French-speaking Switzerland—flanking a great river (the
Rhône) and facing the Alps' highest peak (Mont Blanc), no other
one-word description is more apt. Any objective observer of European cities is bound to conclude that of those in the
medium-size category, Geneva ranks with Germany's rich and
ritzy Düsseldorf (see *Germany at Its Best*) and Italy's ancient and
art-filled Florence (see *Italy at Its Best*).

Arrive today and the long Geneva centuries fall effortlessly
into place. Geneva is at once supremely Swiss—precise, orderly,
immaculate. And, although it is no less reserved with
foreigners—praise be—than Italian-speaking towns like
Locarno and Lugano (Chapters 11 and 12), it is more relaxed
and spontaneous than German-speaking urban counterparts,
also-cosmopolitan Zürich (Chapter 20) and smaller Lucerne
(Chapter 12) happily excepted.

This likable, outgoing quality is hardly surprising, you are
likely to retort, what with France—exuberant, Latin-
Mediterranean France—just next door and its language, cuisine,

and lifestyle so obviously influential. But Geneva knew non-Gallic influences in its formative early centuries. Ancient Celts dubbed it *Genua* in the eighth century B.C., colonizing Romans followed, with Alpine-origin Burgundians, Germanic Franks, and the Holy Roman Empire succeeding.

It was during the Empire's heyday that Catholic bishops replaced Counts of Geneva as arbitrary temporal rulers who became increasingly unpopular with an increasingly wealthy mercantile elite. In the thirteenth century, they pledged allegiance to the Dukes of Savoy. In the fourteenth, they had achieved a measure of self-government, but as the fifteenth century became the sixteenth, Savoy dukes—by then in cahoots with still-on-scene bishops—had become autocratic to the point that unhappy Genevans, joining forces with a pair of Swiss cantons (Bern and Fribourg), rejected the bishops and almost simultaneously accepted the Reformation.

The year was 1535. And the roles played by a pair of Frenchmen—anything but exuberantly Gallic—not only transformed Geneva into an austere, hardly frivolous seat of the Reformation—a Protestant Rome, it has been called—but formulated a concept that resulted in what came to be called the Protestant work ethic, upon which, its adherents insist, modern capitalism is based.

I say two Frenchman because the first—fervently anti-Catholic Guillaume Farel, who had based himself in Geneva and was largely responsible for expulsion of the bishops—brought in the second—Paris-educated Jean Calvin, whose treatise, *Institutes of the Christian Religion*, was to become a Reformation credo. Calvin's sermons, preached from the originally Catholic Cathedral of St.-Pierre, were far-reaching, to be sure, but of immediate impact in Geneva, which came to be ruled—and regulated—by Calvin.

Two contemporary Geneva hotels, in felicitously written histories of the city which they give to guests, describe Calvin's Geneva. "The *Ordonnances* of 1560," according to Geneviève Armleder and Pierre Bertrand's text, as published by the Richemond Hôtel, "demanded modesty and austerity of the inhabitants. That is what marked the face of Geneva: no jewels or gold ornaments, nor silk clothes. Women and girls were forbidden any curling, pinning, or twisting of hair."

And the book produced by Jacques Clavel for the De La Paix Hôtel states that Calvin "tried to transform the town into a saintly city by means of a strict moral regimentation which became more and more severe. So now this town, gay and frankly ribald, becomes austere. The church police have the right to enter any citizen's home at any hour of the day or night to see if they honor the Lord properly. Having a card game in an inn could lead to the stocks, playing the violin could merit a solo in jail, a smile during a sermon could cost three days in prison."

Well, so much for the stereotype of French frivolity. Calvin died in 1564 at the age of fifty-five. The philosophy adopted by his Reform movement traveled all through Europe, later crossing the Atlantic with England's Puritans. His influence remained a factor in the lifestyle of Geneva's upper classes. It was the bourgeoisie and the craftsmen—not least of which were the watchmakers who, with their successors, made Geneva the world's watch capital—whose example led the city to abandon Calvin's excessively harsh, narrowly defined moralism.

By the eighteenth century Geneva's ambience was at once sophisticated and intellectual. It was the city of author-philosopher-composer Jean Jacques Rousseau, the son of a Geneva watchmaker; of Jacques Necker, also Geneva-born, who, as Treasurer of France, provided French financial aid for the American Revolution; and of Geneva-born Albert Gallatin, who became Secretary of the U.S. Treasury under Presidents Jefferson and Madison. Voltaire, the French philosopher, was first of a considerable group of foreigners to settle in Geneva, where he became a controversial figure. Byron, Shelley (and his wife, Mary, who wrote her *Frankenstein* tales in Geneva), Hugo, Liszt, George Sand—all became fond of Geneva. Annexed to France between 1798 and 1813, the city joined Switzerland as seat of a canton in 1815–the very last to become part of the Confederation.

One of Geneva's citizens, Henri Dunant, organized a volunteer group of medical and nursing workers to care for the wounded of the mid-nineteenth-century Battle of Solferino, thereby laying groundwork for establishment of the Red

Cross—and for Geneva's hospitality toward headquartering international organizations and hosting international conferences, the most notable of the latter that between America's Reagan and the Soviet Union's Gorbachev in 1985. Indeed, the dateline "Geneva" appears so often in the world press that non-Genevan Swiss—possibly envious of its global repute—often tend to pass it off rather patronizingly as more "international" than Swiss. Nothing of the sort. Geneva is the kind of city that could flourish only in Switzerland. It represents what all Switzerland might well aspire to be: truly multilingual, culturally rich, as architecturally arresting as it is splendidly situated, as amusing as it is edifying.

ON SCENE
Lay of the Land: Geneva comes in two parts: *Rive Droite*, or Right Bank, west of *Lac Léman* (a.k.a. Lac de Genève or Lake Geneva) and *Rive Gauche* or Left Bank, east of the lake, which joins the *Rhône River* at *Pont du Mont Blanc*, northernmost of several bridges spanning the two banks. Geneva's principal landmark is on neither bank, but rather *in* the lake; it's the striking fountain, *Jet d'Eau*, whose spray rises 460 feet. When you're ambling about interior precincts of either bank, look for *Jet d'Eau* to guide you back to the waterfront.

Walks on *Rive Gauche/Left Bank* should take you inland from the lakefront quais to the city's smartest shopping street, *Rue du Rhône*, a block inland from *Quai Général Guisan*, which it parallels. It, in turn, is paralleled by also-mercantile *Rue du Marché* (which becomes *Rue de la Croix d'Or* as it extends east). From this bustling area, you are a hop and a skip—albeit uphill—to Geneva's enchanting *Vieille Ville*, or Old Town. *Rue de la Cité* leads from the shopping district into *Grande Rue* (indeed the grandest of Vieille Ville's streets), with one of the superbly facaded old houses lining it (No. 40) the birthplace of Rousseau, and both the *Cathedral of St.-Pierre* (below) and *Hôtel de Ville*, the Renaissance-baroque city hall (with the open-to-visitors room in which the Red Cross was created in 1864). Take your time wandering about this quarter—noting such architecturally rich squares as *Place du Bourg de Four* and *Place du Grand Mezel* and streets leading from them. *Place Neuve*, just west of La

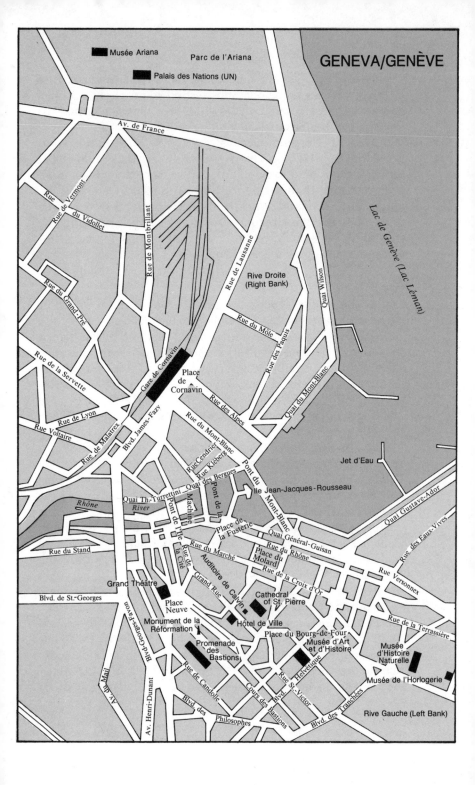

GENEVA/GENÈVE

Musée Ariana

Parc de l'Ariana

Palais des Nations (UN)

Av. de France

Rue de Vermont

Rue du Vidollet

Rue de Montbrillant

Rue de Lausanne

Lac de Genève (Lac Léman)

Rue du Grand-Pré

Quai Wilson

Rive Droite
(Right Bank)

Rue de la Servette

Rue du Môle

Rue des Pâquis

Gare de Cornavin

Place de Cornavin

Rue de Lyon

Blvd. James-Fazy

Rue des Alpes

Quai du Mont-Blanc

Rue Voltaire

Rue de Malatrex

Rue du Mont-Blanc

Jet d'Eau

Rhône
River

Quai Th.-Turrettini

Rue Cendrier

Rue Kléberg

Quai des Bergues

Pont du Mont-Blanc

Ile Jean-Jacques-Rousseau

Machine

Pont de l'Ile

Pont de la

Quai Gustave-Ador

Rue du Stand

Place de la Fusterie

Quai Général-Guisan

Rue des Eaux-Vives

Rue Versonnex

Grand Théâtre

Rue du Marché

Rue du Rhône

Place du Molard

Rue de la Croix-d'Or

Blvd. de St.-Georges

Auditoire de Calvin

Rue de la Cité

Grand'Rue

Place Neuve

Cathedral of St. Pierre

Rue de la Terrassière

Monument de la Réformation

Hôtel de Ville

Place du Bourg-de-Four

Blvd. Georges-Favon

Promenade des Bastions

Musée d'Art et d'Histoire

Musée d'Histoire Naturelle

Av. du Mail

Av. Henri-Dunant

Rue de Candolle

Cours des Bastions

Rue St.-Victor

Blvd. Helvétique

Musée de l'Horlogerie

Blvd. des Philosophes

Blvd. des Tranchées

Rive Gauche (Left Bank)

Vieille Ville, is the site of the *Grand-Théâtre*, Geneva's late nineteenth-century opera house. *Promenade des Bastions*, contiguous with *Place Neuve*, to its south, is the site of *Monument de la Réformation*—a monolithic wall nearly 330 feet long, centered by sculptures of Calvin, Guillaume Farel, John Knox (Mary Queen of Scots' fiery antagonist who took refuge in Geneva), and Theodore de Bèze, a theologian-collaborator of Calvin and his successor as rector of the Calvin-founded academy which became the University of Geneva.

Rive Droite/Right Bank, lined by a quai backed by facades of a number of grand hotels, successively named—in its core—*Quai Turrettini, Quai des Bergues*, and *Quai du Mont Blanc*—has as its main street *Rue du Mont Blanc*, which cuts inland from Quai du Mont Blanc as far as *Place du Cornavin*, passing the Gothic Revival *Église Anglaise* (Anglican) to *Gare de Cornavin*, the railway station. Other Rive Droite shopping streets—*Rue Kléberg* and *Rue Cendrier* among them—lead from Rue du Mont Blanc. *Parc d'Ariana* is one of several parks to the north that more or less enclose the complex of *Palais des Nations*—European headquarters of the United Nations—and a number of other international organization headquarters (below).

Cathedral of St.-Pierre (Place de la Taconnerie)—high on a hill and a Geneva landmark these many centuries—is visitworthy, first because it is where Calvin (above) preached to the Genevans nearly four and a half centuries ago (you may see his chair—designated as *La Chaise de Calvin*—*1535* and quite as spindly and uncomfortable-appearing as you would expect— just before you reach the transept, on the left; and second, because it is such an interesting architectural mix. The span is extraordinary, with walls of the nave twelfth-century Romanesque; its west (or principal) front (out back, if you've entered on the side, from Place de la Taconnerie), a surprising eighteenth-century classic-style portico supported by five Corinthian columns; the interior of its eastern portion—transept, high altar, side chapels—essentially Gothic; its towers fourteenth-sixteenth centuries and its steeple, turn of the twentieth century—replacing a Gothic original. The cathedral is at its best, certainly for me, in the nave, flanked by Gothic arches and

topped by Gothic vaults. Although I have to add that the neoclassic west entrance—built to replace the then-crumbling
original facade, at a time when medieval architecture was
looked at askance—works very well indeed. It is important to
note, too, that the area excavated in the course of the cathedral's
recent decade-long restoration (1976–1986) is an archeological
museum embracing the entire area beneath the building,
chockablock with treasures—sculpture, architectural fragments, and the like—that span much of the city's history.

Auditoire de Calvin (Place de la Taconnerie)—the cathedral's
next-door neighbor—is an originally Gothic structure that has
been heavily restored, and is an overseas property of the Church
of Scotland (Edinburgh's John Knox lived in Geneva, as I point
out above) with a plaque within that reads, in translation: "In
this nave, Jean Calvin taught theology from 1552 to 1564, and
his doctrine illuminated the entire world." The hall is now
multifunction, concerts among these.

Musée d'Art et d'Histoire (Rue Charles Galland)—occupying
an impressive Beaux-Arts building with Ionic capitals topping
the dozen pilasters of its facade—is one of Switzerland's Big
Four, right up there with Basel's Kunstmuseum (Chapter 2),
Zürich's Kunsthaus (Chapter 20), and Lugano's Collection
Thyssen Bornemisza (Chapter 13). It abounds in special treats.
Period rooms for starters: a seventeenth-century paneled salon;
still another brimming with Baroque Italian furniture; the reception room of a nearby château transported *in toto*—crystal
chandeliers, walls of gray-hued *boiserie*, an entire suite of gray-
upholstered Louis XVI furniture; and—among others—Salle du
Conseil, council chamber of Hôtel de Ville, the City Hall, its
walls Beauvais-tapestried, its furniture Louis XVI, its paintings
by Largillière and Nattier, the ensemble constituting one of the
loveliest such of any that I know in Europe's museums. Paintings, then. The French, right next door to Geneva, are well
represented. *Sabina Poppaea*, a beautiful woman painted—from
the waist up and attired only in transparent gauze—by an unknown School of Fontainebleau painter of the sixteenth century,
is museum mascot. On hand, too, are Philippe de Champaigne,

Simon Vouet, Quentin de La Tour from the Renaissance; pre-Impressionists including Corot, Delacroix, and Géricault; Boudin, Sisley, and Renoir representing the Impressionists; Bonnard, Vuillard, Dufy, Roualt, and Picasso from among their successors. The Dutch come on strong: a Rembrandt of the artist's mother, Maes and Pourbus, Avercamp and Hobbema. But you remember, as well, Veronese's *Entombment of Christ,* Juan de Flandes's *St. John the Baptist,* and Conrad Witz's *Miracle of the Fishermen.* Swiss work represents a veritable survey of painting in the Confederation. If you haven't encountered them already, you get to know Cuno Amiet and Giovanni Giacometti. And I suspect not even Bern's Kunstmuseum does as well by diversely talented Ferdinand Hodler, who was born in Bern in 1853, and died in Geneva in 1918; his *Lac de Thoune*—with the mountains above Lake Thun reflected in its waters—is probably the most celebrated of his Geneva works. Sculpture is hardly neglected—a rich cache of Rodin figures, a Lemoyne bust of onetime Geneva resident Voltaire, a Houdon head of Geneva-born Necker, a Pradier bust of native son Jean Jacques Rousseau. And the galleries of ancient Egyptian, Greek, Roman art—beautiful installations the lot of them—are the most impressive such in Switzerland.

Musée du Petit Palais (2 Terrasse St.-Victor) is accorded space at this point principally because of its location a couple of blocks to the rear of Musée d'Art et d'Histoire (above). This is a private collection (you pay to enter) in a multistory townhouse, and although anticlimactic—to understate—after the Art and History Museum, it is not without familiar masters' works. There's a sprinkling of Impressionists, including Renoir, Cézanne, and Toulouse-Lautrec, somewhat later French artists like Utrillo, Marquet, and Marie Laurencin, and more recent masters, including Van Dongen, Soutine, Dufy, and Picasso.

Musée de l'Horlogerie (15 Route de Malagnou): Watches in museums—even lovely antique watches—have a way of looking like merchandise in curio shops. Geneva's Watch Museum is an exception to this rule: an enchanting spot that charms from without—setting is Villa Malagnou, an early nineteenth-century mock-Palladian villa—and contains a series of galleries, the lot of them intimate in scale and a perfect foil for a collection (originally housed in Musée d'Art et d'Histoire) that is at once scientifically significant and perfectly beautiful. Time span is late sixteenth through late nineteenth centuries, the collection mostly but not entirely Genevan. The museum's goal—achieved in spades—is to show how watchmaking developed in the mid-sixteenth century with the advent of the Reformation, when the city drew skilled artisan-Protestants fleeing not only France but other European lands, as well. Because Calvinist authorities forbade the manufacture of "crosses, chalices and other instruments serving popery or idolatry"—to quote the museum's English-language catalogue—they turned to watches, in cases "that were superb pieces of jewelry." And so began Geneva's watchmaking industry. You'll see a 1580 table clock and a covered pocket watch of the same era, a watch embedded in a gold cross with a hinged rock-crystal cover; exquisitely enameled cases for eighteenth-century movements; a series of complex astronomical clocks, a clutch of wall clocks, including one from Paris in gilt bronze and green tortoiseshell, dated 1780, that's a museum masterwork. The early nineteenth century work becomes neoclassical, assuming mock-Rococo contours in later decades. And the enamels—snuffboxes and miniature portraits, especially—are winners, too.

Musée d'Histoire Naturelle (a.k.a. just plain *Museum;* Route de Malagnou, next door to *Musée de l'Horlogerie,* above): I said before I visited this museum's counterpart in Bern (Chapter 3) that natural history museums are for kids—and had to eat my words, so absolutely fabulous are its animal dioramas. I must say ditto, with respect to similar exhibits in this boldly contemporary museum. Range is fauna of Africa (towering giraffes) through animals of Europe (also-towering bears), beyond to smaller-scaled birds, *chouettes,* or owls, especially. Cafeteria.

Musée Voltaire (25 Rue des Délices) is quartered in the handsome house where Voltaire lived for a full decade, 1755–1765. You go first if you are a Voltaire enthusiast, second if you're an enthusiast of the eighteenth century. There are two rooms brimming with furniture of that era (including Voltaire's desk, with a look-alike mannequin of the philosopher seated at it, and dressed in a Voltaire costume). There are as well interpretations of Voltaire in a bust by Houdon and a portrait by Largillière, with first editions and other Voltairiana in an adjacent library.

Musée Jean Jacques Rousseau et Musée Historique de la Réformation share quarters in Salle Lullin, a room in the public library, or Bibliothèque Publique, on *Promenade des Bastions*. The former is indicated for Rousseau buffs, with manuscripts, correspondence, first editions, prints, and— Exhibit No. 1—Rousseau's death mask. The latter features portraits of Calvin, painted during his lifetime, and of his contemporaries in the Reform movement, along with mementos, medals, and manuscripts.

Musée Ariana (Avenue de la Paix; Parc de l'Ariana) is a palatial neoclassic pavilion—centered by a two-story *galerie*, dome-topped. It's situated in the park taking its name and shelters an all-Europe ranker of a porcelain collection: a blue and white coffee service, each piece of which is rimmed in gold—from early nineteenth-century Paris; a gaily embellished Delft cow, its neck garlanded with painted flowers, its rump accented in shades of blue; Swiss mid-nineteenth century tableware, the dinner plates embellished with black-and-white scenes of city squares. And a bonus of massive and magnificent porcelain stoves.

Musée d'Éthnographie (65 Boulevard Carl Vogt) may or may not be of interest; you've seen ethnographic collections at home, no doubt, but if you're game for more—some 17,000 objects— Indonesian masks through Thai Buddhas—from Africa, the Americas, Asia, the South Pacific, and the folk cultures of Europe as well, the Ethnographic Museum is visitworthy.

Musée Rath (Place Neuve) is a veritable Greek temple, heart-of-town, that is not so much a museum as a space for temporary art exhibitions. Hotel concierges and *La Semaine à Genève*—the weekly what's-on guide—will have details on the current show, if any.

International Organizations are quartered north of the center in the neighborhood of Parc de l'Ariana (above). *Palais des Nations*—built to house the League of Nations in the early 1930s, and since the end of World War II European headquarters of the United Nations—closed its doors to visitors in the mid-1980s, during the Secretary Generalship of Javier Perez de Cuellar. Should it have reopened by the time of your visit, you'll no doubt follow a tour guide who will take you through Salle des Pas Perdus, the lobby, with smashing views from it of Lac Léman and Mont Blanc; the 1,800-seat Assembly Hall, Council Chamber with murals by the Spanish painter José María Sert, other of whose murals line the walls of the big lobby of 30 Rockefeller Plaza in New York's Rockefeller Center, and a pair of museums, one devoted to the history of the ill-fated League of Nations, the other to stamps—those of the UN in particular. The globelike sculpture out front was a gift to the League of Nations in 1939 from the Woodrow Wilson Foundation, in memory of the American president who founded the League; its design represents signs of the zodiac and it's the work of the late U.S. sculptor, Paul Manship.

Among other international organizations in this quarter are the open-to-visitors *International Committee of the Red Cross* (with the look of a rather grand turn-of-century hotel, at 7 Avenue de la Paix), *International Labor Office* (4 Route des Morillons), *World Health Organization* (20 Avenue Appia), and *World Council of Churches* (150 Route de Ferne). *Missions to the UN* of both the *United States* and of the *Soviet Union* are in the neighborhood (you can identify each by the flags) with that of the USSR—hardly celebrated for its contemporary architecture—surprisingly the better looking of the pair.

SETTLING IN

RIVE DROITE/RIGHT BANK

De La Paix Hôtel (11 Quai du Mont Blanc; Phone 32-61-50) is at once an enchanter of a period piece—erected to the plans of an

Italian architect in 1865—and a sprightly, of-this-very-moment hostelry. What dazzles the just-arrived guest is the atrium-lobby, marble-columned and hung with a giant crystal chandelier that extends from the ceiling six stories downward. Lounges adjacent charm with original nineteenth-century furnishings. There are 106 rooms and ten suites, pleasantly traditional, no two of them alike. Some overlook verdant Square du Mont Blanc; others—the ones to aim for, in my view—give onto Jet d'Eau in the lake, with the mountains beyond. There's a delightful bar, adjacent salon (where drinks are also served), restaurant worthy of comment on a later page, and a staff—mostly long on scene—that is alert, attentive, and agreeable. Special. Member, Leading Hotels of the World. *Luxury.*

Le Richemond Hôtel (Jardin Brunswick at Quai du Mont Blanc; Phone 31-14-00): The high proportion of suites to rooms—30 of the former against 75 of the latter—gives you an idea of what the Richemond is all about. It's been operated by successive generations of the Armleder family since it opened in 1875, just a decade after its across-the-square neighbor, the De La Paix (above). I suspect that if there's an Armleder motto, it's "Attention to Detail" translated into Latin and inscribed on a coat of arms. The doorman greets every guest who enters with a smile. A coffered ceiling, in the style of the Renaissance, frames the humming lobby. Decor style and color varies in public areas—spacious lounge that's red-walled and red-upholstered; bar in tones of mahogany, brown, and gold; restaurant (later evaluated and one of several including a terrace-café) that is a classy variation on a theme of paisley. Corridor walls are surfaced in pink-and-red toile, a foil for red velvet panels on doors leading into rooms. All accommodations that I've inspected—standard singles through sumptuous suites—are winners, their baths included. Member, Leading Hotels of the World. *Luxury.*

Du Rhône Hôtel (Quai Turrettini; Phone 31-98-31)—long, sleek, and low-slung—borders the Right Bank of the Rhône, and manages to combine extraordinary creativity—its own solar energy installation, a Staff Training Center that is an all-Switzerland model of its kind, ingeniously designed minibars in its rooms that are slid through wall openings into corridors for daily refills, obviating the need for attendants to enter rooms in the course of daily rounds. This is a modishly modern 280-room house. Interesting color accents combine with burled wood, brass lamps, and tasteful textiles in both suites and rooms, the most desirable of which face the water, with the mountains as a backdrop. There are a pair of respected restaurants, lobby-lounge with striking semiabstract tapestries, and a terrace-café. Member, Leading Hotels of the World. *Luxury.*

Des Bergues Hôtel (33 Quai des Bergues; Phone 31-50-50)— not unlike the De La Paix and Le Richemond (above) and the Beau Rivage (below)—is a pioneer of the grand-hotels cluster facing the lake on the Right Bank. It goes all the way back to the third decade of the last century. Trusthouse Forte Hotels, its Britain-based operators, deserve high marks for the skill with which they have remodeled it, stem to stern, in the style—Biedermeier/Regency, you might call it—of its period of construction. Management tells me that the most popular of its 120 rooms and suites are the compact singles favored by business travelers, apparently the bulk of its clientele. There are, of course, larger accommodations—doubles and suites—as well, understatedly good-looking in subdued tones of green, beige, and brown, with those to aim for in the front—facing the lake and Mont Blanc. Amphitryon, the principal restaurant and later evaluated, is one of Geneva's best-looking interior spaces; there are, as well, a casual café and a bar whose *plats du jour* are locally esteemed. A Trusthouse Forte Exclusive Division hotel. *Luxury.*

Beau Rivage Hôtel (13 Quai du Mont Blanc; Phone 31-02-21) takes its history seriously enough to have created an on-premises museum whose exhibits delineate its background—extending over a century and a quarter. A component part of the early-bird waterfront group—along with the De La Paix, Richemond, and Des Bergues—it has managed to update where essential—superb baths, for example—the while retaining, despite periodic refurbishings, style and ambience of the last century. Not unlike the De La Paix, it greets guests in a lobby that's a spectacular six-story atrium. Public spaces, still with much of their original furniture, are a pleasure: the bar is dark-paneled; Louis XIV-style chairs with tapestrylike covering surround tables of Le Chat Botté Restaurant; there's a café—Quai 13—for casual sustenance (it's reviewed on a later page); and 120 no-two-alike rooms and suites. Those I have inspected are good-size and good-looking, with front ones—facing the lake and the Alps—the most desirable. *Luxury.*

Président Hôtel (47 Quai Wilson; Phone 31-10-00) is located on the Right Bank waterfront thoroughfare that's an extension of closer-to-the-center Quai du Mont Blanc. You don't expect the interior of a hotel with so modern a facade to sport traditional interiors that so evoke earlier Geneva eras. Massive brass chandeliers cast just the proper amount of illumination on antique tapestries which embellish paneled walls of an especially felicitous lobby. There's a pair of restaurants (picture-windowed Grill Room, wickery Café La Palmeraie), a bar with satin-upholstered easy chairs, and accommodations—160 rooms, 30 suites, with super baths—whose decor is based on Louis XV- and Louis XVI-style furnishings. A link of the Swissôtel chain, a subsidiary of Swissair. *Luxury.*

Inter-Continental Genève Hôtel (7 Chemin du Petit Saconnex; Phone 34-60-91) is the closest of the luxury hotels to the United Nations/International Organizations quarter. It serves—and very well—as a home away from home for heads of state, diplomats, assorted international bigwigs, and just plain travelers who enjoy headquartering in this absorbing part of the city. This is a big house—eighteen stories, with broadly scaled public spaces—you ascend to the main lobby by means of a pair of escalators—that include a softly lit, nicely rambling bar-lounge, pair of restaurants (oak-paneled, crystal-chandeliered Louis XV-furnished Les Continents, sprightly La Pergola [try its buffet Wednesday evenings]), as well as a jumbo swimming pool-cum-café in the garden. The extraordinary Presidential Suite is comprised of a living room that could be a ballroom, pair of oversized bedrooms, one of whose baths has a giant sunken tub, formal dining room, several baths, and kitchen. The remaining 31 suites are somewhat less gala, and there are, as well, 321 rooms, relatively recently refurbished in smart period style. *Luxury.*

Ramada Renaissance Hôtel (Rue de Zürich; Phone 31-02-41) —inland from the lake—catches one up with its sleek mirrored facade. Inside is something else again—a big peachy-buff lobby based on traditional motifs, off which lead a stylish bar and a pair of worth-knowing-about restaurants, one of which—later reviewed—is celebrated for buffet dinners. Those of the 219 rooms and suites I've inspected successfully mix classic motifs with modern, and they're spacious. Friendly. *Luxury.*

Ambassador Hôtel (21 Quai des Bergues; Phone 31-72-00) is nicely located on the Right Bank waterfront. A good-value restaurant and bar lead from the big lobby, and those of the 92 rooms I have inspected—those facing lake and mountains especially—are pleasant. *First Class.*

D'Angleterre Hôtel (17 Quai de Mont Blanc; Phone 32-81-80) is a satisfactorily updated oldie, lakefront, with bright public spaces, and 45 rooms; those giving onto the water are preferred. Restaurant, bar. *First Class.*

Du Midi Hôtel (Place Chevelu; Phone 31-78-00), a bit in from the lake, is attractively modern, with 85 plaid-accented rooms, small but inviting, and several restaurants including a brasserie that moves to umbrella-covered tables out front in good weather. Nice. *First Class.*

Warwick Hôtel (14 Rue de Lausanne; Phone 31-62-50) is the Geneva outpost of the chain whose name it takes; you may know the New York Warwick or the Paris Warwick. This one— just opposite the railway station and Swissair terminal—is relatively recently refurbished, with close to 120 well-planned (if not overlarge) rooms with excellent baths, a pair of restaurants (Les Quatre Saisons features nouvelle cuisine; the other's a brasserie with good-value prix-fixe menus) and a lively piano bar. The staff is one of Geneva's most engaging. *First Class.*

Cristal Hôtel (4 Rue Pradier; Phone 31-34-00) is a near neighbor of the railway station and Rue du Mont Blanc shops. There is a light, bright look to this house, both in public spaces (including a white-walled restaurant with white-painted bentwood chairs) and in those of the 59 rooms I have inspected. *First Class.*

Epsom Hôtel (18 Rue Richemond; Phone 32-08-35) is a fair distance away from the center, on a nondescript street off Quai Wilson. Public spaces include a restaurant and bar, and are generous size if not inviting; those of the 165 rooms I inspected are hardly more felicitous, and reception staff is the least accommodating I have encountered in Geneva; groups, traditionally from the U.S. and Spain, comprise the bulk of the clientele. I can't recommend this one. *First Class.*

Savoy Hotel (8 Place Cornavin; Phone 32-22-31) is adequate for overnight if you require accommodation near the train station, just opposite. Forty rooms, restaurant, bar. So-so. *First Class.*

Alba Hôtel (19 Rue du Mont Blanc; Phone 32-68-51) is at its best with respect to location; fronting the pedestrian section of Rue du Mont Blanc, and near the train station. Those of the 50 rooms I have inspected are satisfactory. Bar and breakfast but no restaurant. *First Class.*

California Hôtel (1 Rue Gevray; Phone 31-50-50)—on a quiet street a block inland from Quai du Mont Blanc, is well worth the walk to the waterfront; those of the 40 rooms I have inspected are colorfully contemporary, and some have kitchenettes. The roof garden is a pleasure in summer, and there's a bar but no restaurant. *Moderate.*

Strasbourg-Univers Hôtel (10 Rue Pradier; Phone 31-39-20) offers 40 neat rooms, a cozy lounge-bar, and a convenient restaurant, with location just opposite the train station, off Rue du Mont Blanc. *Moderate.*

Balzac Hôtel (14 Rue de l'Ancien Port; Phone 31-01-60) is convenient for visitors to the UN/International Organizations area, a couple of blocks from Quai Wilson and the lake. There are just 40 rooms, nicely furnished and mostly spacious. Bar and breakfast but no restaurant. *Moderate.*

RIVE GAUCHE/LEFT BANK

Metropole Hôtel (34 Quai Général Guisan; Phone 21-13-44) is Grande Dame of the Left Bank—a Belle Époque beauty that emerged in the early 1980s, after a $17 million renovation-refurbishing directed by General Manager André Hauri and his wife, Malihé, following a struggle—by concerned citizens—of nearly two decades to preserve it. A marble stairway leads into the lobby, with ceilings of stained glass. The cocktail lounge is an Art Deco dazzler. There's a pair of restaurants—smart Arlequin (later reviewed) and amusing Café Grand Quai. Those of the 140 rooms and suites that I have inspected stun with smartness. Suites, in pastel tones accented by contemporary textiles, are furnished in a marvelous mélange, the range formal Regency through brass bedsteads. The distinctively decorated rooms, based on Louis XV and Louis XVI, are similarly bright and inventive. And views can be either of the Old Town or the lake and mountains. Distinguished Hotels/Robert F. Warner. *Luxury.*

Les Armures Hôtel (1 Rue Puits-St.-Pierre; Phone 28-91-72)—known as much for its restaurant (below) as its rooms—is small but choice. Les Armures is an instant transplant to the seventeenth century, with location appropriately in the Old Town. The lobby-lounge/bar, with its painted ceiling, sets the tone. Rooms—only 28 of them—feature wood-beamed ceilings and Baroque-style furnishings. And the restaurant warrants comment in a later paragraph. Friendly. *Luxury.*

De La Cigogne Hôtel (17 Place Longemalle; Phone 21-42-42) is heart of the Left Bank, off shop-lined Rue du Rhône. It occupies a pair of contiguous townhouses, relatively recently converted to their present use. The lobby is antique-dotted and charming, with an intimate restaurant and bar, and the half a hundred rooms are in a range of periods—some Baroque with four-poster beds, others in the style of the eighteenth century. *Luxury.*

Touring Balance Hôtel (Place Longemalle; Phone 28-71-22) is enviably well situated—on a square between the waterfront and the Old Town, a hop and a skip from shops of Rue du Rhône. Despite its aged facade, the look within is contemporary, with half a hundred functional rooms and an up-a-flight restaurant. *Moderate.*

DAILY BREAD

RIVE DROITE/RIGHT BANK

La Mère Royaume (41 Rue des Corps Saints; Phone 20-08-07) is visitable as much for its ambience—high ceilings, wood-beamed, with immense windows of stained glass—and its name (La Mère Royaume was folk heroine of an early seventeenth-century battle in which Genevans were victors against the Duke of Savoy's troops), as for its cuisine. The à la carte—based on classic French fare with Swiss overtones—is extensive. But the prix-fixe menu is better value. You might open with a crayfish salad or, if it's in season, asparagus dressed with a delicious *Mousseline* sauce; go on to broiled lamb chops, rosemary-scented, or the day's fish, concluding with cheeses offered from a big platter, or a choice of pastries. Zippy service. *First Class.*

Au Fin Bec (Rue de Berne 55; Phone 32-29-19) has for long been as popular with Genevans as with visitors. Comfortably old school, it makes a point of traditional dishes deliciously cooked and graciously served. Dinner might open with *quenelles de brochet*—minced fresh fish in fingersized timbales, expertly sauced; follow with veal steak and French fries, concluding with a rich dessert. Friendly. *First Class.*

De La Paix Hôtel Restaurant (11 Quai du Mont Blanc; Phone 32-61-60) is the prototypical grand hotel dining room, illuminated by crystal chandeliers, with a central buffet brimming with hors d'oeuvres and salads to tickle your palate, caned Louis XV-style chairs surrounding tables centered by bowls of red roses. The time to go is lunch—when the well-priced prix-fixe menu tempts. A salad based on *confit de canard*—preserved duck—might serve as appetizer, a *friture* of lake fish might follow, with roast beef generously garnished (a *gratin* of leeks is one of the chef's vegetable specialties) as an entrée, and desserts as selected by you—from a groaning chariot. *First Class* for the prix-fixe lunch; *Luxury* otherwise.

Amphitryon (Des Bergues Hôtel; 33 Quai des Bergues; Phone 31-50-50)—relatively recently redecorated in the style of the nineteenth century's earlier decades, and with paintings of art-gallery caliber—does not disappoint, with respect to either ambience or cuisine. The chef comes up with daily specials—terrine of duck liver or seafood-stuffed ravioli as openers; truffled breast of chicken or fennel-flavored lamb as entrées. And the regular à la carte is authentically French. Especially festive at dinner. *Luxury.*

Bistrot du Gentilhomme (Le Richemond Hôtel, Jardin Brunswick; Phone 31-14-00) is the restaurant which adjoins the Richemond's No. 1 eatery, Le Gentilhomme, but has a bill of fare of its own, and with lower tabs. It's fun to have a glass of wine at the bar first with, perhaps, steak tartare to accompany. If it's lunchtime, roast beef, generously garnished, is reasonably priced and tasty. But there are other options, omelets through pasta. (And if the day is warm and sunny, consider still another Richemond restaurant—the less expensive *Le Jardin,* with tables outside on its terrace.) Both are *First Class.*

Quai Treize (Beau Rivage Hôtel, 13 Quai du Mont Blanc; Phone 31-02-21): Clientele is heavily local—Genevans at midday come for the bargain-priced and delicious lunch-only buffet. At that time, *Moderate;* otherwise, *First Class.*

Vieux Bois (12 Avenue de la Paix; Phone 33-03-30) is a sensible lunchtime choice (it is open only for the midday meal, usually from noon to 3:00 P.M.) in the course of a morning ambling about the International Organizations neighborhood. It's a branch of the Geneva Hotel School; chefs and waiters are all in training, under close supervision, with the result reasonable tabs and invariably delicious vittles. Attractive. *First Class.*

Mövenpick Cendrier (17 Rue du Cendrier; Phone 32-50-30) is a link of the Switzerland-wide chain, with its up-a-flight restaurant specializing in U.S.-imported beef; order it traditionally roasted or—tasty, this—*steak au poivre*, pepper-sauced and accompanied by *gratin Dauphinois*. Sprightly service. *First Class.*

La Cortile (Ramada Renaissance Hôtel, Rue de Zürich; Phone 31-02-41): The draw here—a handsome room in a handsome hotel—is the copious buffet, its range salads in profusion through hot entrées of beef, poultry, and seafood, with a generous choice of desserts as well. Go with an appetite. *First Class.*

Manora (Rue Cornavin; Phone 31-31-46) might fill the bill for, say, a quick lunch prior to departure by train from the nearby station. This is a cafeteria with a gardenlike decor, and chockablock with good-looking and good-tasting things to eat, appetizers through sweets. *Moderate.*

Chez Pouly (2 Rue Rousseau; Phone 32-08-89) is one of a number of Pouly outlets around town; prime lure is pastry, in tandem with coffee or to conclude a light lunch. *Moderate.*

RIVE GAUCHE/LEFT BANK

Eaux Vives (Parc des Eaux Vives, a 10- or 12-minute drive from the center; Phone 35-41-40): Select a sunny day for this one. Your destination is a honey of an eighteenth-century house in a verdant park edging the lake. If it's warm, an aperitif on the lawn is in order. Then order from one of a number of prix-fixe menus. Best buys are at lunch, when you might open with a crab and shrimp salad, continue with sautéed frogs' legs (an Eaux Vives specialty), continuing with a filet of beef deliciously garnished, and concluding with one of a choice of spectacular sweets. Service can be patronizing, but the setting is so idyllic, the antiques-filled interiors so tasteful, and the food so good, that I consider this one of Switzerland's best restaurants. *First Class/Luxury.*

Les Armures (1 Rue Puits-St.-Pierre; Phone 28-91-72)—heart of the Old Town and in an above-counseled hotel of the same name—is as good a choice as I know for a typically Swiss dinner. Open with *raclette*, sliced heated cheese served with boiled potatoes and sour gherkins. Follow with a fish course—Les Armures is proud of its filet of perch—or *émincé de veau à la crème*—Switzerland's beloved veal specialty, served with *rösti* potatoes. An option, though, is *fondue* as a main course; each member of your party dips chunks of French bread, affixed to long forks, into the hot melted cheese centered on the table. Mind that the bread does not fall off the fork into the *fondue;* if it does, tradition decrees that you buy a round of drinks for your party. *First Class.*

L'Arlequin (Metropole Hôtel, 34 Quai Général Guisan; Phone 21-13-44)—illuminated by silk-shaded chandeliers, with blue candles in silver sticks centering its tables—is a gala venue for a River Gauche dinner. Captains start guests off with *amuse-gueules*—a plateful of tiny hot canapes to whet your appetite. Choose either the prix-fixe menu—opening, for example, with lobster salad, with a chicken casserole as entrée, and a choice of desserts. Or zero in on L'Arlequin's No. 1 favorite: Roast beef sliced from a wagon wheeled to table and served with *gratin Dauphinois* and the day's fresh vegetables. Service is cordial. *First Class.*

Roberto (10 Rue Pierre-Fatio; Phone 21-80-80): Restaurants specializing in Italian food don't appear to be as prevalent in Geneva as in other major Swiss cities. No matter; Roberto—near the east end of Rue du Rhône—compensates. Open with *antipasto misto* or any of a number of pastas, selecting a veal entrée and concluding, if you've appetite enough, with a typical dessert like *zabaione*. Congenial. *First Class.*

Brasserie aux Maîtres (6 Rue de la Fontaine; Phone 21-97-58) is an atmospheric Old Town source of steak—prepared half a dozen ways, with salad to accompany. Caveat: no credit cards. *Moderate.*

Grand Passage (Rue du Rhône; Phone 20-66-11): Geneva's No. 1 department store will feed you in its waitress-service *Restaurant* (with good-value prix-fixe menus), its less pricey *Snack,* or its *Pizzeria.* The first mentioned is especially pleasant. *Moderate.*

Le Béarn (4 Quai de la Poste; Phone 21-00-28) occupies a pair of not especially distinguished appearing rooms—one is red and white; the other with walls covered in floral-design paper—and offers the choice of ordering from its very costly prix-fixe menu (embracing, for example, *foie gras* as an opener, the day's fish, a duck entrée with cheese and a sweet) or à la carte. A house specialty, raw salmon *tartare,* is offered as an *amuse-gueule* or appetizer (you have to like raw fish in an oily sauce to find this appetizing). The cream of asparagus soup is satisfactory, as are fish entrées. One wants to be *really* into nouvelle cuisine to be a Béarn fan; I am not. And service, though efficient, is on the chilly side. *Luxury.*

Chocolaterie du Rhône (3 Rue de la Confédération; Phone 21-56-14) is nicely situated—on an extension of central Rue du Marché—as a stopping point for coffee or tea with pastry. You may—or may not—be able to escape without purchasing a box of house-made chocolates. Excepting the chocolates (which are expensive): *Moderate.*

SOUND OF MUSIC
Grand Théâtre (Place Neuve) is Geneva's evocatively Belle Époque opera house—*Tannhäuser* through *Falstaff.* It's the setting, as well, for performances by its own dance troupe, *Ballet du Grand Théâtre,* and other entertainment. And mini-concerts and recitals are held in its *Foyer.*

Victoria Hall (Boulevard Georges Favon) is still another nineteenth-century spectacular, a near neighbor of Grand Théâtre (above) and home base—in its marvelously mock-Baroque auditorium—of *Orchestre de la Suisse Romande,* the Geneva symphony which gained global fame during the long conductorship of the late Ernest Ansermet (and which visits other Swiss cities on tours).

The same orchestra plays at other Geneva locales, including *Grand Casino* (Quai du Mont Blanc), which hosts visiting orchestras and ballet companies. Other concert venues include *Cathédrale Saint-Pierre*, its neighbor, *Auditoire de Calvin*, and in summer, *Cour de l'Hôtel de Ville* (the City Hall courtyard). *What's on in Geneva*, a monthly English-language giveaway (available at the tourist office, below) and *Geneva News*, a monthly English-language magazine, publish schedules.

SHOPPER'S GENEVA

The No. 1 department store, *Grand Passage*, is on the Left Bank's main shopping street, Rue du Rhône, and goes through to the parallel street, Rue du Marché. You'll find inexpensive watches and chocolate, as well as a souvenir department on main, a supermarket on two; there are excellent clothing, home furnishings, and housewares departments as well, and several restaurants (above). Another department store, *Placette*, is on the Right Bank's Rue de Coutance. Because it is in the Confederation's principal watchmaking region, and because it abounds in moneybags visitors, Geneva is Switzerland's No. 1 source of *watches*. If I were to have a look at one of the flossiest stores, it would be that in the headquarters building of *Patek Philippe* (22 Quai Général Guisan), where you're comfortably seated and attended to by one of a gracious multilingual staff, happy to take all of the time you may require to purchase one of that firm's extravagant timepieces. Other interesting watch sources include *Les Ambassadeurs* (20 Quai Général Guisan and other locations), with Audemars, Piguet, and Omega among its specialties, and with good-value lesser-price watches with its own label; *B & B*, (10 Quai du Mont Blanc) with Cartier watches; *Bücherer* (45 Rue du Rhône and other locations), a link of the nationwide chain, with many makes including its own, which tend to be lower in cost; *Golay Fils & Stahl* (1 Place des Bergues—with jewelry as well); and *Vacheron Constantin* (1 Rue des Moulins en l'Île). This is, as well, a *jewelry* city of special—if I may say so— brilliance. Consider such sources as *Adler, Alexandre Reza, Eric Beathaud, Boucheron* (all on Rue du Rhône); *Chayto* (31 Quai du Général Guisan), *Van Cleef & Arpels* (12 Quai du Général Guisan and other locations, including New York), *Via Gioielli* (17 Rue de la Rôtisserie), and *Marina B* (Place du Molard, and with a New York branch).

Clothing stores are hardly in short supply. Walk down Rue du Rhône and you'll come across *Valentino, Claude Montana, Christian Dior, Chanel, Lanvin, Chlöe, Céline, Blue Marine,* and *Gianfranco Ferre*—among others. On nearby Rue du Marché and streets leading from it, there are such shops as *Bally* and *Charles Jourdan* (both for shoes); *Franz Carl Weber* (toys); *Gucci* (clothes, leather accessories); *Collet* (silver); *Bon Génie* (women's clothes); and *L'Homme* (for men). Other noteworthy stores include *Naville* (books, including English language, Place Gorcière); *Sturzenegger* (embroideries and linens, 19 Rue du Rhône); *Frette* (Italian linens, 5 Rue Céard); *Jenny* (Rue Kléberg) and *Rohr* (42 Rue du Rhône)—both for chocolate; *Touzeau* (porcelain and crystal, 3 Rue du Mont Blanc); *Fauchon* (a branch of the Paris-based fancy-food chain, 6 Cours de Rive); *Impérial Fourrures* (furs, 35 Rue de Rhône); *Fontaine* (15 Rue de la Confédération, with Christofle French silver and Limoges porcelain); *Souleiado* (2 Grand Rue, a branch of a French textile chain with Provençal cotton prints); and *Christie's* (8 Place de la Taconnerie), a branch of the London-based auction house, with jewelry its principal specialty.

INCIDENTAL INTELLIGENCE

Swissair flies to Geneva's Aéroport de Genève-Cointrin, from which there is direct train service (with frequent departures from a futuristic rail terminal that opened in mid-1987) not only to Geneva's central Gare Cornavin (travel time: six minutes), but to the neighboring lakeshore cities of Lausanne (Chapter 10) and Montreux (Chapter 14), as well as Bern (Chapter 3), the federal capital. The tourist office (below) has timetables of Compagnie Générale de Navigation and other boat operators which operate excursion steamers to various Lac Léman points, including Lausanne and Montreux. *Further information:* Office de Tourisme, Tour de l'Île, Geneva, and with an accommodations counter in Gare Cornavin.

7

Grindelwald
Gateway to the Jungfrau

BACKGROUND BRIEFING

Fascination with the plethora of peaks in the Bernese Oberland—that area of west-central Switzerland as richly endowed with azure lakes and verdant valleys as with magnificent mountains—dates back several centuries. Only in the early decades of the nineteenth, though, did a pair of determined Swiss brothers, Meyer by name, succeed in climbing the 13,642-foot Jungfrau. The year was 1811.

The 12,409-foot summit of the not-far-distant Breithorn was reached a few years later. Only in 1858 was the 13,025-foot summit of Mt. Eiger conquered. Before long, the intrepid English were on scene, basing themselves in the neighborhood of the Alpine village called Grindelwald, a mixed bag of climbers (men ascending the lower peaks on horseback, women being toted about by porters in mountain-style sedan chairs), painters, and even poets.

Then, in the early 1890s, the railways' brilliant engineer-designer teams set to work with extraordinary success. The first section of the Jungfrau Railway was operating in 1898, and by 1912 it had reached Jungfraujoch, the Jungfrau's satellite peak, at an elevation of 13,333 feet. It was then—and remains today—Europe's highest railway station. And it opened the region to the nonmountaineer visitor. All you needed to do was board a train to reach one of the more exalted of the Alpine summits.

Happily, that is still the case. And succeeding decades have seen Grindelwald become the takeoff point—by means of cable cars, chair lifts and, for that matter, roads—for Kleine Scheidegg (the hotel-equipped mountain station midpoint between Grindelwald and Jungfraujoch); First (gained by a fabulous, half-hour duration chairlift for winter skiing and summer strolls); Pfingstegg (via a swift, seven-minute cableway, with views from its observation terrace of Grindelwald's massive Oberer and Unterer glaciers—within hiking distance); Grindelwald Glacier Gorge (a natural wonderland seen from a deck high above the Lütchine River); the attractive resort villages of Mürren (beneath nearly 10,000-foot Mt. Schilthorn) and Wengen (a near neighbor of Mt. Männlichen, 7,300-feet plus); and—last but hardly least—Jungfraujoch, just beneath Jungfrau proper—the region's highest peak.

ON SCENE

Lay of the Land: Consider Grindelwald an essentially one-street town. Running west to east, *Haupstrasse*'s landmarks are the *Bahnhof* near its west end, *Sportzentrum*—a massive and modern complex boasting a giant swimming pool, gargantuan ice rink, curling hall, fitness and games rooms, sauna, and massage; along with the *Post Office* (a major congregating venue), restaurants, cafés, and shops in the center; and—at the east end, next to the pretty single-steeple Protestant church, *Grindelwald Museum* (in traditional chalet-style quarters, with the range of exhibits regional furniture, crafts, and household implements through to historic displays recounting area eminence in mountaineering and skiing). Most hotels are in the village, although some lie beyond it. The tourist office, which celebrated its 100th anniversary in 1985 and can, therefore, claim some expertise, reckons that with Grindelwald's facilities for skiers—a pair of cable cars, 7 chair lifts, 9 cogwheel trains, and 22 ski lifts—the total lift capacity is 26,800 persons per hour. And summer visitors are not neglected; there are some 25 splendidly scenic miles of walking paths.

An excursion sampler: A day-long excursion to *Jungfraujoch* is without any question the most requisite, and for that matter, the most effortless. You go up the coward's way—by train. It's a leisurely ascent from the village with a stop halfway up at *Kleine Scheidegg*, where there's a pair of old-fashioned Alpine hotels, cafés, shops, fine skiing, and an extraordinary viewing area, for vistas of Mt. Eiger and the Jungfrau. Journey's end is Europe's highest railway station, hacked out of Jungfraujoch rock; you make your way through chambers of the *Ice Palace*, so named because it is actually created from natural ice formations, even to its carved ice furnishings. Take a lift to the so-called *Sphinx observation terrace*, for a 360-degree view that—with clear weather—is one of the most memorable in Switzerland, with the *Aletsch Glacier*—the Alps' longest—virtually at your feet. Allow time for a brief journey by sleds pulled by resident huskies, and for lunch in a restaurant, all of whose food is hauled many thousands of feet upward from the valley. The half-hour chair-lift ride (Europe's longest such, in four sections, at an average altitude of 3,600 feet) from Grindelwald to *First*—a peak of some 6,500 feet—is a Grindelwald adventure of consequence. At journey's end, there is a range of ski options, not to mention restaurants with sun terraces and, in summer, 50 miles of walkers' paths and mountain trails.

Männlichen, at an elevation of just over 7,300 feet, is a 30-minute gondola-cableway journey from Grindelwald, but closer to the beautifully situated hotel-dotted village of *Wengen;* excellent ski facilities and ravishing views. By bus, you may reach *Oberer (Upper) Grindelwald Glacier*—one of the Alps' largest, constantly expanding in size, and *Grindelwald Glacier Gorge,* high above foamy waters of the Lütschine River, and viewable from an observation platform.

Pfinstegg, at an elevation of some 3,500 feet, is gained by a swift seven-minute cableway, and affords views from its observation terrace of both the Oberer (Upper) and the Unterer (Lower) glaciers—within hiking distance, if you're up to it. *Mürren* (autofree and 5,412 feet high) has a wide range of hotels and is reached by cable car from the village of *Stechelberg,* also the cable-car takeoff point for 9,744-foot *Mt. Schilthorn* (a.k.a. *Piz Gloria*), with a revolving restaurant (below) you may recall from the James Bond film, *On Her Majesty's Secret Service.* Both Piz Gloria and lower-down, 6,273-foot *Mt. Allmendhubel* (a five-minute funicular ride from Mürren, just below it) make for delightful excursions, whether one's mission is skiing, hiking, sunning, lunch, or a combination thereof. And *Interlaken,* principal town of the region—and locale of the world-class Victoria-Jungfrau Hotel—is but 40 minutes from Grindelwald via frequently departing trains; it is the subject of Chapter 9.

SETTLING IN
Regina Hotel (Phone 54-54-55): Grindelwald's sole luxury-category house has undertaken a long-range room-refurbishment project. Those of the relatively recently redone rooms and suites that I have inspected are generous in size and with big two-sink baths; there are 120, all told. Public spaces—including a rambling lobby-lounge and a restaurant about which I write more on a succeeding page—are attractive, and you may stay in shape by means of swims in both indoor and outdoor pools, gym, and sauna. Caveat: no credit cards. Member, Leading Hotels of the World. *Luxury.*

Belvedere Hotel (Phone 54-54-34) is nondescript of facade, but pleasing within. By that I mean the double rooms—certainly those I have inspected—are big and bright (although singles can be small). The traditional-style lobby—with picture windows giving onto a warm-weather terrace and the mountains—is pleasant, as indeed is the restaurant, later evaluated. There's a satellite eatery for cheese dishes—*fondue* and *raclette*—as well as a cozy bar and a swimming pool/fitness center. *First Class.*

Sunstar Adler Hotel (Phone 54-54-17)—Grindelwald's largest, with 160 rooms and suites—has had the good sense and/or fortune to retain an interior designer able to create interiors that, though with a chalet motif, merge with contemporary style, in tones of brown, beige, and gold. There are two restaurants, bar-lounge, terrace café, swimming pool, tennis, and fitness center. *First Class.*

Schweizerhof Hotel (Phone 53-22-02): Virtually every Swiss town has a Schweizerhof—although they are independent and not part of a chain by that name. Grindelwald's Schweizerhof is distinguished by the bright red facade fronting its pretty garden. Indoors is a traditional/modern mix, with 35 spotless rooms, a pair of restaurants, cocktail lounge with over-upholstered chairs surrounding tables, and welcoming lounge. There's an indoor pool alongside a fitness center, and even a bowling alley. *First Class.*

Weisses Kreuz & Post Hotel (Phone 58-54-92) embraces a pair of joined structures totaling 40 rooms. Rooms in the older building are being nicely refurbished. Those in the newer part have fair-sized balconies. There are a pair of well-regarded restaurants and a congenial bar, not to mention an indoor pool. Heart of town. *First Class.*

Spinne Hotel (Phone 53-23-41): Those of the 35 rooms of this centrally situated hotel that I have inspected are so small—and their beds so narrow—that I can recommend only the Spinne's several restaurants and cafés (see Daily Bread). *Moderate.*

Eiger Hotel (Phone 53-21-21) is a two-building, 50-room complex, with rooms of the newer section—capacious and attractive if those I have inspected are typical—somewhat pricier. One of the two restaurants features steak and is later counseled. *Moderate.*

Derby Hotel (Phone 54-54-61) appears to have as its prime plus an opposite-the-Bahnhof location. Standard-rate rooms I have inspected are small, but I am told there are costlier accommodations that are larger. My reception was unsmiling. Restaurant, café, bar. *Moderate.*

Alpina Hotel (Phone 53-33-33) is an agreeable chalet-style, 30-room house with a hillside albeit central situation, clean-lined rooms, convenient restaurant, café-cum-terrace, and bar. *Moderate.*

Central Hotel Wolter (Phone 53-22-33) is indeed central, has baths in 33 of its neat-as-a-pin rooms, curtained and bed-spreaded in brown-and-tan plaid. The restaurant-cum-Hauptstrasse café is good value. *Moderate.*

Scheidegg Hotels (Kleine Scheidegg; Phone 55-12-12) are a pair of adjacent-to-each-other nineteenth-century hostelries, with cozy lounges, bars, and restaurants. Some rooms are with baths, some without. Okay for overnight. *Moderate.*

Park Hotel (Wengen; Phone 56-51-61) is a nicely refurbished, long-on-scene house, straddling a hill overlooking the village, with 45 comfortable rooms and a restaurant worth knowing about for lunch, in the course of an excursion from Grindelwald. *First Class.*

Eiger Hotel (Mürren; Phone 55-13-31) is an attractive 40-room house with inviting public spaces, fitness center that comprises gym, pool, and sauna, bar-lounge, and a reliable restaurant to which you might repair for lunch while on a day's outing. *Luxury.*

DAILY BREAD
Regina Hotel Restaurant (Phone 54-54-55): Grindelwald's dressiest eatery (gentlemen, you're asked to wear jacket and tie at dinner) has an especially tempting à la carte, with oysters on the half shell, *steak tartare*, and deliciously sauced snails as starters; filet of beef, grilled lamb chops, and corking good fresh fish among entrées. And there's a prix-fixe menu of four or five

courses, as you prefer. Book in advance if you're not a hotel guest. Caveat: no credit cards. *Luxury.*

Spinne Hotel restaurants (Phone 53-23-41): *Mercato* calls itself a pizzeria, but there are quite as many pasta dishes—including delicious cream-sauced *tortellini alla penna, gnocchi al gorgonzola,* and an authentic lasagne—as there are choices of pizza. Expertly dressed green salad is counseled to accompany, as is a bottle of, say, Orvieto or Chianti Classico. In the *Rotisserie,* tables are set with red linen that contrasts with brown leather banquettes, and the five-course prix-fixe, based perhaps on an entrée of sautéed *médaillons* of veal, is a winner. The *Spycher* specializes in *fondue* and *raclette.* All are *First Class.*

Belevedere Hotel Restaurant (Phone 54-54-34) is a mix of dark woods, silk-shaded chandeliers, and—at dinner—red candles. The prix-fixe evening meal might run to oxtail soup, followed by asparagus stalks wrapped in thin-sliced ham, salads to which you help yourself from a bountiful buffet, veal *cordon bleu* nicely garnished, a choice of cheeses, and of desserts. *First Class.*

Steak House (Eiger Hotel; Phone 53-21-21) is indicated when you long for a thick U.S. sirloin. There are two sizes; both come with baked potatoes or French fries. And there are other beef options, including *Châteaubriand* served with Béarnaise sauce. Friendly. *First Class.*

Restaurant Sportzentrum (in the Sportzentrum; Phone 53-32-77) is convenient for the *plat du jour* at lunch, or a good-value prix-fixe in the evening. Veal dishes are good here; ditto *bratwurst mit rösti. Moderate.*

Spinet (Hauptstrasse, opposite the Eiger Hotel but operated by the nearby Spinne Hotel) is just the ticket for midmorning coffee, a light lunch, or afternoon tea-cum-pastries, at which time it's an all-Grindelwald congregating spot. *Moderate.*

Jungfraujoch Restaurant (Jungfraujoch): If there's a requisite lunch destination in the Grindelwald area, it's this spot. Plan your day's outing to Jungfraujoch so that you arrive midday, to partake of a meal all the ingredients of which will have been painstakingly transported up from the valley. *Moderate.*

Bahnhof Buffet (Bahnhof, Kleine Scheidegg): Give yourself some time between trains en route to or from Grindelwald, or to or from Jungfraujoch, to amble about Kleine Scheidegg, stopping here for coffee or a snack. *Moderate.*

Piz Gloria Restaurant (atop Mt. Schilthorn a.k.a. Piz Gloria and reached by cable car from Stechelberg, itself reached by train from Lauterbrunnen): You've seen the movie; now have lunch in the restaurant. By that I mean this circular, picture-windowed eatery—the world's highest revolving restaurant—had its moment of glory when scenes were shot in it for the James Bond film, *On Her Majesty's Secret Service.* The Alpine views—you move the full 360 degrees in just under an hour—are the thing here, but fare is hearty—soups, sausages, and veal entrées, rich desserts—and satisfying. *First Class.*

INCIDENTAL INTELLIGENCE

The tourist office (below) offers a variety of packages, both winter (primarily for skiers and including Ski School instruction if desired) and summer (for hikers, wildlife buffs, and the like). *Further information:* Verkehrsbüro, Hauptstrasse, Grindelwald.

8

Gstaad
Jewel of the Bernese Oberland

BACKGROUND BRIEFING

It was not, to be sure, intentional. But surely a case can be made for the premise that Gstaad's peculiar name—oddly spelled and pronounced [G'h-*shtahd*] has been a factor in its success as quite the smartest of the Swiss mountain resorts.

Gstaad, ever proud of its beginnings as an unpretentious mountain village, has kept itself small, the while relying largely on word of mouth—by that I mean satisfied customers who *do* know how to pronounce it properly—to establish its image.

Not part of a resort cluster—in the manner of such close-to-each-other spots as easterly Arosa, Davos, and Klosters (Chapter 5), westerly Gstaad's grandeur (a few satellite villages excepted) is solitary. It occupies a Bernese Oberland valley framed by nearby peaks like Oldenhorn, Wildhorn, Wispile, Rellerlie, and Eggli, from whose summits you may observe the really big ones like Mont Blanc and Dent du Midi.

Gstaad's go-getters realized, as the nineteenth century was about to become the twentieth, that only the railroad could link it with the contemporary world. For some time, though, the village was considered too small for inclusion on a planned train route, even though a deviation of but a couple of miles was all that was required. What would today be termed a Gstaad Rail

Lobby was ultimately convincing; on December 20, 1904, the first train steamed into the village's just-completed station.

Within ten years, ten hotels had gone up. Decades between the two World Wars saw the resort lure such vacationers as Belgium's King Leopold II and America's Mary Pickford, the while carefully designed facilities—ski lifts, tennis courts, golf courses, swimming pools—were constructed. More recently, Gstaad's Yehudi Menuhin-led summer music festivals have brought it cultural eminence.

All along the way, though, its growth has been regulated by the authorities. Designs for all new construction, hotels of course included, must conform to rigid regulations based on the traditional style of the region. Gstaad's quiet conservatism has attracted a substantial sprinkling of affluent regulars, many of them resident the winter long in their own or rented chalets. And its main street—studded with branches of famous shops—is a kind of bucolic Bond Street/Madison Avenue/Rue du Faubourg St.-Honoré.

Still, eminence has not led to arrogance. Gstaad remains not only small but cozy. Villagers and guests get to know—and often befriend—one another. The short-term holidaymaker—summer as well as winter—is regarded with the same goodwill as, say, the titled moneybags back for an entire season.

ON SCENE
Lay of the Land: Couldn't be simpler. *Hauptstrasse,* the main street, runs the length of the village core, and is lined by good-looking chalet-style buildings sheltering shops (see Shopper's Gstaad), cafés (see Daily Bread), the occasional hotel, and the *Bahnhof.* The Hauptstrasse's slim-steepled *Niklauskapelle* is charming, tiny, and Anglican (with services in English every Sunday at 10:00 A.M.). Nearby are the town's *Kunsteishalle,* the indoor ice rink; *Eisbahn* (the outdoor rink); *Hallenbad*—a glass-walled, heated swimming pool-cum-sauna and café: *Tennishalle,* with a trio of indoor courts, 16 clay and hard outdoor tennis courts; covered *Riding School,* and even a *Curling Hall. Cable cars* lead to *Mt. Eggli* (5,000 feet), *Höhe Wispile* (6,500 feet), and—from the nearby village of *Col du Pillon*—to the *Diablerets Glacier* (9,800 feet)—with utterly breathtaking views

and as beautiful in summer as in winter. All told, there are more than 60 area ski lifts.

Nearby villages make for agreeable excursions. Besides *Col du Pillon* (above), the take-off point for Diablerets Glacier, they include *Gruyères*—not as well known, perhaps, as the cheese taking its name but with an enchanting open-to-visitors fifteenth-century castle and a dairy where you can watch cheese being made; *Château d'Oeux,* whose *Musée du Vieux Pays d'Enhaut's* regional historical exhibits are at their best in a series of period rooms; and *Aigle,* where you want to inspect both *Musée de la Vigne* (subject is the neighborhood's reputed white wine) and *Musée du Sel* (about locally mined salt) in turreted, medieval Château de St.-Maurice, concluding with a stroll along Ruelle de Jérusalem, a core-of-town street flanked by wooden galleries. Golfers may well want to play Gstaad's *Golfplatz,* an idyllically situated nine-hole links at an altitude of 4,200 feet, high above the nearby village of Saanmöser.

SETTLING IN
Palace Hotel (Phone 831-31): You've probably come across them as indeed have I—resort towns with a single luxury hotel whose management and staff, for lack of any competition in their exalted category, become spoiled and cocky. Gstaad's Palace *could* be such a hotel; it's the only five-star house in town. But that's not the style of the owning Scherz family, or their management colleagues, Hansruedi Schaerer and Gianni Biggi. This half-century-old 138 room establishment appears never to stop trying harder. It's possible to feel a newcomer the first day or two of one's stay. Beyond that, though, and you find the concierge (on hand nearly three decades) calling you by name; the chief barman (with the Palace for almost as long) remembering your favorite drink, even to brand designation; the maître d'hôtel (a 20-year Palace veteran) leading you with a smile to your regular table. Look of the Palace? It does not intimidate. Decor is of the region. High ceilings are pine-paneled. Chandeliers and sconces are brass. Furniture is generously upholstered with textiles—chairs and sofas as well as draperies—warm and soft. Attention is paid to details; bathrooms, for example, are

fabulous; housekeeping is meticulous. And facilities are extraordinary: quite grand restaurant (especially gala on black-tie evenings), and a dressy à la carte grill (evaluated in a later paragraph), Sans Cravate (translating as "without necktie" and meaning casual as you like), Fromagerie (another informal spot, with *fondue* and *raclette* as specialties), snack bar adjacent to the indoor swimming pool. There's a big outdoor pool for summer, disco, gym-sauna, squash court, games room, even an imported-from-Geneva hairdresser. And lessons in everything from skiing to skating. Traditionally closed late March through early June; late September through mid-December. Modified American Plan. Member, Leading Hotels of the World. *Luxury.*

Olden Hotel (Phone 4-34-44)—heart of the village with its painted facade representative of the region—is no less typical within. Pine panels of doors, cupboards, and closets of the dozen guest rooms have been hand-decorated by talented Manager Heidi Donizetti (a professional singer as well as a professional painter). Public spaces are equally handsome— Olden Bar, for drinks and *plats du jour;* La Petite Salle for snacks and sandwiches; La Pinte, the best place in town to meet locals, and La Cave, smart dinner-only, winter-only restaurant that's a major Gstaad congregating place, about which I write more on a later page. A lovely hotel. *First Class.*

Bernerhof Hotel (Phone 8-33-66) is the attractive hotel you spot as you exit the railway station. There are some 40 good-sized, good-looking rooms, several restaurants (including the recommendable Chessi) and bars, adults' and kids' swimming pools, sauna-fitness center. *First Class.*

Alpine Hotel (Phone 4-57-25) stands out because of its situation; a pretty parklike garden elevated enough so as to afford a fine view of the village and the mountains. This is an updated old-timer with 30 rooms, restaurant, bar-lounge, tennis. *First Class.*

Christiania Hotel (Phone 4-51-21), opposite the skating rink and tennis court, has a pleasantly intimate quality. There are not quite 20 nicely furnished and accessorized rooms and duplex suites, inviting public spaces that include a reliable restaurant and comfortable lounge. *First Class.*

Post Hotel Rössli (Phone 4-34-12)—constructed in 1845—is the oldest hotel in town. Thoroughly refurbished in chalet style, it embraces a popular restaurant and café, and 15 functional rooms. Central. *Moderate.*

Arc-en-Ciel Hotel (Phone 9-22-286) is a comfortable house with a trio of restaurants (one of which is later recommended) that's away from the center but a hop and a skip from the Eggli and Wispile cable cars. Those of the 30 rooms I have inspected are adequate, and there are still additional rooms and apartments (larger, more attractive, and with kitchens) in a newer annex across the road. *First Class.*

Gstaaderhof Hotel (Phone 8-33-44) is good sized (70 rustic-modern rooms, some of them duplexes), well equipped (two restaurants and a bar), and central. *Moderate.*

Alphorn Hotel (Phone 4-45-45) is a neighbor of the Arc-en-Ciel (above)—away from the center, near the Wispile cable car station and the Ski School. There are 15 well-planned rooms, most with balconies, and a pair of restaurants, one with cheese specialties. *Moderate.*

DAILY BREAD
Chesery (Phone 4-35-51) appears forbiddingly large from without; a heroically proportioned chalet just off Hauptstrasse, core of the village. Once inside, though, and the atmosphere is one of good cheer, good looks, and good food—lightish, *nouvelle*-influenced dishes, if you like; but more solid vittles—veal steaks, filet of beef, tastily prepared poultry—as well. With super sweets and—following dinner—a considerable crowd drawn by entertainment emanating from the piano bar—through the wee hours. *First Class.*

Chlösterli (Phone 5-10-45)—a 10-minute drive from the center—in the outlying village of Grund, has been on scene close onto four centuries. But contemporary customers are drawn not only by its antique rusticity. Fare is solid and substantial: Swiss specialties—*raclette*, local sausages, *bündnerfleisch* are top-class; so are rotisserie-grilled steaks and chops, and such rib-sticking entrées as Irish stew, Hungarian goulash, and braised beef. Lunch revolves around a tempting buffet based on a variety of salads. *First Class.*

Grill and *Sans Cravate* (Palace Hotel; Phone 8-31-31): The difference between these two contiguous restaurants is clothes. By that I mean that men wear jacket and tie in the Grill, with women correspondingly dressy; but that for dinner in Sans Cravate (with its own entrance as a means of encouraging non-hotel guests) men dispense with ties and women appear in casual attire. Menu—à la carte in contrast to the table d'hôte of the Palace's restaurant—is identical in both rooms, happily—and deliciously—based on French classic cuisine. Splurge with caviar or *foie gras* among openers, opting for considerably less pricey soups or pastas (the calves' liver and mushroom-accented *risotto* is special) to begin. Fish and seafood—*truite au bleu*, grilled lobster, fresh Irish salmon—are exemplary, and the Grill takes its name seriously enough to prepare beef, lamb, and veal any number of ways—and well. *Luxury.*

La Cave (Olden Hotel; Phone 4-34-34)—most celebrated of the Olden's several restaurants—with pine-paneled walls and ceiling—sports draperies in red at its windows, the same color as fat candles that illuminate its tables, dressed in pink linen. Open with the real (not mock) turtle soup, goulash soup, or *raclette*. Veal *piccata*, prepared as you remember it from Italy, and served with a side of spaghetti, is a favored entrée. So is *steak au poivre*. And if you're a party of two or more, the *fondue* is a good bet on a cold evening. Which, chances are, it will be, for La Cave is a winter-only, dinner-only proposition. With post-dinner songs by the proprietor-manager, Heidi Donizetti, invariably joined by whatever showbiz professionals are in attendance. *First Class.*

Post Hotel Rössli Restaurant (Phone 4-34-12) lures both villagers and visitors, for hearty meals—order from the prix-fixe menu—built around entrées of pork and veal; the potato specialty, *rösti*, is delicious here. With a popular pub adjacent. *Moderate.*

Pizzeria (Arc-en-Ciel Hotel; Phone 8-31-91): Forget about the chaletlike ambience. Italian fare here is authentic. And not only the pizzas. Open with antipasto, such soups as *minestrone* or *stracciatella*, following with a choice of pastas, including ravioli (I've had none better in Italy), or a veal entrée. *First Class.*

Charly's Tea Room is a Hauptstrasse institution. Drop in between bouts of shopping, for a light lunch, morning coffee, or afternoon tea. Charly's pastries are delicious. *Moderate.*

Restaurants on High—with adjacent sun terraces—are ideal lunch locales. Take the cable car to *Glacier des Diablerets, Eggli,* and *Wispile. Moderate/First Class.*

SOUND OF MUSIC
Menuhin Festival, organized, directed and invariably participated in by longtime Gstaad resident Yehudi Menuhin, traditionally extends over the month of August, with performances in the lovely old village church in nearby Saanen. Besides performances by students of the Menuhin-directed music school's Chamber Orchestra, a season's program might include London's Royal Philharmonic, the Warsaw Symphony, the English Chamber Orchestra, and the Neues Züricher Streichquartett—to give you an idea. The tourist office (below) organizes week-long festival packages.

SHOPPER'S GSTAAD
I don't know of a small village anywhere with as spectacular a main shopping street as Gstaad's Hauptstrasse. It is not, to be sure, for budgeteers. Excepting an establishment called *Caconau*—with such mundane merchandise as postcards and paperbacks, Hauptstrasse's stakes are high. Jewelry and watches are vended at *Cartier, Beno de Gorski, Williger* (for Patek

Philippe timepieces), and *May* (for Piaget). Clothing: Consider *Valentino, Gianni Versace, May* (for Hermès accessories); *Hermann* (for Daniel Hechter); *Favre* (for Christian Dior); *Hermenjat* (for Cerrutti and Polo); and *Loertscher* (for cashmere). *Sittwer's* floral arrangements are among the most beautiful of any Swiss florist's that I've come upon. And the chocolates at *Oehrli* are hardly to be despised.

Come winter—the months of January and February—glossy jewelers, couturiers, and art galleries set up short-term quarters in hotels like the Palace and the Olden, each remaining on scene several days, to the accompaniment of soirées and galas heralding their arrival. Schedules are published well in advance, so that you know precisely when you can spend your francs or bucks or deutsche marks or pounds sterling on baubles from, say, *Harry Winston, Boucheron, Marina B, Bulgari,* and *Van Cleef & Arpels.*

INCIDENTAL INTELLIGENCE

The tourist office offers packages for skiers (both Alpine and cross-country), walkers/mountaineers, ambulatory botanists/ nature lovers, tennis players, and tennis fans (for the every-July Swiss Open International Tennis Championships). The nearest town of consequence to Gstaad is Montreux (Chapter 14), a scenic hour and a quarter distant by picture-window Panoramic Express trains of the Montreux-Oberland-Bernois Railway, which pioneered the route at the turn of the century. Language note: If French is one of your languages, speak it all you like in Gstaad which, though in German-speaking Switzerland, is close enough to Suisse Romande to be fluent in both languages—as well, of course, as English. *Further information:* Verkehrsbüro, Hauptstrasse, Gstaad.

9

Interlaken
A Room with a View

BACKGROUND BRIEFING
When you get right down to it, the centrally situated village of
Interlaken is essentially a case of a room with a view.

The room, if you can swing it, should be in the Victoria-
Jungfrau, most romantic of the Confederation's remaining
nineteenth-century hotels. The view, obtainable from any number of 80 additional hotels (Interlaken is a bedroom community
of consequence, with 4,500 rentable beds) will be of the legendary 13,642-foot Jungfrau and its only slightly less elevated
neighbors, mounts Eiger (13,026 feet) and Mönch (14,449 feet).

The area of those peaks, along with lower-down Jungfraujoch
and Kleine Scheidegg, among others, is, in my opinion, more
conveniently explored out of Grindelwald, an Alpine village not
far to the southeast, which is the subject of Chapter 7 in this
book. As I see it, the principal reason for an Interlaken interlude
is to exploit its location—as indeed did early Romans (from
whom its name derives) and the medieval monks (whose monastery was the nucleus of the later town)—between two
mountain-backed lakes (Thunersee to the west and Brienzersee
to the east), and make an excursion or two by land or lake steamer into surrounding territory.

ON SCENE

Lay of the Land: This is an east-west town, with the *Aare River* north of the core, separating it from the quarter called *Untersee* whose *Obere Gasse* is the location of the summer-only *Touristik Museum der Jungfrau Region,* with exhibits detailing the town's success story as a visitor center. An indoor-outdoor swimming pool complex is just north of the river. The wide main street, *Höheweg,* south of the river, runs east-west, a good chunk of its southern flank bordered by the green called *Höhematte.* No small town was ever more in need of a single consolidated railway station: Interlaken's two can be confusing. *Bahnhof West,* at the western end of Höheweg at that point called Bahnhofstrasse, is the main station and adjacent to *Schiffstation Thunersee,* the pier for Lake Thun steamers. *Bahnhof Ost,* at the eastern edge of Höheweg, is the one you want for trains into the Jungfrau region due south; it is adjacent to *Schiffstation Brienzersee,* the pier for Lake Brienz steamers. *Kursaal*—the nineteenth-century casino whose elaborate interiors are worth a peek—has a pretty floral clock in its garden and adjoins a modern convention center with an indoor/outdoor *tennis center,* due west. The top two churches—heavily restored Catholic and Protestant—are next door to each other, off *Schlossstrasse,* at the east end of town. Höheweg's relatively few shops—geared to tourists—are supplemented by others to its west, in and about *Zentralplatz;* they include branches of the reliable *Loeb* department store and *Merkur* food and wine chains.

Thun: The multipinnacled tower that dominates the village of Thun, at the northern tip of Thunersee, is of *Schloss Thun,* a marvelously medieval castle operated as a historical museum. State rooms—grandly proportioned with splendidly beamed ceilings and fireplaces two stories in height—are not unexpected in what had been a baron's seat, dating to the twelfth century. But certain of the exhibits come as delightful surprises, including immense pottery plates on which neighborhood farm families traditionally served *rösti,* the national potato dish, for breakfast, and watercolors that charmingly delineate the atmosphere of the area's towns in the eighteenth century. To see, as well: furniture and pewter, costumes and toys, with advertising flyers proclaiming the virtues of the last century's hotels and steamers, surely the most amusing of this castle's contents. Amble about town in the course of your excursion; I suggest a restaurant for lunch on a later page. And if it's summer, consider a visit to near- by *Schloss Hunegg*, whose furnishings celebrate the turn-of- century Belle-Époque era.

Spiez is another Lake Thun castle town midway between Thun and Interlaken. *Schloss Spiez*, its dominant monument, is a mas- terful hybrid whose medieval origins (including an ascendable tower) combine well with Renaissance and baroque embellish- ments. It was during this last-mentioned era—the baroque— that the castle's *Festsaal*, or banqueting room, was created, with notable ceiling stucco work and friezes. Still another state room, *Täfelzimmer*, stuns with its exquisite wood-paneled walls. There are lovely portraits dotted about, mostly eighteenth century. The kitchen is quite as it was in the fifteenth century. And the apse of the adjacent chapel—severely beautiful Renaissance— retains original frescoes.

Brienz is a woodcarvers' village at the far end of Lake Brienz. What you want to do on arrival is check out the plethora of Hauptstrasse shops—some have resident carvers demonstrat- ing their skills—whose shelves are massed with figures and other objects fashioned of wood. A firm called *Jobin*, on scene since 1835, is among the majors. If you have not already ascend- ed your share of area peaks, consider a journey (one hour each way) aboard Switzerland's sole remaining steam-powered rack railway to the summit and restaurant-café of *Mount Brienzer Rothorn*, at an elevation of more than 7,000 feet. Then proceed a few miles north to *Ballenberg*, site of *Schweizerisches Freilichtmuseum*—which translates as "Swiss Open-Air Muse- um of Rural Dwellings and Lifestyle"—and is considerably more enjoyable than its stodgy title implies. This is a 20-acre complex of 50 dwellings which have been transported from areas of the countryside in every region of the Confederation. The museum is recent—1978—and constantly expanding. Allow yourself enough time to take in representative houses— an elaborately half-timbered vintner's house from eastern

Switzerland, dating to the late eighteenth century, a combination barn/residence, from the same region and era; a seventeenth-century dwelling, three stories and basement, from near Interlaken; a substantial country inn of the last century, from around Bern; a Schaffhausen cider press, an apiary and a mill, a granary and a forge. Every aspect of the dwellings' furnished interiors is authentic; in many, craftsmen demonstrate traditional skills. There's an exceptional craft shop and a restaurant (below).

SETTLING IN

Victoria-Jungfrau Hotel (Phone 21-21-71): Its facade—extending over what would be two long city blocks, surmounted by a mock-Renaissance tower, punctuated with wrought-iron balconies under orange-and-yellow-striped awnings, fronted by a parklike formal garden—is the ultimate Interlaken facade. Originally two hotels (the earlier Victoria, inaugurated in 1865, and the somewhat later Jungfrau), they were united at the turn of the century, although their buildings—Victoria on the right, Jungfrau on the left—retain signs so identifying them, and remain separated by narrow Victoriastrasse. Strolling about the V-J's public spaces is a principal Interlaken diversion. Between them, the two buildings' lobby floors shelter a series of lounges, essentially Louis XV-style, off of which lead rooms used for private parties—the Versailles Ballroom most spectacularly—that are unsurpassed by any that I know in Switzerland; and a trio of restaurants. La Terasse, the village's poshest eatery, is evaluated on a later page. There are, as well, the Jungfrau Stube, rustic-casual; and the Racket Club, with picture windows giving onto indoor courts of the adjacent Tennis Center. The indoor pool edges the garden, with chaise longues for summer sunning. There's a trio of late-hours boîtes—Barbarella disco, Western Saloon, Cabaret—with their own entrances. Which leaves accommodations: 233 rooms and suites, no two quite alike, with the range a lavish contemporary duplex in the tower, through traditionally furnished parlor-and-bedroom combinations, spiffy junior suites, and really good-sized bedrooms, whose baths are ultramod. And it all works like a charm, thanks to razor-sharp direction by ever-present General Manager Emanuel Berger. Member, Leading Hotels of the World. *Luxury.*

Beau Rivage Hotel (Phone 21-62-72)—the only luxury hotel in town aside from the Victoria-Jungfrau (above), is a considerably smaller house, turn-of-century albeit handsomely refurbished, and near the eastern edge of Höheweg. Public spaces are a meld of the contemporary with mostly Louis XV-style furnishings, in tones of brown and beige. Those of the suites and bedrooms, mostly pastel-shaded, that I have inspected are good sized and good looking, as indeed are the bar, in dramatic deep red; the Louis XIV-look Bonne Fourchette Restaurant, and a café edging the indoor pool-gym-sauna complex. *Luxury.*

Interlaken Hotel (Phone 21-22-11) dates, in part, to the fifteenth century—which makes it by far Interlaken's oldest; it's a protected monument, and you may still see parts of the old walls in its Taverne Restaurant and Klosterbar. The entire house has been relatively recently renovated. Those of the 61 bedrooms and suites I have inspected are mostly contemporary but some are antiques-accented. There's a pair of restaurants, one Chinese, the other evaluated in a later paragraph. This is a bright, lively, friendly house. *First Class.*

Krebs Hotel (Phone 23-71-61) is a Bahnhofstrasse neighbor of the main railway station with a green-shuttered white facade which is quite the best-looking in town after that of the Victoria-Jungfrau. Attractive public spaces include a striking Louis XVI lounge, and a restaurant that goes outdoors in summer, as well as thoughtfully furnished rooms. *First Class.*

National Hotel (Phone 22-36-21) overlooks Höhematte, the park edging Höheweg. The facade is clean-lined but interiors are a contemporary-traditional mix, and those of the 40 rooms I have inspected are spacious and cheerful. Restaurant, bar-lounge. *First Class.*

Metropole Hotel (Phone 21-21-51) is the graceless Höheweg highrise that strikes otherwise horizontal Interlaken's most jarring architectural note. It went up in the 1960s with approval of the citizenry, at a time, one learns in the course of questioning locals, when Interlaken wanted to make clear that it could be as progressive as its urban neighbors. Think what you will of its profile—and I am anything but a fan—there's no denying that accommodations in this 100-room house, at least those I have inspected, are agreeable; decent-sized; with good baths; and when they are high up, with super views. There are several restaurants and cafés, two evaluated in later paragraphs. Ambassador Swiss/Best Western. *First Class.*

Du Nord Hotel (Phone 22-26-31) is a pleasant house near the east end of Höheweg, with a perky lounge, good-value restaurant, busy bar, and 35 rooms; aim for a corner one, with a Jungfrau view. *First Class.*

Carlton Hotel (Phone 92-31-55) is just opposite the Beau Rivage (above), with 35 neat rooms, pair of restaurants, bar. Okay. *Moderate.*

Stella Hotel (Phone 22-88-71) is a full facility 25-room house a couple of blocks south of Höheweg, by no means elaborate but with cordial management; restaurant, bar, and indoor pool. *Moderate.*

Gasthof Kirschen (Phone 22-15-35) is a venerable inn some blocks south of Höheweg that's reputed more as a restaurant (see Daily Bread, below) than a hotel. It has, nonetheless, a half-dozen no-frills, neat-as-a-pin rooms with bath, and delightful management. *Moderate.*

Belvedere Hotel (Spiez; Phone 54-33-33) is a gracious house in its own lovely garden high above Lake Thun, not far from the center of Spiez village. The 25 rooms—no two quite alike—are attractive and some have two-sink, black-tile baths. The restaurant has picture windows, the better for lake and mountain vistas. And the Belvedere has its own beach on the lake. *First Class.*

Seegarten Hotel (Spiez; Phone 54-67-61) could not be more central—heart of the village, just below the castle (above). This is a friendly 30-room house, with a terraced restaurant that might be just the ticket for lunch in connection with an excursion from Interlaken. *Moderate.*

Krone Hotel (Thun; Phone 22-82-82) is core of the village—on Rathausplatz. A pleasing tower sets off the traditional facade, but interiors might be termed Rustic Contemporary; there are 20 snappy rooms (they have showers rather than tubs in their baths); restaurant, bar, indoor pool. *First Class.*

Beau Rivage Hotel (Thun; Phone 22-22-36) has an enviable situation on the lakefront in the village center. This is an elderly 25-room house (not all rooms have baths) with agreeable lobby-lounge, restaurant, terrace café, and indoor pool. *Moderate.*

Bären Hotel (Brienz; Phone 51-24-12) is a 25-room house (most of them have baths with showers rather than tubs) amidships in the village, with a terraced restaurant, and swimming in the lake, from its pier. *Moderate.*

DAILY BREAD
La Terrasse (Victoria-Jungfrau Hotel; Phone 21-21-71) looks quite as it should, given its name: white wrought-iron tables and chairs on a picture-window terrace give onto the hotel's garden, with the Jungfrau beyond. This is Interlaken's classiest restaurant. The prix-fixe dinner menu embraces four courses, with several choices for each. You might open with authentically Gallic onion soup or a bracing consommé, followed by the day's pasta or, if it's the season, asparagus dressed with Hollandaise sauce, opting for poached salmon; sage-scented veal scallopine; or roast veal as an entrée, with desserts selected from a tempting trolley. And there's an impressive à la carte, classically French, as well. *Luxury.*

Taverne (Interlaken Hotel; Phone 21-22-11) can be quite the most animated eatery in town, come the height of the dinner hour. Smiling captain and waiters dart about, the while General Manager Peter Kerkhof chats up guests at their tables. There are good value prix-fixe menus built around tasty entrées of veal, pork, and poultry, not to mention first-rate *bratwurst* and *rösti*, preceded by such appetizers as prosciutto and melon or shrimp cocktail, and followed with baked-on-premises pastries among the desserts. *First Class.*

Le Charolais (Metropole Hotel; Phone 21-21-51) compensates with the quality of the fare for what it lacks in altitude; it's on the second floor of Interlaken's solo skyscraper hotel. (A café is rooftop.) Still, prix-fixe lunches and dinners are tasty, service skilled and smiling. You might open with mussels *marinière* or a cream soup, with such entrées as roast pork and *gratin Dauphinois*, or a lamb or veal specialty. An unexpected sherry trifle is among the desserts. *First Class.*

Hirschen (Phone 22-15-45) is a honey of a seventeenth-century house in the Matten quarter south of Höheweg, an easy walk on a fine day. Walls are lined with smartly framed antique prints. Red candles in brass sticks illuminate tables, set with immaculate white linen. You are graciously welcomed and you do well to order from the prix-fixe menu, which might open with *consommé printanier* and continue with the house's delicious *pâté* served with Cumberland sauce. If you're lucky, the entrée will be a juicy grilled steak accompanied by ever so crisp French fries, fresh vegetables, and a green salad. Conclude with a sweet. Satisfying. *First Class.*

Des Alpes (Phone 22-23-23): The heavily tourist-trafficked Höheweg restaurants and cafés do not all appeal. Des Alpes is, however, worth knowing about for its well-priced prix-fixe menus, opening with soup or melon, featuring mixed grill or another meat entrée, and concluding with an ice cream or pastry dessert. *Moderate.*

Pizzeria Ticino (Central Continental Hotel: Phone 22-10-33) may or may not call to mind the Italian-speaking canton of Ticino. But this Bahnhofstrasse spot is most certainly to be counseled for its good choice not only of pizzas but of pastas, too. And it's open until midnight. *Moderate/First Class.*

Chalet (Chalet Hotel Oberland; Phone 22-94-31) is a busy spot in a busy—and centrally situated—hotel on Centralplatz, where the name of the game is Swiss specialties; here's where you may order *fondue* and *fondue Bourguignonne*, with steaks and other grills as well. *First Class.*

Schuh (Phone 22-94-41) is Interlaken's grand old *konditorei*; it occupies a house of its own on Höheweg. Go for midmorning pastries and coffee or afternoon tea. And Schuh serves well-priced prix-fixe meals. Attractive. *Moderate/First Class.*

Panoramic Café (Metropole Hotel): Much as I dislike the way this vertical hotel intrudes itself upon low-slung Interlaken, there is no gainsaying the panoramic advantages of its aptly titled rooftop café. Go for a drink, preferably during the day, when you can see more. *Moderate.*

Wirsthaus Bären (Schweizerisches Freilichtmuseum, Ballenburg; Phone 51-29-02), occupying a historic building of its own on the museum "campus," makes for a convenient lunch break; you've a choice of three prix-fixe menus built around such entrées as veal or ham steak. Caveat: no credit cards. *Moderate.*

Bären Hotel (Brienz; Phone 52-24-12) is an attractive alternative to lunch at the nearby Ballenburg museum (above). You're at an engaging lakefront hotel here. The prix-fixe menu, built perhaps around fresh lake fish, is good value and tasty. *First Class.*

Krone Hotel (Thun; Phone 22-82-82) offers competent fare in an attractive rustic setting, center of the village. Select from the prix-fixe menu. *First Class.*

SOUND OF MUSIC

Interlaken Festwochen is an annual classical music festival, usually occurring over a 12-day August span, with such guests as the Bern Symphony and the Ballet du Nord, from Lille in France; venue is the Kursaal's Konzerthall. Other entertainments—folklore evenings and band concerts—take place in the Kursaal as well; the tourist office (below) publishes a monthly program. There are about a dozen evening performances, usually in July, of an annual pageant enacting the William Tell legend at the open-air Freilichtspiele.

Schloss Thun—the castle in Thun (above) is the principal site of an annual classical concert season—usually two and a half weeks in June; still other concerts, in other venues, at other times.

INCIDENTAL INTELLIGENCE

Interlaken Golf Club's 18-hole, par 72 course is two miles west of town and is restaurant-equipped. *Further information:* Verkehrsbüro, Höheweg, Interlaken; Verkehrsbüro, Hauptstrasse, Thun; Verkehrsbüro, Hauptstrasse, Brienz; Verkehrsbüro, Hauptstrasse, Spiez.

10

Lausanne
Suisse Romande's Cathedral City

BACKGROUND BRIEFING

It lacks the excitement of Geneva (Chapter 6), its bigger Lac Léman neighbor to the southwest, but it is, at the same time, livelier and with a more urban flavor than smaller, quieter Montreux (Chapter 14), on the shore of the same lake, but due west. Lausanne—actually No. 5 in size of the Swiss cities, with a population of some 140,000—is, at one and the same time handsome (its deftly sited cathedral is a Gothic masterwork), hard-working (as a port, rail terminal, commercial entrepôt) and—I must caution at the outset—hilly.

The earliest settlers, without the convenience of a Métro to join the lakeshore with elevated terrain—as enjoyed by their descendants today—first settled at the water's edge. Celts preceded Romans who named their colony *Losonna*, and operated a thriving port in the quarter called Vidy, remnants of which remain in an on-site archeological museum.

As it prospered on crossroads linking Italy to Gaul, and the Mediterranean to the Rhine, it became more mercantile—and richer. Passing migrants' designs on it impelled moves upward as early as the third century, onto a more easily defended hill. By the sixth century the town had become wealthy enough for the Catholic Church to have designated it an episcopal see. Before

long, bishops were styled *prince* bishops, adding temporal powers to spiritual authority. They ruled (from a cathedral which
dates back to the twelfth century) well into the sixteenth century, when Lausanne, conquered by the Protestant Bernese, had
no choice but to accept the Reformation.

The eighteenth century was a kind of Golden Age; Voltaire
and Rousseau settled in, the social scene was sparkling, intellectual activity was at high pitch. The Bernese were ousted in
1798 and in 1803 Lausanne became capital of the newly created canton of Vaud. Its place in history is assured as site of a
trio of history-book treaties—Peace of Ouchy (1912) between
Turkey and Italy; Treaty of Lausanne (1920), between Turkey
and the World War I Allies; and the 1922 World War I Repara-
tions Conference.

At least as important in the contemporary scheme of things is
the site in Lausanne of what is surely the most celebrated of
Hotel Training Colleges. Its alumni—general managers, food
and beverage directors, head chefs—are based not only in
prominent hotels and restaurants throughout Switzerland, but
all around the world. *Vive Lausanne!*

ON SCENE
Lay of the Land: Setting is super—on the shores of Lac Léman
(a.k.a. Lake Geneva)—Western Europe's largest, backed by Alps of
the Savoie, with vineyards both east and west, and—in the
north—3,000-foot high *Mt. Jurat.* The city center is at an altitude of
about 1,600 feet. Its core is *Place St. François,* named for the originally Gothic albeit heavily restored church edging it. Two
pedestrian streets, *Rue St.-François* and the No. 1 shopping street,
Rue de Bourg, lead from the square. Walk north on nearby *Rue
Caroline* and you soon reach the bridge—*Pont Bessières*—which
will take you into Lausanne's *Cité*—the name it gave to its Old
Town many centuries back. It is dominated by the cathedral
(below) on *Place de la Cathédrale.* A pair of parallel streets—
interestingly named *Rue Cité-Devant* ("Front of the Cité Street"),
and *Rue Cité-Derrière* ("Behind the Cité Street")—converge upon
Place du Château, named for the fourteenth-century quadruple-
towered *Château St.-Maire* overlooking it; a onetime seat of
bishops, later of Bernese bailiffs, now of Cantonal officials, its

terrace affords fine views. Lausanne's city hall, *Hôtel de Ville*, is on *Place de la Palud* southwest of the cathedral. The northern terminus of the city's one-line Métro system, which bills itself as Europe's smallest (although I believe that of Budapest comes close) is at *Place de la Gare* (site as well of *Gare Centrale*, the main train station). The Métro leads downhill past a quartet of stops to *Ouchy*, Lausanne's delightful lakefront quarter, from where—at *Debarcadère d'Ouchy*—lake steamers sail regularly for *Évian*, France (see *France at Its Best*) and other excursion points along both the Swiss and French shores of the mountain-backed lake. The medieval castle in the center of Ouchy is the former *Château d'Ouchy*, now a hotel (below). Relaxing cafés are all about, on *Place du Port* and the lakeside quais.

Cathédrale de Lausanne (Place de la Cathédrale), a single delicate steeple rising from one of its half-dozen variously shaped towers, looms large over the Cité. Along with counterparts in Bern (Chapter 3) and in Basel (Chapter 2) it is quite the most spectacularly sited such structure in Switzerland. It is, as well, the largest. And in my view, quite the most beautiful. It's at its oldest in an apse distinguished by flying buttresses (1160), and its newest at its main, or west entrance—completed in the succeeding century. This is an early Gothic masterwork with a pair of prime attributes: the jumble of felicitous verticals that constitute its exterior and splendid scale within. The south, or so-called Painted, portal is a symphony in carved stone, no longer painted but with sculpted prophets on the columns to the left, apostles and evangelists to the right. The nave's vaults are surfaced in severe brick. But the detail of the transept's rose window compensates, as do other aspects of the cathedral—intricately carved wood of the choir stalls, stained glass in mint condition, capitals of columns, floors studded with tombs. You will want to return.

Musée de l'Ancien Évêché (Place de la Cathédrale): The former Bishop's Palace, adjacent to the cathedral, houses a pair of smallish museums. One is devoted to the cathedral, principally as a repository of sculpture that had graced its exterior, including statues of Moses, David, and such saints as Anthony, Anne,

Sebastian, and John the Baptist; with other bits and pieces, a pair of bishop's shoes, made almost seven centuries ago, among them. The other museum is a Lausanne historic hodgepodge—coins and maps, old furniture and fragments of old walls; even a reconstructed medieval kitchen.

Musée Cantonal des Beaux-Arts (6 Place de la Riponne) is by no means among the larger of the Swiss art museums, but it has some fine paintings. Best-known artists represented are French—a self-portrait of Largillière in a velvet smock, brush in hand; a black-robed duchess by Rigaud; Impressionist works by the likes of Degas, Cézanne, and Renoir; later masters like Bonnard, Vuillard, Marquet, Derain, and Utrillo. And the prolific and multitalented Ferdinand Hodler is the best known of the Swiss represented.

Musée Archéologique Cantonal (6 Place de la Riponne), in the same building as Beaux-Arts (above) is at its best with Roman works, most spectacularly a gold bust of Marcus Aurelius. (Not to be confused with the mainly-for-students *Musée d'Histoire Naturelle*, also in the same building.)

Musée Romain de Pully (Place du Prieuré, in the adjacent lakefront village of Pully, just east of Lausanne, whose lures include a beach and pool) is visitable for its restored Roman villa, discovered as recently as 1921, with a 60-foot-long fresco, and other souvenirs of Roman Lausanne—going back some 2,000 years.

Musée Romain de Vidy (Château du Bois-de-Vaux, in Vidy, on the lake just west of Lausanne) is a mix of objects excavated on the site of ancient Vidy, which had been the port of the Romans' *Losonna*—including pottery and coins.

Fondation de l'Hermitage (2 Route du Signal, away from the center), a country house in its own park, is brought to your attention because it is, from time to time, the site of first-rate temporary art exhibitions; the tourist office (below) will know if anything is on during the course of your visit.

SETTLING IN

Lausanne Palace Hôtel (7 Rue du Grand Chêne; Phone 29-37-11) had the most central location in town when it opened in 1915—and it still does. Recent seasons have seen it meticulously refurbished. Its colonnaded lobby—high-ceilinged, ballroom-size, and hung with crystal chandeliers—is one of the best-looking in the Confederation. There are 167 rooms and suites—motifs are mostly Louis XV and Louis XVI—with excellent baths; a pair of restaurants, each with its lakeview terrace for summer, one of which I evaluate on a later page; and a striking, red-walled bar-lounge with leather chairs surrounding tables. There's a pleasantly perky feeling to the Palace. Service—concierges through cashiers—is as swift and cordial as ambience is easy and winning. A Swissôtel that is a member of Leading Hotels of the World. *Luxury.*

Beau Rivage Palace Hôtel (Chemin du Beau Rivage in the Ouchy quarter; Phone 26-38-31) is at once a lavish Belle Époque city hotel—among the more sumptuous in Europe—and a country resort set in a ten-acre park with a big indoor-outdoor swimming pool, pair of tennis courts, and its own jogging trails in Ouchy, on the shore of Lac Léman. The hotel is a two-building complex. The original structure, Beau Rivage, with the heroic scale and stucco work of its public spaces—Terrasse Rotonde restaurant, Bar Anglais, and ballroom especially—unsurpassed on the continent, went up in 1861. Its connected annex, the Palace, dates to 1906. All told, there are 204 rooms, including 15 fabulous suites, with the look traditional except in premium *chambres de luxe*, where Directeur Général Maurice Urech's talented designers have created a mod-traditional meld. Le Wellingtonia, with its own lively bar-cum-dancing, warrants additional comment in a later paragraph. Member, Leading Hotels of the World. *Luxury.*

De la Paix Hôtel (5 Avenue Benjamin Constant; Phone 29-71-71) is Old School without, contemporary—it has been completely refurbished—within. And tastefully. Those of the 80 rooms and suites I have inspected are good size and with good baths; try and book a higher-up one with a lakeview terrace. There's a pair of restaurants (one later evaluated) and a bar-lounge. Central. *First Class.*

Royal Savoy Hôtel (40 Avenue d'Ouchy; Phone 26-42-01) is midway between the center of the city and Ouchy, set in a capacious garden with swimming pool. It's a rambling turn-of-century house, updated, to be sure, but retaining the essence of its original decor. Those of the rooms and suites—110 all told—I have inspected are lovely, and most have terraces. There are two restaurants, one later reviewed, and a honey of a bar. Alert management. *First Class.*

Continental Hôtel (2 Place de la Gare; Phone 20-15-51) is noteworthy because of its proximity to the railway station and the center of town. It's a clean-lined modern house of 121 functional rooms, with one of its restaurants—this too is worth knowing—open till midnight. Bar-lounge. *First Class.*

Château d'Ouchy Hôtel (Quai Dapple; Phone 26-74-51) is accurately named. It's housed in Ouchy's originally twelfth-century castle. A half-dozen of the 35 rooms are in the original château tower and are quite the most romantic in the house. There are several restaurants, the most appealing of which is an indoor/outdoor terrace facing the lake. *First Class.*

Mirabeau Hôtel (31 Avenue de la Gare; Phone 20-62-31) is near the train station and an easy walk to the center. Public spaces, including a restaurant and bar, are satisfactory, and those of the 30 rooms I have inspected are adequate. *Moderate.*

Crystal Hôtel (5 Rue Chaucreu; Phone 28-28-31) is central—on a pedestrian street albeit with police authorization for its guests' cars to pull up—and with baths in 32 of its 38 rooms. Neat as a pin. Breakfast only. *Moderate.*

DAILY BREAD
Le Wellingtonia (Beau Rivage Palace Hôtel, Chemin du Beau Rivage, and with its own entrance at the lakefront end of the

hotel; Phone 28-38-31) sounds, from its title, neither especially Swiss nor especially French. It is, however, an engaging blend of the two, in a space more intimate than most in the Beau Rivage—good paintings on paneled walls, soft lighting with candles at dinner, tuxedoed staff expertly orchestrated, delicious things to eat. You might, for example, begin with the surprisingly tasty eel terrine (opting if you prefer for *foie gras* with asparagus tips under a bed of delicious puff pastry). Grilled red snapper is a wise fish choice. Beef filet sauced with Béarnaise is tasty, but sautéed breast of pigeon is more interesting. Normandy's celebrated apple upside-down cake—*Tarte Tatin*—is, believe me, no better on France's Channel coast. And Le Wellingtonia's hot chocolate *soufflé* is a masterwork. In my experience one of Switzerland's best restaurants. *Luxury.*

La Grappe d'Or (3 Cheneau de Bourg; Phone 23-07-60) combines the virtues of style (its red, black, and brass look is tasteful) and comfort (you are not intimidated by the decor). The welcome is cordial and the nouvelle-accented choice is ample, from either of two prix-fixe *menus du jour.* The less steeply tabbed might start you off with a salad of turbot dressed with passion-fruit juice, and served *tiède,* or warm. Grilled salmon steak, garnished with also-grilled tomatoes would follow. Your entrée might be lamb filet in a *Pinot Noir* sauce. A giant *plateau* of cheeses would tempt you as the succeeding course. And you would terminate with a choice of desserts from a multitiered *chariot. Luxury.*

Le Relais (Lausanne Palace Hôtel, 7 Rue du Grand Chêne; Phone 20-37-11): Cheers to the Palace management for allocating its best-situated public space to this Louis XV-decor restaurant. It's flanked by picture windows that afford sublime vistas of the lake and mountains. (And in summer it moves to an al fresco terrace.) If you're two or more and famished, you could do worse than to select the Menu Gourmand—a five-course prix-fixe built around such entrées as truffle-accented breast of turkey and *médaillons* of veal accompanied by *tagliatelle verde* (this restaurant's pastas are noteworthy). But the à la carte is extensive. Among starters, quail salad and cabbage stuffed with crayfish and caviar stand out. And the beef entrée billed as *Entrecôte Américain* is a thick steak served with green pepper sauce. Dessert? You skip *Millefeuille de Pommes au Caramel* at your peril. Super service. *Luxury.*

La Voile d'Or (9 Avenue Jacques-Dalcroz; Phone 27-80-11) is just the ticket for a gala lakeside lunch. This is a sleek contemporary pavilion whose immense windows give onto the water. There's an à la carte, but the weekday-only, lunchtime-only prix-fixe menu makes better sense. You might begin with the day's salad or soup, preparatory to an entrée of either fish (I recall a tasty *ragoût de lotte*) or meat (Dijon mustard-spiked filet of beef, served with the house's own noodles), and the day's dessert. *First Class* (with a *Moderate*-category café adjacent, that goes al fresco in sunny weather).

Plaza (28 Rue de Bourg; Phone 23-74-01) is central (on the main shopping street), sprightly (it's busy with gossipy regulars, especially at noon), and tasty (the range is well-priced, pasta-centered prix-fixe menus, or a lengthy à la carte which includes pizza as well as *bistecca Fiorentina*—a Florentine steak). Open from 11:30 A.M. to 1:00 A.M. Caveat: no credit cards. *Moderate/First Class.*

Churrasco (51 Rue de Bourg; Phone 20-67-45) is the Lausanne link of a chain celebrating the barbecue prowess of Argentina, and indicated for a meal centered on beef—the range of steaks and other cuts is wide—ideally accompanied by *frites* and a salad. *Moderate/First Class.*

Café de la Paix (De la Paix Hôtel; 5 Avenue Benjamin Constant; Phone 26-42-01): The menu (with a collector's-item photo of the hotel, its limousine, and a group of guests, snapped in 1910) offers day-long snacks and drinks, club sandwiches through *cappuccino*, as well as *plats du jour* (the local sausage baked in a *brioche*, for example). *Moderate/First Class.*

Savoy (Royal-Savoy Hôtel, 40 Avenue d'Ouchy; Phone 26-42-01): With walls paneled in beige and gold and illumination from crystal sconces, the Savoy is a looker. The three-course prix-fixe lunch—*vitello tonnato*, fresh grilled trout, dessert, for example—is very good, and dinner—to which you help yourself to all you like from a buffet brimming with salads, hot dishes, and sweets—is a treat. *First Class.*

White Horse Pub (66 Avenue d'Ouchy; Phone 26-75-75) has the beamed and paneled look of an English pub. But it's solidly Swiss, with daily specials—*carpaccio, coq au vin,* a variety of salads—chalked on a blackboard. *Moderate/First Class.*

Terrasse (Château d'Ouchy Hôtel, Quai Dapple; Phone 26-74-51) is strategically situated, with respect to the views it affords of Ouchy's lakeside strollers. Prix-fixe menus—*quiche Lorraine,* rosemary-flavored roast chicken, *coupe Melba*—are counseled at lunch or dinner. Snacks and drinks, too. *Moderate/First Class.*

Café Manuel (Place St. François) is center of the action. Take a table on the square for coffee or tea with pastry, or a casual lunch. *Moderate.*

Le Chalet Suisse (Signal de Sauvabelin; Phone 22-23-12) is indicated as a destination in the course of an excursion from Lausanne to the mountains high above it. Setting is verdant Bois de Sauvabelin. The beamed dining room is cheery, but you want to go on a clear and sunny day, for lunch—Swiss veal specialties are indicated—on the terrace. *First Class.*

Girardet (Route d'Yvardon, in Crissier, 3 miles northwest of Lausanne; Phone 34-15-14): I save what is surely Switzerland's most celebrated (and among its most expensive) restaurants for last, because it's a bit out of town and because, very often, advance booking must be made *way* in advance (before you arrive in Lausanne, unless your visit is to be an extended one). Named for its chef-proprietor, in the manner of the nouvelle-cuisine restaurants of neighboring France, Girardet is attractively quartered in a substantial three-story structure, dating to the turn of the century, that was the Crissier *Hôtel de Ville*, or Town Hall, before Fredy Girdardet took it over some years back. You have a choice of two prix-fixe menus, one less costly than the other but hardly what you would call budget. Or order à la carte. Everything that I have tasted has been delicious, imaginatively presented, and impeccably served. Girardet, who happily does not eschew such ingredients as butter or cream, as do many *nouvelle* cooks, does interesting things with *foie gras de canard*, poached fattened duck liver, with which he combines truffles and asparagus or other vegetables in a minicasserole; and with lobster tails, which he sauces in a variety of ways. His kidney and sweetbreads preparations make fans of long-confirmed antikidney, antisweetbreads diners. His desserts—*gratin d'orange Madame France, mille-feuille aux fraises,* passion-fruit soufflé, sorbet scented with Swiss-made *poire William eau-de-vie*—are masterful. And he makes a point of emphasizing Swiss wines. In my experience, one of Switzerland's best restaurants. *Luxury.*

SOUND OF MUSIC

Théâtre Municipal (Avenue du Théâtre)—Lausanne's opera house—presents an engaging mix of opera, concerts (by Lausanne's noted Orchestre de Chambre and the Geneva-based Orchestre de la Suisse Romande), ballet, and musical comedy. *Palais de Beaulieu* (the Centre des Congrès, or convention hall, on Avenue des Bergières) is, as well, a venue for opera, concerts, ballet, and other entertainment.

SHOPPER'S LAUSANNE

Innovation, the major department store, and with a remarkable grocery and wine department, is on Rue St. François; *Placette,* another department store, is on Rue St. Laurent; and there's a big branch of *Migros* just off Place de la Riponne. *Bon Génie,* with extensive clothing and shoe selections, is on Place St. François. Rue de Bourg emporia include *Franz Carl Weber* (toys); *Divarese* (an Italian moderate-priced shoe chain); *Cartier* (jewelry and watches); *Payot* (link of a bookstore chain); *Blondel* (chocolates); *Théorème* (china, linens, paper goods); *Albion House* (with Hermès and Lanvin clothes, accessories); *Cléo* (with Céline clothes, accessories); *Charles Jourdan* (women's shoes, clothes); *Christofle* (crystal, silver); and *Alain Manoukian* (women's clothes). Note, too, that on Wednesdays and Saturdays Rue de Bourg is the site of an open flower and produce market that's fun to stroll.

INCIDENTAL INTELLIGENCE

Ask the tourist office (below,) for the current timetable of Compagnie Générale de Navigation sur le Lac Léman—so that you can plan an excursion or two on Lake Geneva. Note that fast trains linking Lausanne and Geneva's intercontinental Aéroport de Genève-Cointrin depart frequently the day long. *Further information:* Office du Tourisme, 60 Avenue d'Ouchy, Lausanne.

11

Locarno
Lake Maggiore's Beauty Spot

BACKGROUND BRIEFING

Extraordinary natural beauty does not always favor a town. Nonetheless, Locarno, second city of Ticino—Switzerland's southeasterly Italian-speaking canton—had no trouble either with very early Celts (who may, or may not, have provided its name from the presumed Celtic term for waterside settlement) or later Romans (who created glass in quantity enough for there to be considerable specimens open to contemporary public view).

Locarno's adversaries came later—beginning in the early Middle Ages when Lombard nobles—first lured to a splendidly sited pilgrimage church on a mountain over the town— began to covet Locarno for strategic purposes, with the opening of the not-far-distant St. Gotthard Pass, through the high Alps, due north.

In the late twelfth century, Holy Roman Emperor Frederick Barbarossa decreed Locarno—by then ruled from Lombardy—a territory of the empire. The following century an army from nearby Como largely destroyed the town. Not long after, Milanese troops paddled up Lake Maggiore to Locarno— at its northern tip—and its leaders gained control, remaining for two centuries.

Armies of the southern Swiss cantons, by then united, ousted the Milanese in 1512. But they were hardly bearers of good tidings or goodwill. The town's first century under Swiss auspices saw military destruction, repeated floods, the deadly plague, and the exodus of half a hundred of the most powerful family-clans, as a consequence of the Reformation.

Subsequently, Locarno has fared better. Association with the Confederation occurred in 1803, and the modern era saw Locarno accorded a place in history books as site of the signing in 1925 of the Locarno Pact—a mix of post–World War I treaties and arbitration agreements between Germany (Hitler renounced them a decade later) and its wartime enemies.

Today's Locarno—good humored and good looking—thrives on tourism. German-speaking Swiss are attracted to its delightful Italianate style and ambience. Italians from just over the frontier are drawn by the anomaly of a canton of the Swiss Confederation which is the only territory beyond Italy (the micro-states of San Marino and, only partially, the Vatican excepted) where Italian is the principal official language, and where the culture is an artful Italo-Swiss blend. That leaves the rest of us—non-Swiss and non-Italians. Too often, Locarno (as well as larger Lugano [Chapter 13], Ticino's other "L" city) is bypassed. It's time we mended our ways in this respect. Locarno is lovely.

ON SCENE

Lay of the Land: You walk virtually everywhere in this charmer of a town—and with pleasure. Backed by mountains and fronted by the natural indentation of a *Lake Maggiore* bay, Locarno's core is edged by a garden-fringed waterfront promenade called *Lungolago Giuseppe Motte;* it begins at the western edge of the town and extends eastward into the quarter called *Muralto.* At a point between the two, *Largo Zorri* leads inland to the elongated square—its mostly eighteenth-century buildings are lined with graceful arcades—that is *Piazza Grande,* Locarno's handsome, huge, and humming nerve center, an animated jumble of restaurants and businesses, palm trees and department stores, that lies at the entrance to *Città Vecchia,* the architecturally noteworthy sixteenth- and seventeeth-century Old Town, dominated by the

Municipio—a graceful palazzo of that period that is the City Hall. *Via della Pace*, with its landmark the *Pretorio* or courthouse, wherein the Locarno Pact was signed in 1925—leads south from Piazza Grande. *Piazza Stazione*, site of the main railway station, is due east, and a near neighbor of *Stazione Funicolare*, from where trains depart for the elevated pilgrimage *Church of Madonna del Sasso* (below) and cable cars reaching even higher mountain points above the city. *Fiume Maggia*, the Maggia River, which flows from the mountains into the lake, marks Locarno's western frontier and is the demarcation point between it and the little next-door resort town of *Ascona*, essentially low down, alongside the lake, and without the dramatic elevations of Locarno, albeit popular with German vacationers.

Castello Visconti (Piazza Costello) is Locarno's single most romantic structure—a small but cohesive portion of what had been a much larger medieval castle named for the Milanese clan which long ago ruled the town. The red and blue flag of Ticino Canton flies from it today, but once you step into the arcaded courtyard you're back in the Middle Ages—frescoed walls, venerable furniture, coats of arms, beamed ceilings, and in a pair of museums—utterly beautiful glassware made a couple of millennia back by Romans in local residence, and, contrastingly, a considerable collection of modern art donated by the sculptor Jean Arp (who for a time lived in Locarno), including some 40 of his own works. Museum No. 3 of the castello complex is in a kind of annex building (that, I should warn, is not always open) and shelters a couple of thousand prints and drawings and a hundred-odd paintings, the lot of them relatively contemporary, with Picasso, Chagall, and Utrillo among the artists.

Church of San Antonio (Piazza San Antonio): There is no cathedral in this dominantly Catholic town but San Antonio, the principal parish church, is a Baroque beauty with an immense and elaborate high altar and pretty side chapels. *Via San Antonio*, which leads from the square, is among the more attractive Città Vecchia streets; have a look in the craft and antique shops and peek into courtyards and gardens.

Church of San Francesco (Piazza San Francesco), originally Romanesque, was rebuilt by Franciscans during the Renaissance. Still, the apse and cupola pre-date that era, and side altars are later Baroque. Withal, San Francesco comes together beautifully.

Chiesa Nuova (on Via Cappuccini—one of Città Vecchia's finest streets) is an exuberant Baroque church that was *nuova*, or new, in 1630. A sculpted, larger-than-life St. Christopher dominates its stuccoed facade. But the interior is no less striking. And the rector's residence next door is of the period and similarly striking.

Church of San Vittore (Via della Collegiata, behind the main railway station) is distinguished by its imposing campanile, or bell tower, sixteenth century and with a sculpted equestrian St. Victor. Within, the marble altar is Baroque, but San Vittore is essentially twelfth-century Romanesque—considered among the finest churches of that epoch in Switzerland, and architecturally the finest church of any epoch in church-packed Locarno. You want not to miss the distinctive capitals of columns in the severe but splendid crypt; the frescoed apse, the choir carved of pearwood, and the beautiful wooden ceiling.

Church of Madonna del Sasso (Orselina, above Locarno and reached by funicular from Stazione Funicolare, on Piazza Stazione) straddles a rocky eminence marking the site where, in the late fifteenth century, the Virgin Mary is said to have appeared before a local monk. The church, which dates from that time, is noteworthy for the nonpilgrim visitor because of its spectacular location. There is one especially lovely painting— Bramantino's *Flight into Egypt*, and a museum having to do with pilgrimages over the centuries. But it's the view of town and lake you'll most remember. From Madonna del Sasso you may ascend via cable car (there are four steep flights to climb in the cable car station) to *Mt. Cardada*, at an elevation of 4,200 feet, with a restaurant-café (below) at which you may pause for a drink or lunch before returning to town, taking a walk on the mountain, or ascending even higher—this time via chairlift—to restaurant-equipped *Mt. Cimetta*, just over 5,000 feet.

Ascona, the resort village next door to Locarno, backs a lakefront promenade called simply *Piazza*, and lined with cafés, restaurants, and hotels. An 18-hole golf course and still additional hotels lie beyond the center, many of them along the lake. *Museo d'Arte Moderna* (Via Borgo) has works by such Swiss painters as Paul Klee and Cuno Amiet, and modern foreigners, as well. Visit, as well, a pair of Renaissance Ascona churches: *Pietro e Paolo* (Via Borgo), the main parish church, extensively frescoed, and *Santa Maria della Misericordia* (Via Papio), parts of which are older than Pietro e Paolo and rich in sixteenth-century art.

Bellinzona (11 miles east of Locarno, and an absorbing excursion destination) is the seat of Ticino's cantonal government, and, of respectably advanced age, with a lot to show for its longevity. How many small towns do you know with not one but a trio of walled medieval castles (two housing museums) and as many outstanding churches? *Castel Grande* (by foot uphill from Piazza Collegiata in the center, by car along Via Orico) is, in part at least, as old as the fourth century, with a pair of towers and a courtyard that could be a set from an Errol Flynn movie, and super vistas. *Castello di Montebello* surmounts the hill taking its name, considerably above Castel Grande (above). Dating to the thirteenth century, its dungeon houses *Museo Civico*—a contemporarily created celebration of Bellinzona's past—sculpture fragments, arms, ceramics, jewelry. *Castello di Sasso Corbaro* (Via Ospedale), highest up of the castle trio, is derring-do in the manner of the fifteenth century, and is home—in its dungeon—to a museum whose theme is domestic life in Ticino, over the centuries—costumes and stamps, coins and furniture. *Church of the Collegiata* (Piazza Collegiata, in the center) dates to the Renaissance but its art and artifacts are from later centuries as well—baroque stucco work, eighteenth-century frescoes and pulpit. *Church of Santa Maria delle Grazie* (Via Convento) was Franciscan-built in the fifteenth century; you want to see the massive wall fresco, painted in the Renaissance, of the Crucifixion, and still other splendid frescoes in the first left and first right chapels. *Church of San Biaggio* (in the adjacent village of Ravecchia) is the oldest of the trio, with parts of it dating to the twelfth century. Its bell tower and exterior frescoes are standouts; the interior is art-filled—wall frescoes, painted columns, and chapel altars.

SETTLING IN

Palma au Lac Hotel (Viale Verbano; Phone 33-01-71) takes pride in being Locarno's only five-star house. The staff is at once proficient and cordial. Public spaces are smartly traditional—brown-and-beige lobby, red leather-accented bar, pair of terraced restaurants (one of which I evaluate on a later page). There's an indoor pool with an adjacent solarium/sauna, private beach, and best of all, all 75 balconied rooms and suites—some Art Deco, some traditional, all lakeview. *Luxury.*

Muralto Hotel (Piazza Stazione; Phone 33-01-81) has the most convenient location in town—opposite the train station and heart of everything. Half of its 40-plus rooms are lakeview, terraced, good-sized, and good-looking; they're the ones you want to aim for. Public spaces—up a flight from the compact reception area—include a rambling lobby-bar-lounge and a reliable restaurant. And service is pleasant. Ambassador Swiss/Best Western. *First Class.*

Reber au Lac Hotel (Via alla Riva; Phone 33-02-02): You're away from the center at the Reber but this lovely family-run house—it turned a young 100 in 1986—is charming. You're directly on the lake and there's a big outdoor pool, private beach and tennis court, as well as a pair of good restaurants and a cozy bar. Some of the single rooms (50 all told) are small but the doubles—decor is Louis XV or Louis XVI—I have inspected are spacious and handsome. *First Class.*

Grand Hotel (Via Sempione; Phone 33-02-82) is indeed grand of facade (massive and well-detailed in the manner of the late nineteenth century), of setting (it is fronted by a walled parklike lawn, heart of the city), and of scale (public spaces are as high ceilinged as they are generous sized). Bedrooms are the big surprise. Most of the total of 83, including suites, have been daringly refurbished in sleek contemporary style, with furniture by such internationally known designers as Mies van der Rohe, Charles Eames, Harry Bettoia, and Le Corbusier. But the lobby (with a multitiered chandelier hanging in its atrium) and restaurant remain mostly traditional. There are, as well, a bar-lounge, terrace café, outdoor pool, and tennis court. Not surprisingly, it was the Grand that housed delegates (including Italy's Mussolini and Britain's Neville Chamberlain) at the 1925 Locarno Pact conference, many of whose meetings took place within. *First Class.*

Beau Rivage Hotel (Viale Verbano; Phone 33-13-55)—a next-door neighbor of the Palma au Lac (above)—is an agreeable 40-room house, whose attractive front rooms—all of them with white wrought-iron terraces—face the lake. The inviting restaurant becomes al fresco in summer. Nice. *Moderate.*

Quisisana Hotel (Via del Sole; Phone 33-01-41) is quite central, with comfortable public spaces, competent restaurant, indoor pool and sundeck, and balconies on those of its 45 rooms which face the lake. *Moderate.*

Arcadia al Lago Hotel (Lungolago Guisseppe Motta; Phone 31-02-82) is rather cold contemporary, and a fairish walk from the center. But it is lakefront and all 80 rooms have terraces as well as kitchens. Indoor-outdoor restaurant, bar, and pool. *First Class.*

Rosa Seegarten Hotel (Viale Verbano; Phone 33-87-31) is a central and smallish (25 rooms) house with terraces on its lakefront rooms, restaurant that moves outdoors in summer, and showers rather than tubs in baths. *Moderate.*

Dellavalle Hotel (in Brione, a pretty village high above Locarno, accessible via car along Via Brione, or by means of the funicular linking Locarno with Madonna del Sasso [above];

Phone 33-01-21): This is a get-away-from-it-all hotel, with top-of-the-world views of Locarno, the lake, and the mountains beyond; comfortable rooms with terraces; welcoming ambience; splendidly sited outdoor pool; bar-lounge; and pair of restaurants, one of which is evaluated in a later paragraph. *First Class.*

Orselina Hotel (Orselina, a village above Locarno, even closer to the Madonna del Sasso funicular than Brione [above] and also accessible by way of Via Canovacca from Locarno; Phone 33-02-32) is one of the best-looking contemporary hotels I have encountered in Switzerland. Public spaces, in soft tones of brown and beige, are traditional with antique touches; their picture windows give onto terraces, the better for sweeping panoramic views. The 100 rooms and suites are mostly good-sized. There are a pair of restaurants, a big outdoor pool, and a congenial staff. *First Class.*

DAILY BREAD

Panorama Restaurant (Dellavalle Hotel, Brione; Phone 33-01-21): The excellent-value prix-fixe lunch opens with an extraordinary buffet—scrumptious salads, cold meats, treats galore—that is, to my knowledge, unsurpassed anywhere in the Confederation. Continue with a meal that might embrace the day's soup; such entrée choices as grilled salmon, *escallope* of veal or *entrecôte* served with Bordelaise sauce, concluding with the chef's *vacherin glacé*—a masterful sweet—or a choice of delicious house-baked pastries. Lovely service, sweeping views. In my experience, one of Switzerland's best restaurants. *First Class.*

Centenario (17 Lungolago; Phone 33-82-22) is not overlarge. You are welcomed cordially, and seated at a flower-centered table from which you observe that paintings on the walls of this smallish, intimate restaurant are contemporary and of quite as high caliber as the fare. Open with crayfish salad. Trout from a nearby stream is masterfully prepared. So is roast lamb, either with an accent of rosemary or mustard-seasoned. And roast pigeon, tarragon-flavored, is special. Conclude with Centenario's celebrated hot dessert, *gratin d'orange*, sorbet-topped. *Luxury.*

Le Petit Champignon (8 Via alla Motte, a 5-minute drive from the center; Phone 31-23-54) is low-key in look, and with a kindly staff. The relatively limited menu, changed weekly, offers a good value prix-fixe at lunch and a much costlier seven course *menu gourmand,* available at dinner only if everyone at your table orders it. Or dine à la carte, perhaps beginning with frogs legs sautéed in Sauterne or crab-stuffed ravioli. Grilled lamb chops and port-sauced filet of beef are favored entrées. And desserts are as inventive as they are delicious. *First Class/Luxury.*

Citadella (Via Citadella; Phone 31-58-85) is surely Locarno's most atmospheric restaurant. Setting is a centuries-old house just opposite Chiesa Nuova (above)—on one of the handsomer of Città Vecchia's streets. Opt for either the main floor dining room or up a flight—with beamed ceilings and fine old paintings. Open with a pasta (ravioli is rewarding, but so are variations on the theme of spaghetti), and select grilled swordfish from among the seafood entrées for which this restaurant is noted. *First Class.*

Coq d'Or (La Palma au Lac Hotel, Viale Verbano; Phone 33-01-71) is arguably the most elegant dining environment in town. You lunch or dine under painted ceilings in a room whose paneled walls are hung with creditable paintings. Face in the right direction and you're watching chefs at work in the open grill-kitchen. If you're two or more—and really famished—the nine (yes, *nine!*) course *menu gastronomique* may suit. Chances are you'll settle for two or three à la carte dishes—fish soup or a nouvelle-inspired duck salad to start, the house's own mussel and crayfish casserole or truffled breast of turkey as possible entrées, with a dessert masterwork—*crêpes soufflées aux poires, sauce Willamine*—missed at your peril. Skilled service. *Luxury.*

Svizzera (Piazza Grande; Phone 31-28-74) is an apt choice for lunch on a sunny day when you do well to select an outdoor table on the square. Pizza is the specialty, but you're in Switzerland (the restaurant's name is the way it is spelled in the Italian language), so that *bratwurst mit rösti*—the national standby—is available as well. *Moderate.*

Mövenpick Oldrati (Viale Verbano; Phone 33-85-44) is strategically situated on the lakefront near the steamer pier. Sit on the terrace of this attractive link of a national chain, for a gooey ice cream concoction or a drink. Order a meal indoors and you want to open it with selections from the salad buffet. Fresh fish is a favored entrée. *Moderate/First Class.*

Buffet Stazione (Piazza Stazione): Call it what you will—Bahnhof Buffet, Buffet de la Gare, or by its Italian title—Locarno's station restaurant—plaid cloths on its tables, wood-paneled walls—serves up reasonably priced prix-fixe menus—built around *osso bucco* or roast veal, to name two entrées—and à la carte plates as well. *Moderate.*

Caffè Ravelli (Piazza Grande) is locally celebrated, and not without reason, for the species of cookie called *amaretti* and a range of pastries. Have coffee or tea in conjunction. Other Piazza Grande caffès include *Paolino* and *Varenna*, ideal for people-watching. All are *Moderate.*

Caffè Al Porto (on the Viale Verbano side of the Muralto Hotel): Order *cappuccino*, a glass of wine, ice cream, or a snack. And watch lakeside crowds pass in review. *Moderate.*

Caffè Elvezia (Piazza Ascona) is indicated for refreshments or a casual lunch pause in the course of an Ascona foray. *Moderate.*

Cardada Hotel Restaurant/Caffè (a hop and a skip from the Cardada cable car station, above Locarno): You've come for the view. It looks even better from a table on the terrace of the Cardada Hotel, in conjunction with coffee, a drink, or a tasty lunch. *Moderate.*

Unione Hotel Restaurant (Via Général Guisan, Bellinzona; Phone 22-55-77) is a sensible choice for lunch in the course of

Bellinzona exploration. Choose the prix-fixe menu or order pasta and salad à la carte. *Moderate/First Class.*

SOUND OF MUSIC
Concerti di Locarno take place spring through summer, in the Church of San Francesco and the auditorium of *Societè Elettrice Sopracenerina.* Settimane Musicale, or Musical Weeks, occur late August through mid-October; Locarno's Church of San Francesco is a venue, along with Ascona's Collegio Papio Church; performances are by visiting symphonies, chamber orchestras, and other musical groups, the range London's Academy of St. Martin's in the Fields through Yugoslavia's Slovenia Philharmonic.

Festival Internazionale del Film: Locarno's celebrated annual movie festival—approaching its fourth decade—takes place for three August weeks, traditionally opening, al fresco, in Piazza Grande.

SHOPPER'S LOCARNO
Piazza Grande and satellite streets constitute the mercantile core of town. *Jelmoli* and *Innovazione*—the top department stores— are both on the square, along with *Bücherer* (watches, jewelry); *Monn* (men's and women's clothes); *Franz Carl Weber* (toys); and *Bosto & Franconi* (fancy groceries, wine), to cite a few. And there are many shops in pedestrians-only Via Ramognia.

INCIDENTAL INTELLIGENCE

Hydrofoil boats depart Locarno for Stresa/Isola Bella in Italy, and there are halfday excursions from Locarno to other Italian points, including Como, Bellagio, and Milan (see *Italy at Its Best*). Still other hydrofoils link Locarno with nearby Italian towns like Luino, Cannobio, and Intra; ask the tourist office (below) for the *orario* (timetable) of Navigazione Lago Maggiore. If your approach to Locarno is via train from western or west-central Switzerland, you will no doubt travel to Brig where there is a change of trains and a trip through one of the world's longest rail tunnels—the 12¼-mile Simplon—to Domodossola, in Italy.

You'll go through entry customs at the Italian town of Iselle, and departure customs at the Italian town of Ribellasca, at which point the train returns to Swiss territory, stopping at Camedo for minimal Swiss entry formalities. *Further information:* Ente Turistico di Locarno e Valli, 2 Viale Balli, Locarno; Ente Turistico di Bellinzona, Via Camminati, Bellinzona.

Lucerne/Luzern

The Quintessential Switzerland

BACKGROUND BRIEFING

Lucerne is arguably the quintessential Swiss town—small enough to be downright homey and eminently walkable; large enough to be endowed with cultural facilities, superior hotels, eating places, and after-dark options; splendidly enough sited—on an idyllic lake and Alp-surrounded—to offer as smashingly scenic an urban environment as is to be found in the Confederation. If it is without the sophistication of the Big Two cities, Geneva and Zürich, its easy charm certainly surpasses that of, say, smaller and less diverting Interlaken or larger but less spontaneous Basel.

Credit the sound esthetics of a band of Benedictine monks for what came to be Lucerne. They established a monastery—as long ago as the middle decades of the eighth century—at the point where the Reuss River meets Vierwaldstättersee (a.k.a. Lake Lucerne), in central Switzerland. An adjacent settlement evolved into a regional trade center, given its proximity to the increasingly trafficked St. Gotthard Pass, which opened in the thirteenth century. The pass was responsible for increasing commerce between Lucerne and Italy, to the point where powerful Habsburg emperors annexed Lucerne by means of outright purchase from an absentee ruler, the abbot of a monastery in distant Alsace. Not at all happy with the authoritarian Habsburgs,

Lucerners joined the newly created Swiss Confederation—three cantons which had liberated themselves from the Austrians in 1332.

Increasingly prosperous over the Renaissance and baroque eras, the eighteenth century saw Lucerne become capital of the French-backed, short-lived (1798–1803) Helvetia Republic. Half a century later, it joined the modern Swiss state. And as the nineteenth century became the twentieth, pleasure visitors arrived. The grand hotels that were built on or within view of its mountain-backed lake happily remain today.

ON SCENE
Lay of the Land: This is an easy walking city; you're never far from the lake or the mountains. Lucerne's northern and southern quarters are bisected by the *Reuss River,* as it flows easterly into *Lake Lucerne.* The south side is not without significant points—railway station on *Bahnhofplatz,* an important shopping street, *Pilatusstrasse* (leading south from Bahnhofplatz), nearby docks for lake steamers and neighboring *Kongresshaus* (which shelters the fine-arts museum, below), important churches later described, and *Mt. Gütsch,* reached by a funicular whose lower terminus is on *Gütschstrasse.*

By and large, though, visitor's Lucerne is north of the water, based on *Schwanenplatz,* which flanks *Seebrücke,* widest of six bridges connecting the two segments of town. *Nationalquai* leads east from Schwanenplatz, following the lake to the *Kursaal,* or Casino (with low-stakes gambling, places to dine, drink, and be entertained) and several palatial hotels. *Grebdekstrasse* takes one northwest from Schwanenplatz into the *Altstadt,* or Old Town, and its trendy boutiques, cafés, and restaurants. Not far north is *Museggstrasse,* paralleling *Museggmauer*—a section of Lucerne's extraordinary medieval wall, blessedly preserved and punctuated by no less than nine superb towers; three of these, *Männli, Zeit,* and *Schirmer,* are open in summer. *Löwenplatz,* northwest of Museggstrasse, edges the landmark *Löwendenkmal,* a larger-than-life and somnolent lion designed by the Danish sculptor Thorvaldsen in 1819 (but actually carved into sandstone by his pupils) as a memorial to Swiss troops killed in the French Revolution. It edges *Gletschergarten,* the so-called Glacier Garden, a geological

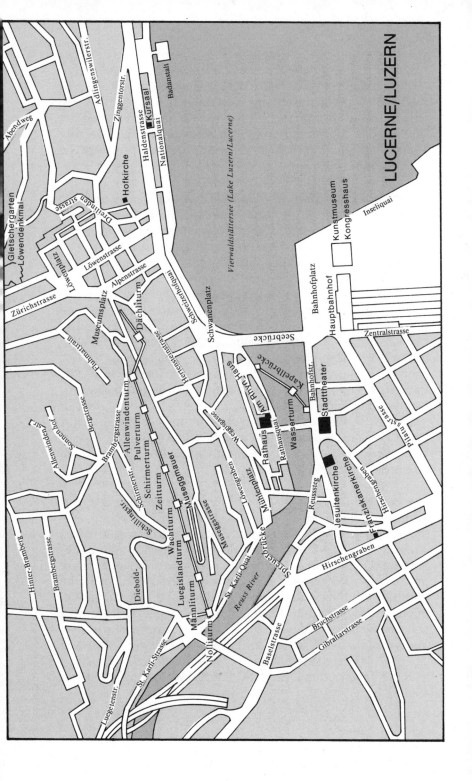

curiosity with an adjacent museum. It is from *Rathausquai,* named for the *Rathaus* or Town Hall (below) that one gains *Kapellbrücke,* better known of the two frame footbridges (below) spanning the river; the other, *Spreuerbrücke,* is reached from westerly *Mühlenplatz.* Most significant of the museums, *Verkehrshaus der Schweiz* (below) is a fair distance east of the core on *Haldenstrasse.*

Bird's-eye view from Mt. Pilatus: There are four points to be made about Pilatus. First, its elevation—7,000 feet—assures (in clear weather, at least) unforgettable views not only of Lucerne and the lake, but of the Alps considerably distant, and of closer-to-sea-level Swiss territory, as well. Second: You may go one way, return another. It's exciting to approach by means of cable car; you start at Kriens, 12 miles by bus from Lucerne, ascending to Frakmüntegg, transfer point to another cable car to the summit. Plan your journey so as to arrive for lunch and relaxation on the sun terrace. Then descend (except in winter) by train—the route is a remarkable engineering achievement—from the station at Pilatus-Kulm to Alpnachstad, at the base of the mountain, lakeside, from where a steamer will transport you—comfortably and scenically—back to town. (Alternatively, or additionally—if you collect mountaintops—consider excursions via a series of conveyances to 6,900-foot *Mt. Rigi,* and/or *Mt. Titlus,* at 10,000 feet the most elevated of our trio, high above the eternal snow line.)

Verkehrshaus der Schweiz (which translates as *Swiss Transport Museum* and is entered from Lidostrasse, off Haldenstrasse, a bus or taxi ride east of the center): Sound like a drag to transport yourself from downtown to trek through a museum whose subject matter is transportation? Well, that's what I thought, before my first visit. What you would be missing, if you didn't make the journey, would be an all-Switzerland leader of a museum. Exhibits are housed in a striking campus of a complex, lakefront, in a dozen sleekly styled pavilions. Idea is to convey achievements of transportation in its various forms—surface, water, air, and space. A landing strip is home to historic Swissair planes, including a pioneering DC-3 (and there's an amusing display of

Swissair crew uniforms, over the decades). Rail locomotives, antique and contemporary, are on scene: you may walk through
interiors of train coaches, including some from the nineteenth
century, of the same vintage as those in London's considerably
less ambitious Transport Museum (see *Britain at Its Best*). Arrive
at the proper time and you may take a ride on a train. There are
old trolleys, too, and exhibits of varying species of transport, the
range sleighs, sedan chairs, and skis through scooters, bikes,
motorcycles, cable cars, even including toy hobbyhorses. Miss
the planetarium if you must, but on no account skip a showing
of Swissorama, an in-the-round film that's a 360-degree panorama projection depicting the national landscape, starting,
appropriately enough, with the view you will no doubt have had
from Mt. Pilatus (above). Restaurant.

Historic bridges: What is most extraordinary about this pair of
wooden footbridges spanning the Reuss River is that, despite
advanced age, they are used by Lucerners—and by visitors—
as a means of pedestrian transport, quite as functional as they
have been since they were constructed. In the case of the more
celebrated *Kapellbrücke*—with its distinctive octagon of a stone
tower—the date was 1333. *Sprauerbrücke* followed, in 1408.
You want to make at least one crossing on each, to take in overhead paintings, the lot of them seventeenth century;
Kapelbrücke's depict bright moments in Lucerne history.
Sprauerbrücke's—curious these—have as their cheerless
theme "The Dance of Death."

Jesuitenkirche (Bahnhofstrasse)—built by the Jesuits in 1663
and still operated by them—has quite the most beautiful interior
of any church in town. Indeed, this light and lovely Baroque
church is an all-Swiss leader, not unlike counterparts in Munich
and throughout Bavaria (see *Germany at Its Best*)—splendidly
proportioned and extravagantly decorated, its barrel-vaulted
ceilings are a symphony of pink and white stucco, with gilt
frames enclosing frescoes, gilt capitals atop pilasters, a brilliant
high altar, a pulpit topped with a gilded angel, richly frescoed
side chapels, and an organ of special beauty.

Hofkirche (Stiftsstrasse, a short walk east from Schwanenplatz): This church's two severely pointed steeples contrast boldly with the twin onion-steeples of the Jesuitenkirche (above). The Hofkirche, although rebuilt at about the same time as the Jesuits' church, is an architectural hybrid, part medieval (the Gothic steeples), part Baroque (that part of the facade between the steeples), part Renaissance, or at least in the style of the Renaissance. Details of the interior stand out more than the church overall. Have a look at beautifully carved stalls of the choir, wooden frame of the organ, spiral stairway leading to the pulpit, high altar in black marble, and painting- and sculpture-filled side chapels.

Rathaus (Rathausquai): The old Town Hall is a late Renaissance masterwork whose facade—galleries at street level, extending to a broadly pitched roof over its third floor—is set off by waters of the Reuss. Ascend to the second floor for inspection of a series of paneled rooms, with original parquet floors quite as impressive as walls and ceilings. One room, originally the municipal archives, has drawers, each elaborately embellished, surfacing its four walls, each of which is surmounted by a carved-wood gallery.

Am Rhyn Haus (Furrengasse, near the Rathaus [above]) is a late Renaissance townhouse, built in the early seventeenth century, that is a perfect foil for an up-a-flight cache of paintings, lithographs, and ceramics by Pablo Picasso—*Picasso-Sammlung der Stadt Luzern*—that were given to the city by a public-spirited couple, Siegfried and Angela Rosengart, on the occasion of its 800th anniversary in 1978. This is mostly late Picasso—1950s and 1960s. Exceptions include a 1939 gouache, *Standing Nude,* and a 1933 drawing, *Minotaur and Nude.* But your eye will be caught, as well, by the later *Woman Dressing Her Hair, Luncheon on the Grass* (based on the Manet painting, *Déjeuner sur l'herbe*), two witty variations on the theme of *A Woman with a Hat,* and an exquisitely sculpted *Blue Dove.*

Franziskanerkirche (Hirschengraben) is a treasure of a Gothic church built by Franciscans at the turn of the thirteenth century, embellished in the Baroque era, and the subject of contemporary restoration. Original frescoes, surfacing the wall separating nave from chancel, and surmounting the high altar, are striking. The seventeenth-century carved-wood choir and pulpit are noteworthy, too.

Kunstmuseum (Zündstrasse, near the Bahnhof and a part of the Kongresshaus complex) has a proclivity for special exhibitions which are all well and good, except that they displace substantial segments of the permanent collection. If you visit the museum when it is devoid of temporary shows, you'll come upon considerable Swiss work—gifted and prolific Ferdinand Hodler (1853–1918), the earlier Arnold Böcklin, and Anton Graf are three such. There is, as well, a sampling of medieval and Renaissance paintings—and of such modern foreigners as Dufy, Vlaminck, and Soutine.

Richard Wagner Museum (at the tip of a parklike peninsula in the Triebschen quarter): You have to be a dedicated Wagner disciple to want to make the journey—a good distance from the center—to this undeniably attractive—and attractively situated—nineteenth-century house. It's where Wagner created *Siegfried,* and it contains original scores; pictures of the composer; his wife, Cosima (Franz Liszt's daughter); and of demented King Ludwig II of Bavaria, who idolized Wagner to the point of heavily subsidizing him (see *Germany at Its Best*). There's a collection of musical instruments, and the views are pretty—you look across the water to the hotel-dotted plateau of Burgenstock (below). In summer there is boat service from near the Bahnhof, in town, but the rest of the year you take a pricey cab or approach via bus, with the house a ten- to twelve-minute walk from the nearest stop.

Panorama (Löwenplatz) is a 12,000 square-foot painting—it covers the circular wall of the second floor of the nondescript building in which it is situated—meticulously detailing a battle between the French and the Swiss during the Franco-Prussian War in 1870–71. It was the work of seven artists, a chap named

Castres dominantly, with Ferdinand Hodler among the supplementary six. If you grew up with platoons of toy soldiers or are a battle buff, this is for you.

SETTLING IN

Palace Hotel (10 Haldenstrasse; Phone 50-22-22) went up in the closing years of the last century, in the exuberant style of the Belle Époque (with not only a central tower but a side one, as well, in case you miss the first), and sweeping public spaces. Recent years have seen it redecorated throughout with notable flair. Picture windows now constitute the terraced lakeside wall of the main lounge, furnished and accessorized in shades of salmon and pale green, with antique tapestries to provide interest. The principal restaurant (worthy of an evaluation on a later page) is Louis XVI but with sprightly touches of color and accent. Deep brown leather chairs surround tables in the cozy bar. A café occupies the terrace during warm weather months. The 170 rooms and suites are—in my not inconsiderable experience of such—quite the most consistently good-looking of any hotel that I know in Switzerland; aim for a balconied one facing the lake. Those that I have either inhabited or inspected are a mix of eighteenth-century style furniture, brass bedside lamps, crystal chandeliers, sumptuous textiles in delicious combinations of color and pattern. And separate stall showers supplement tubs in baths of bigger rooms and suites. Congenial General Manager Jürg Reinshagen is on scene breakfast through postdinner, seeing that his guests are happy. And central Schwanenplatz is a pleasurable five-minute stroll along the lake. Member, Leading Hotels of the World. *Luxury.*

Schweizerhof Hotel (Schweizerhofquai; Phone 50-22-11): It is not every hotel that is positioned on a street which is named for it. Which is nothing less than the heart-of-town Schweizerhof deserves; its central building goes all the way back to 1846. The stadium-size lobby-lounge contains original furnishings. Paneling, chandeliers, sconces, stucco work, paintings throughout date to early Schweizerhof days. Fruitwood chairs enclose tables in the welcoming bar and the restaurant, reviewed on a later page, is handsome. Each of the 148 rooms and suites is one of a

kind; in many, original furniture remains, with crystal chandeliers and chaise longues not uncommon; accommodations to aim
for are those affording a view of the lake and Mt. Pilatus. The
Schweizerhof staff—every guest meets cordial General Manager Kurt Alchenberger—are pros, and they smile. Distinguished Hotels/Robert F. Warner. *Luxury.*

Grand National Hotel (4 Haldenstrasse; Phone 50-11-11):
César Ritz and Auguste Escoffier managed the Grand
National—the former out front, the latter in the kitchen—for a
dozen of its formative years. This imposing lakefront house,
opened in 1871, has been thoughtfully updated and is expertly
managed. There are 75 traditionally furnished rooms and suites
(those with brass beds are special), several restaurants, including one that embraces a lakefront terrace and is evaluated on a
subsequent page, a lively bar, and an up-to-the-minute swimming pool/sauna/gym. Central. *Luxury.*

Carlton Tivoli Hotel (57 Haldenstrasse; Phone 51-30-51) is the
most distant from the center of the luxury houses, set in its own
garden, across Haldenstrasse from the lakefront promenade.
There are a hundred rooms and suites, their look traditional,
their sizes varying; inviting lobby; pair of restaurants (one formal, one in a detached pavilion edging the lake); and a pair of
chatty bars. This is a friendly, well-operated house. Ambassador
Swiss/Best Western. *Luxury.*

Wilden Mann Hotel (30 Bahnhofstrasse; Phone 23-16-66) is a
50-room hostelry occupying no less than seven contiguous
houses, the lot of them dating to the early sixteenth century,
with the same owning family for the last 150 years. Those of the
accommodations I have inspected—especially including a junior suite—are attractive and often antique-accented, and with
partially beamed ceilings. The rustic bar is friendly and there are
a pair of restaurants (one later reviewed). The alert staff is head-
ed by Susan Rick, pioneering as a female hotel manager in a
country where males (or, more often, males assisted by their
wives) dominate the field. *First Class.*

Balances & Bellevue Hotel (7 Metzgerranie; Phone 51-18-51)
—long on scene and relatively recently reopened after a
stem-to-stern refurbishing—borders the Reuss River and has 80
rooms (riverside ones, especially those with balconies, are the
most desirable), pair of restaurants (one with a riverside café),
bar-lounge. Ambassador Swiss/Best Western. *First Class.*

Union Hotel (16 Löwenstrasse; Phone 22-34-78) is at its best
with respect to location (central) and public spaces (high
ceilinged and handsome with an absolutely fabulous ballroom).
There are two restaurants (Pony Snack is convenient for well-
priced lunches), a bar frequented by neighborhood regulars and
70 okay rooms, mostly contemporary. *First Class.*

Château Gütsch Hotel (Kanonenstrasse; Phone 22-02-72) is
ideal for honeymooners or for that matter any travelers who
want to be isolated from—and atop—the city. You gain this
tower-topped nineteenth-century *schloss* via funicular, from
Gütschstrasse, way below. Queen Victoria was a guest in the
current building's predecessor. There are 40 rooms and suites—
those I have inspected are pleasant—as well as a restaurant
(later counseled as a dinner excursion destination). *First Class.*

Eden Hotel (47 Haldenstrasse; Phone 51-38-06) is a near neighbor of the Palace (above), a nineteenth-century house with its
higher-up lakeview rooms preferred. There are 30 rooms all
told. Restaurant, bar. Good value. *Moderate.*

Des Alpes Hotel (5 Rathausquai; Phone 53-58-25) has a super
central location, facing the Reuss River, core of town. There are
30 adequate rooms and—the Des Alpes at its best—a restaurant
with a waterfront view. *Moderate.*

Kolping Hotel (8 Friedenstrasse; Phone 51-58-25) is well situated, just up Löwenstrasse from the landmark Hofkirche (above).
There are 70 functional rooms, restaurant, and bar. *Moderate.*

Bürgenstock Hotels (on Bürgenstock, a 3,000-foot mountain
that's a half-hour's drive from Lucerne, which it overlooks) is a

unique complex of three alongside-each-other hostelries sharing owner-management, as well as the Bürgenstock Club (with
indoor/outdoor swimming pool, sauna, solarium, gym, restaurant, and bars), nine-hole golf course, chapel, wee-hours disco,
post office, and a funicular connecting the plateau with the lake
(there is a paved, all-weather road as well). *Grand* (Phone 64-12-
12) is quite the grandest of the hotel trio with 62 rooms and
suites. It and the *Palace* (Phone 66-11-22), with 68 rooms and
suites, and the bulk of the complex's convention and meeting facilities, are both *Luxury* category, while the attractive *Park*
(Phone 64-13-31) is *First Class.* Decor throughout, the modern
Bürgenstock Club excepted, is traditional with lobbies veritable
Old Masters art galleries. Tintoretto, Rubens (his enormous
Diana and the Hunt), Snyders, Magnasco, Maes, Panini, and
Anton Graf are among painters whose works I have noted, and
there are many more. Those of the bedrooms and suites I have
inspected are as tasteful as they are impeccably maintained. Bar-
lounges are animated and restaurants range from dressy (black
tie upon occasion) to the rustic *Taverne*, where *fondue, raclette,*
and Swiss veal dishes are specialties. And if you've stayed at the
Flüela Hotel in Davos (Chapter 5), you'll see familiar faces; the
Flüela (closed in summer) and Bürgenstock (closed in winter)
staffs (but not, of course, managements) interchange. Member,
Leading Hotels of the World.

DAILY BREAD
Chez Marianne (a.k.a. Zum Raben; 5 Kornmarkt; Phone 51-51-
25) is the multichambered restaurant of a cookbook author who
is, as well, a gifted chef. And who knows a thing or two about
decor. Each of the four component parts of this restaurant—
paneled Weinstübe, Renaissance-look Schultheissenstübe, rustic Beizli, posh Reuss Stübe—is attractive in its way. But the
fare's the thing. Marianne deftly melds traditional French and
Swiss cuisines with imaginative contemporary touches. Her
prix-fixe gourmet menu is as good-value as it is good-tasting; it
might open with a beautifully composed, deliciously dressed
seasonal salad, proceed with a dumpling-dotted fish soup,
which would be preparatory to sherry-sauced breast of duck,
garnished with spinach and noodles that have been cooked with

morilles. Her fish, beef, and chicken entrées are exemplary, too. Dessert? Select house-made strawberry sherbet topped with fresh berries, the lot buried under Marianne's own strawberry sauce. Charming waitresses. In my experience, one of Switzerland's best restaurants. *First Class*.

Old Swiss House (4 Löwenplatz; Phone 51-61-71) is indeed an old Swiss house, owned and operated by the Bucholzer family since it went up in 1859. At first glance, the look from without is ominously *Hansel and Gretel*, its half-timbering scarlet-hued rather than in its natural state, and the facade almost too freshly painted. Go inside, though, and you like what you see—antique windows, shelves with aged Meissen, Baroque pewter, oak doors weathered over long centuries, Renaissance coats of arms in stained-glass windows. Tables are handsomely set, there are roses in the silver bud vases, and you tuck into the day's *menu du marché*—shrimp-studded avocado as an opener, cream of mushroom soup following; Hollandaise-sauced asparagus as the next course, with U.S.-imported *steak au poivre* the entrée. Super service. *Luxury*.

Mignon Grill (Palace Hotel, 10 Haldenstrasse; Phone 50-22-22): You could be in your club. A pale green hue has been worked into the paneling, the same color as the velvet of the Louis XVI chairs at widely spaced tables set in pink linen. A tuxedoed captain takes your order: *mousseline* of trout with a red caviar and wine sauce as a starter; *médaillons de lapin* (rabbit as you've not known it), thyme-sauced, with a mixed fresh vegetable garnish to follow. The trolley comes to table with two levels of desserts; you weaken, selecting chocolate cake. Lovely. *Luxury*.

La Rotonde (Schweizerhof Hotel, Schweizerhofquai; Phone 50-22-11) embraces two levels; the upper, crystal-chandeliered, the lower, more contemporary with picture windows giving onto the square. Tables are set in pink. There's a prix-fixe menu and an extensive à la carte. The chef's *pâté* is a standout; so are snails prepared in classic Burgundy style. Filet of pork or veal steak are favored entrées. The traditional *apfelkuchen* and chocolate mousse are but two dessert tempters. Everything is delicious, carefully presented, graciously served. *First Class/Luxury.*

Barbatti (Töpferstrasse 10; Phone 51-13-41) occupies a pair of felicitous rooms in smartly styled nineteenth-century quarters. Choose the forward room and the look is Venetian crystal chandeliers and framed Swiss art; opt for the back, and your eye is on one of Signor Barbatti's antique clocks and a mass of equestrian etchings. Why not be the first on your block to have sampled Barbatti's *spaghetti al Caviale* (the sauce is flecked with caviar)? Opt, if you prefer, for more prosaic *tortellini* or *rigatoni,* following with veal *piccata* or roast chicken, and concluding with the house's celebrated chocolate mousse. Convivial and delicious. *Luxury.*

Promenade (Grand National Hotel, 4 Haldenstrasse: Phone 50-11-11) is indicated on a sunny day. Take a table on the terrace, fronting the lakefront promenade, ordering the *plat du jour* or an à la carte lunch that might open with choice of salads from the buffet, continue with *Wiener Backhendl*—fried chicken, Vienna-style—concluding with an ice cream dessert. *First Class.*

Wilden Mann Hotel Restaurant (30 Bahnhofstrasse; Phone 23-16-66) offers good value with its prix-fixe menu—five courses with the range salad, the day's soup, a seafood casserole, *entrecôte* steak or a pork or veal entrée nicely garnished, with an ice cream dessert topped with fresh fruit, to conclude. Friendly. *First Class.*

Mt. Pilatus restaurants (Phone 96-12-55): Take your choice of the big, *Moderate* category cafeteria, the also *Moderate* terrace, or the *First Class* Taverne in the Bellevue Hotel. In the adjacent Pilatus Kulm Hotel, Sun Terrace and Stübli are both *Moderate,* while the Pilatus Restaurant is *First Class.* Fare ranges from *bratwurst mit rösti*—the reliable all-Swiss standby—through prix-fixe menus embracing soup, such entrées as *veal cordon bleu* or *entrecôte* steak, followed by salad and a sweet. No charge for the view.

Château Gütsch Hotel Restaurant (Gütsch; Phone 22-02-72) is indicated for a romantic dinner, with vistas of the city from a terrace bathed in moonlight. The five-course menu—consommé, an appetizer followed by a salad and a choice of entrées (veal steak, pork chops), with a super dessert—is good-value and nicely served. *First Class.*

Mövenpick (4 Pilatusstrasse; Phone 23-62-50)—Lucerne link of a commendable chain—runs its usual wide gamut here—burgers and pastas, steaks and salads. With lavish ice cream desserts. *Moderate/First Class.*

City (14 Holbeingasse; Phone 34-39-67) is at once central and temptingly tabbed, with its prix-fixe menu—based perhaps on roast pork, a good buy. *Moderate.*

Hein (24 Hertensteinstrasse) is a big, bustling, and beloved Lucerne *konditorei*. Go for coffee and pastry or a casual lunch. *Moderate.*

Mr. Pickwick (18 Rathaus Quai): You're thirsty and you crave something cold, the while resting tired tootsies? Have a beer with Herr Pickwick. Outdoor tables. *Moderate.*

SOUND OF MUSIC

Stadttheater (Bahnhofplatz)—the gracefully neo-classic Opera House facing the Bahnhofplatz side of Kapellbrücke—is the town's principal venue for opera, ballet, concerts, and other entertainment. The tourist office (below) has schedules.

Internationale Musikfestwochen—Lucerne International Music Festival—takes place annually, mid-August through early September, in the Kunst und Kongresshaus (Bahnhofplatz) and other locales, including the Rathaus and Stadttheater. Imported musical organizations are of the caliber of the Berlin Philharmonic, Orchestre de Paris, and London Symphony—all recent performers.

SHOPPER'S LUCERNE

Pilatusstrasse, Lucerne's main shopping street, is the site of *Jelmoli*, No. 1 department store and part of a chain, with a restaurant and grocery as well as fashions and typical souvenirs. *Migros*, also a link of a chain, is moderate category and on Hertensteinstrasse, not far from Schwanenplatz; *EPA*, part of another budget chain, is on Mühlenplatz. If you're in town on a Saturday or a Tuesday, stroll the *open-air markets* in the arcaded streets on either side of the river. And note these interesting shops at various points: *Grieder* (Schweizerhofquai), the very same you may know from Zürich for modish and pricey men's and women's clothes; *Bücherer* (Schwanenplatz), *Gübelin* (Schweizerhofquai), *Les Must de Cartier* (Kappelplatz), *Berreterot* (Löwenstrasse)—but four of many watch stores; *Aux Arts du Feu* (12 Kapellplatz) and *Kristallhaus* (18 Pilatusstrasse)—crystal, silver, and porcelain, including Swiss-made Langenthal china; *Boss* (1 Kramgasse), custom-made gold jewelry; *Heimatwerk* (14 Franziskanerplatz)—ever so costly crafts: textiles, pottery, woodenwares, toys; *Sturzenegger* (7 Schwanenplatz) and *Au Trianon* (2 Leodegarstrasse), embroidered goods; *Bolling-Schneider* (11 Haldenstrasse), Swiss Army knives, dolls, and music boxes; *Bally* (Kappelplatz and 18 Hertensteinstrasse), shoes; *Alte Suidtersche Apotheke* (7 Bahnhofstrasse)—an atmospheric pharmacy in fifteenth-century quarters; *Nordmann* (Schlossergasse), chocolates; and *Robert Räber* (9 Schweizerhofquai), English-language books.

INCIDENTAL INTELLIGENCE

The tourist office (below) has timetables for lake cruises; earmark half a day for an excursion on the water. *Further information:* Verkehrsbüro; 6 Haldenstrasse, Lucerne.

13

Lugano
Pride of Ticino

BACKGROUND BRIEFING

Ascend the funicular to the summit of Monte Salvatore on a day when the sun is strong and the clouds billowy, and your thoughts turn first to Hong Kong; you're atop its celebrated Peak, high above the South China Sea and the adjacent Chinese mainland. No, you say, it could be Sugar Loaf, with Rio de Janeiro and the South Atlantic beneath you. It is, of course, neither. What you observe is Lugano, mini-metropolis of Ticino, Switzerland's remarkable Italian-speaking canton, with the lake taking its name just before it, and two bigger, more celebrated bodies of water—Lago Maggiore on Lugano's west flank, Lago di Como to the east. And as snowy frosting on this scenic cake, a range of Alps—cut through by the St. Gotthard Pass—as a northern backdrop.

It is no wonder, given a situation as strategic—smack between power centers of neighboring Italy and the Teutonic north—as it is splendid, that Lugano, in something like 25 centuries of recorded history, has not escaped attention. There are traces in its neighborhood of settlement, as long ago as the fourth century before Christ, by the Liguri, who came from the east, coexisting with Gauls who migrated from the west. Romans arrived a couple of hundred years later, bringing their well-honed sense of organization, their Latin language, their creative culture. That heritage was to stand the Luganese in good stead during the turmoil of medieval centuries when Lugano was mostly under the thumb of a succession of bishops based in the rich neighboring Italian city of Como, whose hegemony was frequently challenged by also-powerful Dukes of Milan, with occasional incursions of military force by assorted Swiss and French factions, to add not necessarily welcome bits of spice.

In 1512, Lugano became a bailiwick of newly federated Switzerland, the while achieving increased economic clout (churches and mansions, many still standing, were manifestations of newfound wealth), and the beginnings of an Italo-Swiss personality which to this day distinguishes Ticino from Italy on the one hand, and German- and French-speaking Switzerland, on the other.

ON SCENE

Lay of the Land: This is a city of instant charm and sensible geography. It is separated from Lake Lugano by an impeccably maintained park accented by beds of camellias, containing among other things a statue of a chap named Giorgio Washington, erected as a tribute to his adopted land by a son of Lugano who emigrated to the United States in the nineteenth century. (Virtually every family in town, and from throughout Ticino, for that matter, has U.S. [usually California] relatives.) The park contains, as well, an al fresco museum of modern sculpture, a public beach, and a trio of lake-steamer piers. And the promenade flanking it goes by three titles—*Riva Paradiso* (bearing the name of the Paradiso quarter of town immediately south of the center), *Riva Caccia,* and *Riva Vela*—and it is eminently walkable. Running more or less parallel with it, just inland to the west, is Lugano's main shopping street, pedestrians-only *Via Nassa;* it is edged by busy *Piazza della Riforma* (site of the neoclassic *Municipio*—City Hall—dating to 1840) at its north, with pretty *Piazza Battaglini* at midpoint, and *Piazza Luini* named for the Renaissance painter whose frescoes distinguish the square's *Church of Santa Maria degli Angioli* (below). *Via Cattedrale* leads from Via Nassa to *Piazza San Lorenzo,* and Lugano's *cathedral* (below). The world-class *Thyssen-Bornemisza Collection* is housed in a palazzo at the extreme western edge of the water-front. Delightfully strollable older quarters are inland from the lake, based on squares dominated by such historic churches as *Sant' Antonio* (Piazza Dante), *San Rocco* (Piazza Maghetti), and *Loretto* (Piazza Loretto). *Via Pessina* is the shop-lined and cobbled main street of *Città Vecchia*, the Old Town. The railway station fronts *Piazzale della Stazione*, northwest of the core, while the stazione for the funicular to *Monte Salvatore* (below) is at the southern tip of *Via San Salvatore*. And the village of *Gandria*—a visitor requisite (below)—is immediately east of the city.

Monte Salvatore and Monte Bre frame Lugano, the latter to the east, the former—more easy of access—to the west. If you collect mountaintops you'll want to conquer both of these peaks. But settle as a minimum for the rapid ten-minute funicular journey to Monte Salvatore, the better to afford regional perspective. From its summit, just under 3,000 feet, you'll view not only the city and Lake Lugano, but Lakes Maggiore and Como, as well, and if the day is really clear, the Matterhorn will be among visible Alpine peaks. There's a reliable restaurant, should midday coincide with your excursion. A trolley bus will take you from the center of town to the Casserata quarter, and the Monte Bre funicular station. Bre vistas are quite as breathtaking as those from Salvatore; its summit is restaurant-equipped as well.

Collection Thyssen-Bornemisza (occupying Villa Favorita—in the easterly Castagnola quarter—whose main gate, a fair hike from the entrance, may be reached by local bus): If the fine and decorative arts—old master and later paintings, furniture, tapestries, sculpture—hold even a modicum of interest for you, carefully plan to be in Lugano on a Friday, a Saturday, or a Sunday—the only days that this extraordinary museum chooses to open, *except* during certain periods when it is the site of temporary short-term exhibitions and *may* opt to open every day of the week save Monday.

This is a very personal collection of treasures. It was gathered over a ten-year, pre–World War II period by Baron Heinrich Thyssen-Bornemisza, who bought the sumptuous lakefront villa in which it is housed in 1932, promptly building a wing in which to shelter it. We may be unhappy with the old baron's son and heir, Baron Hans Heinrich, for opening only three days a week, but the collection is his to do with as he wishes, and three days, heaven knows, are much better than two or one or none at all.

The old baron's taste was impeccable, and his collecting plan, though ambitious, was eminently sensible. He set out to create a representative survey of European painting, thirteenth through eighteenth centuries. And did he ever succeed. My notes are dotted with exclamation points. The Italian works are stunning-ly beautiful—Bramante's searing *Ecco Homo,* Carpaccio's armored knight before a castle, Lorenzo Costa's *Bentivoglio Family,* Veronese's *Annunciation,* Giovanni Bellini's *Holy Family,* Tiepolo's *Expulsion from the Temple,* Tintoretto's *Paradise,* Titian's *Doge Francesco Venier,* Raphael's *Portrait of a Young Man.* The Dutch are strong: a Steen self-portrait, a domestic scene by Maes, a drinker in a pub by Ostade, landscapes by Cuyp and Van Ruisdael, Rembrandt as painted by himself. There are sub-lime Flemish primitives by Van Eyck (a two-part *Annunciation*), Memling (a long-haired gentleman), and Van der Weyden (a tiny *Virgin and Child),* as well as such later Flemings as Van Dyck (white-ruffed Jacques Le Roy) and Rubens (*Toilet of Venus*—one of a trio). Germans? How about Dürer's *Jesus among the Doctors,* Holbein's *Henry VIII,* a Cranach *Young Lady?* There are Span-iards, too—El Greco, Goya, Zurbarán, Velázquez. And the French—extending from the Renaissance's Clouet and Vouet, through the eighteenth century's Boucher, Chardin, Fragonard, Lancret, Hugo Robert, and Watteau. You will want to return.

Museo Civico (Villa Ciani, in Parco Civico, just east of the cen-ter): The house, first. It's a neoclassic mansion with an octagonal tower surmounting a salmon-hued facade that's an 1839 recon-struction of an earlier mansion. The park contains both a mini-zoo and an aviary and is the setting for daily open-air con-certs the summer long. And Museo Civico's paintings are hardly to be despised. They are mostly but not entirely French—with such Renaissance masters as Manet, Pissarro, and Cézanne rep-resented, as well as later artists like Rousseau and Matisse.

Modern English work by Ben Nicholson and Graham Sutherland is part of the collection, and this is a good place to become acquainted with Ticinese artists, as well.

Church of Santa Maria degli Angioli (Piazza Luini) was built by Franciscans in the fifteenth century. Men who knew the best of the regional painters, they commissioned the very same Bernardino Luini whose *St. Jerome* graces the cathedral in not-far-distant *Como* (see *Italy at Its Best*) to decorate the interior. A leading artist of the Lombard school, he had been a pupil of Leonardo da Vinci. Lugano's Luini is a massive and magnificent fresco—*The Passion of Christ*—which covers a wall that divides the nave from the altar, is centered by the Crucifixion—Jesus is surrounded by a host of angels—comprising a brilliantly detailed blaze of color.

Cathedral of San Lorenzo (Via Cattedrale) is fronted by a hilltop affording fabulous views of the city and the lake. The interior, multiperiod with its vaults busily painted and its columns frescoed, is anticlimactic after the facade—a Renaissance masterwork embracing a trio of elegantly framed portals beneath a stone cornice and a lovely rose window.

Gandria and other nearby villages: Gandria, just east of town at the foot of Monte Bre, is the prototypical Lago di Lugano village—carved into the near-vertical rocky shore of the lake. You may go by boat or car; motorists must park in a lot at the entrance to the village. You amble about then, on hilly stone paths. Principal monument is the essentially Baroque *Church of San Vigilio*, worth a peek. Otherwise, the name of the Gandria game is shopping (myriad emporia in which are vended locally crafted ceramics), with the consumption of lake fish (myriad terraced restaurants-cum-vistas of the water) coming second; it's fun to build your visit around midday, so that you can enjoy a Gandria lunch; I recommend restaurants on a subsequent page.

From Gandria, proceed by boat—the voyage takes five minutes—to *Museo Doganale*, in Cantine di Gandria, a point on the unpopulated side of Lago di Lugano at the border between Switzerland and Italy, and, by reason of location, popular with

smugglers over long centuries. The museum is a onetime customs post; its exhibits explain how smugglers plied their trade.
Bissone, a lakeside village, easily reached by boat from Lugano,
has as its draw *Villa Tencalla*—a seventeenth-century house
seeing service as a museum of Ticino's decorative arts—two
floors of rooms furnished with objects of the last (and earlier)
centuries, with considerable prints and paintings, the most celebrated of which is by the Venetian Renaissance master, Bassano.
I save the prettiest of the villages, *Morcote*, lakefront and seven
miles south of Lugano, for last. At the base of a mountain that
juts into the water, Morcote restaurants and shops hug its shore.
Climb up to the *Church of Santa Maria del Sasso*—you will have
seen its towering campanile if you have approached the village
by boat—a Renaissance-Baroque work, from which views are so
rewarding as to have made the trek worthwhile.

SETTLING IN
Grand Hotel Eden (7 Riva Paradiso; Phone 55-01-21): Happiness in Lugano is terraced lakefront quarters in this superbly
equipped hotel. The look is bright, bold contemporary. There
are 115 rooms and 16 suites in tones of brown and beige or blue
and white, the lot with lakeview balconies and really super
baths. You sink into deep leather chairs in the bar-lounge. The
indoor-outdoor pool's picture windows give onto chaise
longues massed over a broad sundeck at the water's edge.
There's a fitness center-cum-sauna, and a pair of restaurants,
one of which—L'Oasis—is evaluated on a later page. And
there's not a hotel in Switzerland, certainly in my experience,
with a kindlier or more expert staff. Distinguished Hotels/
Robert F. Warner. *Luxury.*

Splendide Royal Hotel (7 Riva Caccia; Phone 54-20-01)—
when I stayed at it on an earlier Lugano visit—occupied a
treasure of a Belle Époque building, lakefront. When the
Splendide's owners decided to expand (the room and suite
count is now 125) they wisely left the original building quite as it
was architecturally, and built a contemporary annex, adjacent; a
passageway links the two. Rooms in the less expensive old part
remain traditional in style, some with original brass beds, but

with up-to-the-minute baths. Rooms in the new section are all lakeview, terraced, and stylishly contemporary. The bar-lounge and restaurant—among Lugano's handsomest environments—happily remain in the original building. And there's an indoor/outdoor pool with a sun terrace. Member, Leading Hotels of the World. *Luxury.*

Castagnola au Lac Hotel (31 Viale Castagnola; Phone 51-22-13) is not, more's the pity, central. But if you've the use of a car and would enjoy a house which evokes grand hotels of the last century—albeit with tasteful updating—consider the Castagnola. It's set in a vast garden—park would be the better term—edging the lake, with its own beach, indoor/outdoor pool and sun terrace, pair of restaurants, bar accented in tones of green; beamed main lounge that could be that of an English country house, and a hundred rooms and suites, most Louis XV- or Louis XVI-style and all those that I have inspected, smartly handsome. *First Class.*

Europa Hotel (1 Via Cattori; Phone 54-36-21) is conveniently central—on the lake and a hop and skip from shops. It's a relatively modern house, impeccably maintained, with a hundred rooms (the twins I have inspected are small but the junior suite I saw was good-size); most lakefront accommodations have terraces. There's an indoor/outdoor pool with sundeck, pair of restaurants (one of which is reviewed in a later paragraph), and a convivial piano bar. *First Class.*

Bellevue au Lac Hotel (10 Riva Caccia; Phone 54-33-33) is a lovely old-fashioned house that's been distinctively refurbished, with 50 rooms (those I have seen are charming), atrium lobby, chandelier-hung restaurant, bar-lounge accented in red and blue, and a honey of an outdoor pool. *First Class.*

Excelsior Hotel (4 Riva Vela; Phone 22-86-61) fronts the lakeshore. There are 80 modern rooms, restaurant, and bar. Conveniently central. *First Class.*

Commodore Hotel (6 Riva Caccia; Phone 54-39-21)—a link in the France-based PLM chain—has an admirable sense of style. Those of the 58 rooms I have inspected are smartly monochromatic—the color is sand—with balconies attached to lakefront accommodations. I like the public spaces—lobby, terraced restaurant—embracing variations on a theme of white. And the bar has a pool table. *First Class.*

De la Paix Hotel (18 Via Cattori; Phone 54-23-31) is atop a hill a little inland from the lake, has 90 rooms (those I have inspected are pleasant), pair of restaurants (one a pizzeria, the other moving to tables around the outdoor pool in summer), and rattan-furnished bar. Attractive. *First Class.*

Meister Hotel (Via San Salvatore; Phone 54-14-12) is a bit inland, but with a swimming pool in its garden as compensation, not to mention agreeable public spaces including a pretty restaurant and a bar-café-cum-terrace, as well as 55 rooms; those I have inspected are very nice indeed. *First Class.*

Dante Hotel (5 Piazza Gloccaro; Phone 22-95-61): You do not expect to come upon a hotel as contemporary as the Dante in the Città Vecchia quarter of town. This fairly recent house has 55 relatively severe but comfortable, well-equipped rooms (most baths have showers but no tubs) and a bar adjacent to its lobby. Breakfast only. Friendly. *First Class.*

Conca d'Oro au Lac Hotel (7 Riva Paradiso; Phone 54-31-31) is a worth-knowing-about house directly on the lake. You want to specify a water-view room; they all have balconies. There's a terraced restaurant, a bar, and a nice pool. *Moderate.*

Canva Riviera au Lac Hotel (18 Riva Paradiso; Phone 54-75-75) embraces half a hundred terraced rooms—neat and functional (specify lakeview), as well as a picture-window restaurant giving onto the lake, and a bar. *Moderate.*

Ticino Hotel (1 Piazza Cioccaro; Phone 22-77-72) is intimate and atmospheric. Setting is a centuries-old Città Vecchia house that has been deftly refurbished in period style. Each of the 23 rooms is distinctive; those I have inspected are inviting, although baths of some have showers but no tubs. And the restaurant, given the central situation, is convenient. *Moderate.*

International au Lac Hotel (68 Via Nassa; Phone 22-75-41). The name is misleading; the International is not on the lake but rather on the main shopping street—a location not to be disparaged. This is an elderly hotel with cozy lounge, inviting restaurant, and baths in most but not all of its 50 rooms. *Moderate.*

DAILY BREAD

L'Oasis (Grand Hotel Eden, 7 Riva Paradiso; Phone 55-01-21): Giant picture windows give onto Lago di Lugano and the mountains. Tables are dressed with navy linen, set with fine porcelain and crystal, surrounded by leather-upholstered chairs. The kitchen is open to view, and the team of chefs—their *toques-blanches* bobbing up as they create your meal—are talented. Order from the extensive à la carte. I counsel opening with *risotto* or one of the pastas—*spaghetti con pomodoro e basilico* (classically sauced with tomato and basil). Continue with a house specialty, crayfish served with an orange-accented *mousseline* sauce; or a really thick veal chop, deliciously grilled, Italian-style. The prix-fixe embraces five courses and might run to truffled artichoke salad, saffron-accented clam chowder, *foie gras de canard,* breast of chicken accompanied by the mushroom species called *morilles,* and a sumptuous dessert. The staff? It operates with symphonic precision and smiles. In my experience, one of Switzerland's best restaurants. *Luxury.*

Bianchi (3 Via Pessina, just off Piazza Riforma; Phone 22-84-79) represents a giant step backward—to the closing decades of the last century. Choose a table in the forward of a pair of main-floor salons—Gothic-arched, with antique pottery decorating paneled walls. Or go back to the inner sanctum, lighter in look, with coffered ceilings. Cuisine throughout Lugano and the rest of Ticino canton is Italian-accented, regardless of restaurant. But Bianchi puts it best foot forward with Italian fare. The day's well-priced prix-fixe menu might open with *macheroni ai quatro formaggi*—the sauce created from four cheeses—or a *minestrone*-type *zuppa di verdura*. *Carpaccio*—sliverlike raw beef delicately sauced, or a filet of lake fish are entrée choices, with that eternal Italian standby, *macedonia di frutta*—fresh fruit cup—among dessert options. But scan the à la carte before you order; there are ten pasta choices and entrées include *costata alla Fiorentina*—the masterful Florentine beefsteak specialty. *First Class.*

Hueginin (1 Riva Albertolli, fronting the lake; Phone 22-88-01) is an ever-popular old timer, grandly neoclassic—stuccoed ceilings and paneled walls, handsomely upholstered armchairs surrounding generously spaced tables, with the option of warm-weather meals al fresco, in an arcade edging the water. Everything I have tasted is delicious: *vitello tonnato* (cold sliced veal enveloped by a chilled tuna sauce), *melone con prosciutto* and a range of pastas among openers; grilled filet of sole or favored Italian entrées like *saltimbocca alla Romana* or *osso bucco* as main courses. Desserts rate a card of their own. How about made-on-premises vodka sorbet or a rich *mousse au chocolat?* *First Class.*

Gambrinus (Piazza Riforma; Phone 23-19-55) is a beloved Piazza Riforma institution. It's inviting and comfortable, waiters are skilled veterans, fare is rib-sticking. A memorable lunch might be comprised of a *terrine de foie gras de canard*, served in tandem with melon and a toasted brioche, and *entrecôte* grilled in a *Marchand du vin* sauce, generously garnished. Desserts are super. On balmy days, tables are set on the square. *First Class.*

Al Portone (3 Viale Casserate; Phone 23-59-95): You're welcomed cordially by Signora Galizzi, the pretty co-owner, and seated in a Louis XIV-style chair covered in mauve velvet, at a table illuminated by candles in silver sticks. The silver motif continues with the waiters' uniforms; they wear black and silver bow ties and similarly hued shirts. There's a pair of prix-fixe menus that change daily; the less pricey (by half) is a lunch-only proposition. But at any time the à la carte is reliable.

Champagne-flavored *risotto* or ravioli are tasty starters. Scampi in a *peperoni* sauce and roast lamb accented with rosemary are winning entrées. *Luxury.*

Grill (Villa Castagnola au Lac Hotel, 31 Viale Castagnola; Phone 51-11-13) makes for an agreeable diversion from city-center dining; you're a car or taxi ride away, here, in a felicitous setting. The à la carte is almost classically French, with such first courses as smoked salmon, caviar, *foie gras*, and *hors d'oeuvres variés* which you select from a trolley. *Truite au bleu* and filet of sole are fish options. *Châteaubriand* and *duck à l'orange* stand out as entrées. And pasta—there are always half a dozen types—is authentic. *Luxury.*

Al Faro's (19 Riva Paradiso; Phone 54-51-41) specialty is seafood. Its pastas are often seafood-based, its fish soup delicious. And entrées—lobsters and crayfish, sole and turbot—are expertly prepared. Lovely service. *First Class.*

Monte Ceneri (44 Via Nassa; Phone 23-33-40) is indicated for a lunch break in the course of exploring Via Nassa shops. Build your meal around an Italian favorite—opening with pasta or *risotto*, with *osso bucco* as an entrée. *Moderate.*

Snack (Europa au Lac Hotel, 1 Via Cattori; Phone 54-36-21) has a lakefront entrance on Riva Paradiso, and fills the bill for coffee, a snack, or a casual lunch based on the *plat du jour*, chicken *cacciatore*, for example. *Moderate.*

Mövenpick Luganella (25 Viale Cattaneo; Phone 23-23-23): This relatively recent link of a reliable Switzerland-wide chain has both self- and waiter-service. Even with the latter, you may open your meal from a buffet of salads and appetizers. Steaks are of U.S.-imported beef, and there's a terrace. *Moderate/First Class.*

Inova (entered from the main floor of Innovazione department store, Piazza Dante) is good-looking and good-value—self-service with a super salad buffet at lunch (caveat: pile your plate high, you may make only one trip) and warm-weather tables in a pretty garden. *Moderate.*

Caffè Vanini has two central locations: Piazza Riforma (with tables on the square, for people watching in the sunshine) and Via Nassa, for breaks when shopping. Go for pastry and coffee, drinks, or lunch. *Moderate.*

Miralago (Gandria; Phone 51-43-61) is a sensible choice for a midday meal in the course of a stroll through this venerable village hugging the shore of Lago di Lugano. Open with soup or a pasta, following with grilled trout or scampi. Lovely views from the terrace. *First Class..*

Carina (Morcote; Phone 69-11-31): It's worth timing exploration of this village on the lake so that you'll be on scene for a pasta and fish lunch at Carina. Visits of the lake and mountains are memorable. *First Class.*

SOUND OF MUSIC
Primavera Concertistica di Lugano translates as Lugano's Spring Concert Season—an annual festival with orchestras (London Symphony, Philharmonica della Scala of Milan, Philharmonica Hungarica of Budapest are three which have played) and other musical groups. Setting is the auditorium of *Palazzo dei Congressi* (Parco Civico). There is, as well, an annual mid-June *New Orleans in Lugano Jazz Festival;* it takes place in several central squares.

SHOPPER'S LUGANO
Innovazione, the top department store, has two locations: at Piazza Dante (with a recommended restaurant [above] and a basement supermarket) and lakefront, on Piazza Manzoni. Shops on the principal shopping street, Via Nassa, include *Martas* (embroidery, linens); *Antioli* (Italian-origin men's and women's clothes); *Bücherer* (a link of the watch store chain); *Casa de Argento* (elderly and antique silver); *Riviera* (Italian shoes); *Andina* (furs); and branches of *Gianfranco Ferre* and

Gianni Versace (pricey Italian clothing, both men's and women's). Note that Via Nassa's *Church of San Carlo*—a tiny Baroque jewel—makes for a refreshing rest stop. Note, too, that the main street of Città Vecchia, the Old Town—Via Pessina—is lined with shops, many of them tempting. And that Via Cattedrale, extending downhill from the cathedral (above), is a maze of boutiques and craft shops; *Ali Baba* (clothing, accessories) and *Casa delle Bombole* (dolls) are two such.

INCIDENTAL INTELLIGENCE ═══════════

Ask the tourist office (below) for the current *orario,* or timetable, of Società Navigazione Lago di Lugano, for cruises to lakeside points. Consider also excursions by bus to such nearby Italian cities as Como, Milan, and Stresa (see *Italy at Its Best*). And consult Chapter 13, whose subject is Locarno, with Ticino and Italian excursions that can be made from it. *Further information:* Ente Turistico Lugano e Dintorni, 5 Riva Albertolli, Lugano.

14

Montreux and Vevey

On the Shore of Lac Léman

BACKGROUND BRIEFING
A modern-day consolidation of a clutch of villages that climb
hills on the north shore of Lake Geneva, Montreux—if one ex-
cepts extensively chronicled Château de Chillon, a much-
restored Gothic church and a small quarter of aged streets—has
precious little to show for a past that saw it variously inhabited
by ancient peoples, medieval Counts of Savoy, later Bernese
bailiffs and such figures of literature and music as Rousseau,
Byron, Mendelssohn and Tchaikovsky.

Withal, its forte is the visitor business. The last century and
the present one have seen this splendidly sited town—Alps to
the rear, a veritable inland sea at its front door, still more Alps on
the horizon—make its reputation in tourism. Montreux puts its
collective best foot forward with its excellent hotels, luring con-
ventions, congresses, and various species of groups to them, and
to its glossy casino. Smaller, neighboring Vevey, by far the more
interesting of the pair of towns, offers the happy contrast of a bit
of intellectual stimulation.

ON SCENE
Lay of the Land: Think of Montreux as running parallel with the
shore of Lac Léman, its southern boundary. *Piscine Publique*, the

city's outdoor swimming pool, edges *Quai des Fleurs,* a lakefront artery, and the flashy restaurant-cafe-boîte-gaming-rooms-equipped *Casino* is its immediate neighbor. (There's a big indoor pool, open to the public, to the west on Rue du Lac.) *Place du Marché,* hub of town, parallels another important thoroughfare, *Avenue des Alpes,* on which the railway station fronts. *Rue du Pont* is the core of *La Vieille Ville*—what remains of old Montreux—whose major monument is a medieval-origin monastery that houses the limited-hours *Musée de Montreux* (with historic mementos) and a restaurant (below). *Château de Chillon,* Montreaux's medieval lakefront landmark, is alongside *Quai Bon Port,* easterly extension of Quai des Fleurs. There are several lake steamer piers, with the principal one—for departures to Geneva, Lausanne, and Évian (across the lake, in France) at *Place Gambetta* just east of *Maison des Congrès,* the convention center/concert hall.

Château de Chillon (Quai Bon Port): Europe abounds in castles with more beautiful interiors. But you've got to give Chillon its due, with respect to location: hugging a rocky eminence on the shore of Lac Léman, its mix of steeply pitched roofs beneath a single tower, flanked by verdant hills due north, the snowy Alpine Dents du Midi to the east, and the lake immediately south. Bigger than it looks—its interiors encircle a trio of courtyards—Chillon is essentially eleventh through thirteenth centuries; Counts of Savoy, who ruled the area, were principal residents. Bernese bailiffs routed the counts in 1536. It was during the period just prior to their takover that Chillon achieved eminence. What happened was that the Catholic Savoy counts, fearful of consequences of the spreading Reformation, imprisoned one of the Reformation's most eloquent clerical champions—François de Bonivard, prior of a monastery in nearby Geneva, who espoused the new Protestanism—in a Chillon dungeon for four years. You will see the pillar to which he was chained during the whole of that time—the fifth from the door as you enter. Following liberation by the Bernese, Bonivard publicly disavowed Catholicism, became a Protestant, was honored by Geneva authorities and—some time later, to be sure—was immortalized (that is not too strong a term) by the poet Byron who, after a visit in the nineteenth century (he autographed the third pillar of the chamber in which Bonivard was imprisoned) wrote "The Prisoner of Chillon." Two noncontiguous rooms are museums: one of medieval spears, swords, and ironwork; the other with models of the castle and predecessor-castles on the site, and with lovely bits of fragmented sculpture. There are several interestingly furnished rooms: Duke's Chamber, Knights' Hall, Grand Hall—with original frescoes and tapestries. There are both a torture chamber and a latrine. And, not to pass unmentioned, there are idyllic views of the lake and mountains from the windows of Chillon. Wear rubber-soled shoes; ascents and descents, along narrow flights of uneven stone steps, are frequent, in the course of a self-guided tour.

Temple St.-Vincent (Rue du Temple)—a Catholic church when it was built in the thirteenth century—has been Protestant (thus the French term, *temple*) since the Reformation. Its lovely Gothic vaults and columns have not been tampered with in the course of restorations. But stained glass has been replaced; it is creditable contemporary work by a designer named Jean Prahin.

Rochers de Naye —at 6,700 feet the highest of the Vaudois Alps peaks backing Montreux—is gained by means of an hour-long cogwheel train journey at whose termination the lures are skiing in winter and, at all times (given a break by the meteorologist), vistas of surrounding mountains, more distant ones even sometimes including Mont Blanc. Arrange to arrive midday for lunch at the summit restaurant.

Vevey and its museums: This pretty lakefront town, due west of Montreux, was for long where Charlie Chaplin made his home, and if you're a Chaplin admirer (who is not?), you'll want to pay your respects at the municipally created statue of *Charlot* (as he was called by French-speaking fans), on *Quai Perdonnet*. The plaque beneath it pays tribute—as translated from the French—"to the genial actor who gave so much pleasure to so much of the world." It is agreeable to stroll Vevey from, say, Quai Perdonnet on the waterfront to central *Grande Place* and beyond to the shops of pedestrians-only *Rue du Lac*, noting the handsome classic-style *Hôtel de Ville*, or City Hall, on *Place Hôtel de Ville*, perhaps checking out Placette department store on busy Place de la Gare, nearby. Then, take in the three principal Vevey museums.

The most charming—*Musée du Vieux Vevey*—occupies a suite of rooms in Château de Vevey (Rue d'Italie), dating to the Renaissance when it was home to Bernese bailiffs. Ring for the long-on-scene curator, a loquacious woman who takes you about, the while offering a French-language commentary on the museum's treasures—pewter and porcelain, prints and paintings, impressive eighteenth- and nineteenth-century furniture, even locally made watches of considerable vintage. Then comes the most surprising of the museums, *Musée des Beaux-Arts* (a.k.a. Jenisch) in generously scaled turn-of-century quarters on Avenue de la Gare. You don't expect a veritable treasure trove of Old Master drawings and watercolors in the fine-arts museum of a town as small as Vevey. Amble about to take in works by such Italians as Palma Il Vecchio and Sebastiano Ricci, Tiepolo (in considerable quality) and Carraci, Vernonese and Guarcino, Tintoretto and Rosa, Del Sarto and Mantegna, with a Michelangelo of a seated Hercules as the Italian clincher. And such French greats as Chardin, Watteau, Robert, and Largillière on hand, too. And an oil of a Lake Léman sunset by Courbet, the No. 1 painting.

Earmark time for the newest of the Vevey museums. It was created in 1986, by the Nestlé chocolate people (their head office and main factory are in Vevey). It goes by the name *Alimentarium*, and occupies quarters in a onetime company office building on Rue du Léman. The installation comprises two floors of creative—and oftentimes witty—exhibits which interpret the theme food and nourishment over the ages. One exhibit is a display of food—fresh, canned, frozen, packaged, liquid—of a typical one-month ration, contemporarily. Another display goes back a couple of centuries, with mockups of a noble family and a farm family, each at table—with a typical meal of their class set out before them. Foods of African, Asian, and Pacific peoples are contrasted with those of the West. There are exhibits of old kitchens and groceries and menus. It's fun.

SETTLING IN

Montreux Palace Hôtel (Grande Rue; Phone 63-53-73) has, to be sure, seen changes since it went up at the turn of the present century as one of the great grand hotels. There are now four restaurants and as many bars, instead of a solitary formal dining room; an enormous swimming pool and tennis in the vast across-the-road garden, connected to the hotel by a tunnel; up-to-the-minute baths attached to the 210 rooms and 30 suites. Still, the original 1906 decor—a pleasant meld of Art Nouveau and mock-eighteenth century, with the stained-glass doors and murals of the former and the crystal chandeliers and stucco work of the latter—happily remains. Public spaces—giant windows dramatically draped, tables massed with fresh flowers, ceilings two stories in height—are monumental. And attention is paid to service (amicable and alert) and food (evaluated on a later page). A Swissôtel that is a member of Leading Hotels of the World. *Luxury.*

Excelsior Hôtel (Quai du Grand Port; Phone 63-32-31) hugs the shore of Lac Léman, and has remained—for more than eight decades—extraordinarily felicitous in the manner of its original designers. By that I mean crystal chandeliers illuminating public rooms whose stuccoed ceilings are supported by marble columns with gilded capitals. All eighty rooms and suites face south, toward the lake and mountains, and although sizes, shapes, and decorative schemes vary, with walls of some surfaced with toile fabric, and certain beds canopied—they all have balconies, indicated for breakfast in the sunshine. Antiques are dotted about—eighteenth-century sedan chairs, a cradle with reputed Napoleonic associations, commodes, mirrors. Still, there's a modern indoor pool (in a connected adjacent building, which houses a health spa/clinic). And I review one of the pair of restaurants in a later paragraph. *Luxury.*

Hyatt Continental Montreux Hôtel (Grande Rue; Phone 63-51-31) is lakefront, and with an agreeable decor that is a successful mix—typifying Hyatt International—of the traditional with the contemporary, against a background of quiet color. Rooms to aim for are those of the 143 (plus a score of suites) that are lakefront, with scrumptious views—and balconies from which to enjoy them. Both restaurants—less pricey *Romance* (where Yank-style hamburgers are always on the menu) and quite grand *Régence* (later reviewed) move to summer terraces. The bar is lively and the pool gives onto a sundeck. *Luxury.*

Suisse et Majestic Hôtel (Avenue des Alpes; Phone 63-51-81) is a beloved oldie that has been expertly and charmingly updated (the lobby, for example, contains a circle of half a dozen original Art Nouveau chairs under an original Art Nouveau chandelier), and that has, moreover, the most central location in town, with entrances on two sides; that on Avenue des Alpes is directly opposite the railway station; that on Grande Rue has you on the main shopping street. The 150 rooms are delightfully traditional; ask for one with a tiny balcony facing the lake. There are two restaurants (one later evaluated) and a broad terrace off the lobby that gives onto the lake and is put to good use for warm weather drinks, barbecues, and dancing. Lovely service. *First Class.*

Eden au Lac Hôtel (Rue du Théâtre; Phone 63-55-11) combines contemporary touches like white rattan furniture with turn-of-century chandeliers and an opulent red-and-white color scheme in public spaces. Sixty of the 105 rooms are lakeview and balconied; those I have inspected are attractive. The two restaurants are lookers, and there's a pool. Ambassador Swiss/Best Western. *First Class.*

Bonivard Hôtel (Rue Bonivard; Phone 63-43-41) is away from the center and a near neighbor of Château de Chillon (above). The name of its game is suites. By that I mean that all 76 rooms consist of a nicely furnished parlor plus at least one bedroom. (Some have two or three.) I like the snazzy public spaces—restaurant, café, bar, and indoor swimming pool-sauna-solarium. Friendly. *First Class.*

Eurotel Hôtel (Grande Rue; Phone 63-49-51) is Montreux's sore thumb of a skyscraper; you see it from everywhere. There are 175 rooms (some with pull-down-from-the-wall beds and some with kitchens) and undeniably super views from those on upper floors; terraced restaurant (with daily barbecue in summer); indoor pool-sauna-solarium. Central. *First Class.*

Helvetia Hôtel (Avenue du Casino; Phone 63-25-51) is an elderly house that has been well maintained. It's heart-of-town (not on the lake) with a big roof terrace that's super for sunning (it has reclining deck chairs), gracious main lounge, honey of a white-wicker restaurant, cozy bar, and 65 rooms with either tub or shower in their baths. Those that I have inspected are very nice indeed. Friendly. *Moderate.*

Europe Hôtel (15 Avenue des Alpes; Phone 65-45-41) is appealing as you approach—orange awnings shade the windows of its 65 rooms, some with showers rather than tubs in their baths. Amenities include both restaurant and bar. Central. *Moderate.*

Victoria Hôtel (in Glion, a village overlooking Montreux; Phone 63-31-31): You want the use of a car for a stay at the Victoria—a quarter-hour drive from town. Compensation is a charming environment—61 rooms in a stylishly updated setting that dates to the time when the queen whose name it takes reigned. Those of the rooms I've inspected are exceptionally attractive. Lobby, terraced restaurant (later evaluated), bar, pool in the garden, smashing views. A pleasure. Member, Relais et Châteaux. *First Class.*

Trois Couronnes Hôtel (Rue d'Italie, Vevey; Phone 51-30-05) has led the Vevey pack since it opened in 1842. It's an all-Swiss *grande dame.* (Russia's Czar Nicholas and Czarina Teodorova stayed for six months more than a century back, Saint-Saens and Paderewski played a two-piano concert in 1913, and the hotel was used in the 1970s film *Daisy Miller.*) Just 65 rooms and suites surround a five-story atrium that anchors the lobby. The bar is a pleasure and the restaurant, with summer terrace (detailed in a later paragraph), is charming. Member, Leading Hotels of the World. *Luxury.*

Du Lac Hôtel (Rue d'Italie, Vevey; Phone 51-10-41) is long on scene and good-looking, in traditional style, with 35 full-facility rooms, restaurant, bar, and outdoor pool. *First Class.*

De Famille Hôtel (Rue des Communaux, Vevey; Phone 51-39-31) is core of Vevey, with 35 neat rooms (not all of which, note, have baths), restaurant, bar, and indoor pool. *Moderate.*

Le Mirador Hôtel (on Mont Pèlerin, accessible by road—20–25 minutes from Vevey, or by funicular from Vevey; Phone 51-35-25): You're more than 2,600 feet upward here, and when the atmosphere is hazefree, vistas of the Vaud Alps and Lac Léman are fabulous. But you have to want to be away from it all. This isolated hotel is, however, good-looking and full-facility—indoor/outdoor pool, big sundeck, tennis, sauna, gym, 65 smartly furnished traditional-style rooms (those I have inspected are, alas, small) and suites, terraced restaurant, bar, poolside café. *Luxury.*

DAILY BREAD

François Doyen (82 Rue de Chillon; Phone 63-64-96) is welcoming—with a smart rustic look—and delicious. You order from either of two menus (but only if all at the table are of the same mind) or from an à la carte which might include such openers as *foie gras de canard,* crayfish salad, or a salad of sautéed frogs legs. Entrées run a deliciously wide gamut—the day's fresh fish variously sauced, filet of beef in a *Pinot Noir* sauce, veal médaillons estragon-accented, roast lamb, or roast pigeon. The house's sherbets and ice creams are created on premises. Or, how about apricot soufflé to conclude? *Luxury.*

Caveau du Musée (40 Rue de la Gare; Phone 63-16-62) occupies quarters in the *caves* of an originally medieval convent, heart of the Vieille Ville. You dine at tables set with red-checked cloths, to share a *fondue* or concentrate on steaks or chops. Late-hours dancing. Dinner only. *First Class.*

Harry's New York Bar (a part of the Montreux Palace Hôtel, but with its own entrance on Grande Rue, just west of the hotel entrance; Phone 63-53-73) is as much eatery as it is for the consumption of drinks. There is, to be sure, a big bar in this modishly contemporary room, with interesting clientele and an interesting bill of fare. You might open with Harry's *hors d'oeuvres sur assiette*—a plateful of tasty nibbles—or the hearty leek soup. There's a *quiche* of the day—*Lundi* through *Dimanche*, imported American sirloin steak, served with a baked potato and, if you like, corn on the cob. And Harry's is proud of its *Salade du Chef* and its *tarte Tatin*, the upside-down warm apple pie that's an import from Normandy. *First Class.*

Suisse et Majestic Hôtel Restaurant (Avenue des Alpes; Phone 63-51-81) serves—in one of the handsomest settings in town—a well-priced four-course menu—the day's soup, filet mignon or roast veal, pastry or ice cream; makes a specialty of lake fish and seafood à la carte, and—on its football-field-size terrace, has a summer barbecue grill with evening dancing. *First Class.*

Excelsior Hôtel Grill (Quai du Grand Port; Phone 63-32-31): Lunch or dine inside and the setting is subdued—in pale blue and beige. Opt for the terrace and tables are set in pink linen, with views of lake and mountains. A prix-fixe meal might include scallops in a port sauce, beef deliciously prepared and garnished, pastry, or a choice of other sweets from a trolley. Extensive à la carte. Smart. *Luxury.*

Régence (Hyatt Continental Hôtel, Grande Rue; Phone 63-51-31) is a good bet at lunch. The deal is its *Buffet du Marché.* You help yourself to appetizers and salads from a generous buffet. You're then served the entrée you've ordered. Back you go to the buffet then, for as many desserts as you can manage. *First Class* (but if you go for dinner, *Luxury*).

Café du Grütli (a.k.a. Chez Stella, Rue du Grand Chêne; Phone 63-42-65): Madame Stella herself will no doubt greet you at this unpretentious Vieille Ville spot. Go in the evening, with a party, to share *fondue*. Convivial. *Moderate.*

La Couronne (102 Avenue des Alpes; Phone 63-35-28) is indicated when nothing but an authentic Italian meal will do. If it's lunchtime, pizza is a good choice. A pasta opener with an Italian-style veal entrée are good dinner selections. Congenial. *First Class.*

Caveau des Vignerons (30 bis Rue Industrielle; Phone 63-25-70) is more central—and therefore convenient—than delicious. The well-priced menu based perhaps on *entrecôte* will, however, be adequate. Cordial service. *Moderate.*

Victoria Hôtel Restaurant (Glion; Phone 63-31-31): You'll need a car for the up-the-mountain location. But on a billowy day you could do worse than be seated at a table on the Victoria's terrace, for the sumptuous buffet lunch—a help-yourself embracing *terrines* and salads, choice of entrées and desserts. *First Class.*

Le Pont du Brent (Brent; Phone 64-52-30) is higher up than the Victoria Hôtel (above). But this restaurant—the look is Elegant Rustic—is indicated for a splurge lunch or dinner when you've plenty of francs to expend on either of two prix-fixe menus. Even the cheaper menu—seafood or rabbit salad, entrées of crayfish, salmon, or duck, cheese platter, sherbet plus dessert—is a tempter. *Luxury.*

Trois Couronnes Hôtel Restaurant (Rue d'Italie, Vevey; Phone 51-30-05): If the weather is fine, a meal on the Trois Couronnes terrace, with the lake and the mountains beyond, is a special Vevey treat. The four-course prix-fixe—soup or a novel appetizer, veal or poultry entrées, desserts from a trolley—is excellent-value and, in my experience, delicious. Old-school service. *First Class.*

Taverne du Château (Rue du Château, Vevey; Phone 51-22-46) occupies space in the same atmospheric building as Musée du

Vieux Vevey (above). The prix-fixe menu—open with asparagus if it's in season, a soup or a salad; continue with grilled lake fish, conclude with a sweet from a wheeled-up *chariot*—is satisfying. *First Class.*

Züricher (Grande Rue, near Place du Marché, Montreux) is known for pastry, combined with coffee or tea in its *salon de thé. Moderate.*

SOUND OF MUSIC

Festival de Musique—a Montreux-Vevey collaboration—takes place late August through early October at Centre des Congrès, in Montreux and several other locations in both towns, with performances by such musical organizations as Orchestre de Paris, Academy of St. Martin's in the Fields, Turin's RAI Symphony and Orchestra de la Chambre Suisse. *Festival International de Jazz* takes place in various Montreux locales, annually in July.

INCIDENTAL INTELLIGENCE

Ask at the tourist office (below) for schedules of Compagnie Générale de Navigation, so that you may plan a cruise or two on Lac Léman, to such points as Lausanne (Chapter 10) and Évian, across the lake in France (see *France at Its Best*). *Further information:* Office du Tourisme, 5 Rue du Théâtre, Montreux; Office du Tourisme, 5 Place de la Gare, Vevey.

15

Neuchâtel
Beneath a Hilltop Castle

BACKGROUND BRIEFING
Its location in French-speaking Switzerland notwithstanding (and with a populace whose spoken French is reputedly the most beautiful such in the Confederation), little Neuchâtel lacks the sparkle and *joie de vivre* so often exported to Suisse Romande from across the frontier in France. Contemporarily wealthy from wine and watches (vineyards climb neighborhood mountain slopes, and the town is a center of research in watch technology), Neuchâtel's unassuming ambience is one of almost stereotypical Swiss reserve. And it could do with a smasher of a first-class hotel or two or three.

What redeems it for the visitor is a situation alongside the lake, which (at five miles by 25) is the largest such lying entirely within the borders of Switzerland, and a reasonably attractive core attesting to an early Golden Age that extended from pre-Renaissance through Baroque centuries. Neuchâtel was successively attached to the powerful Holy Roman Empire, a clan of French nobles, a line of Teutonic monarchs, and—ultimately, in the middle decades of the last century—the Swiss Confederation.

ON SCENE

Lay of the Land: Hilly (there are mountains out back, with the lake out front) but walkable. Several miles of quais—variously known as *Quai Philippe Goden, Quai Osterwald* and *Quai Léopold Robert*—delineate the waterfront, centered by *Place du Port*, overlooking the little café-lined harbor, and leading inland to *Place Paget*, connected by *Rue de l'Hôtel de Ville* with *Rue de l'Hôpital* (a pedestrians-only shopping street) and satellite commercial thoroughfares like *Rue du Seyon*, site of Les Armourins department store (affiliated with the Jelmoli chain) and *Rue du Bassin*. Two historic squares—*Croix du Marché*, edging Rue de l'Hôpital with landmark structures including a late Renaissance mansion, fountain of the same era, and even older tower; and almost contiguous *Places des Halles*, site of turreted *Maison des Halles*, a centuries-old cloth and grain market—constitute the core of Neuchâtel's *Ville Ancienne*, or Old Town. This is agreeable territory for strolls—past colonnaded eighteenth-century *Hôtel de Ville*, the Town Hall, on the street taking its name; a fountain of the same century in the center of *Place de l'Hôtel Communal;* equally aged houses on *Rue du Pommier*, leading uphill to the castle-church-prison-tower complex (below) whose spires and pinnacles pierce the sky.

Neuchâtel from on high: Why not start with a bird's-eye view of the city, *Lac de Neuchâtel*, and the mountains backing them, from the summit of 3,300-foot-high Mont Chaumont? Drive or taxi from the town center to either of two funiculars: *La Doudre*, the closer, is but two miles from town, while the Chaumont station is twice that distance. Not every day is clear enough for Mont Blanc to be visible, but even with a bit of haze—not uncommon—vistas can be dazzlers.

La Collégiale (Rue Rochberg)—originally Romanesque, with Gothic additions, refurbishing following partial damage during the Reformation, additional embellishments in the nineteenth century, and mostly contemporary stained glass—is the high-on-a-hill church that represents Neuchâtel at its most spectacular. Impeccably maintained by the Evangelical Reformed Church (it has been Protestant since the sixteenth century) it is twelfth-century Romanesque out back—a trio of apses retain their original carved-stone decor—and in the choir, albeit with a Gothic nave that is one of the most graceful in Switzerland. Special art treasure is the cenotaph (a memorial to dead persons whose remains are elsewhere) of medieval counts and countesses of Neuchâtel—gaily painted stone statues, a dozen-plus all told, that date to the fourteenth and fifteenth centuries. Have a look at the cloister, too.

Château de Neuchâtel (Rue Hochberg): It has origins quite as ancient (twelfth century) as those of the adjacent Collégiale, but is essentially a fifteenth-century complex that encloses a marvelously asymmetrical courtyard. Credit where it is due: the Canton of Neuchâtel, whose offices are within, sees to it that the château retains a fortresslike ambience, what with a quartet of fabulous towers, oriel windows, formidable walls embellished with coats of arms of a dozen Swiss cantons, an ancient kitchen, and—have a look, if it's open—the imposing Salle du Grand Conseil, or council chamber.

Tour de Diesse (Rue Hochberg) is the third component part of the Château complex, a prison tower whose foundation goes back to the tenth century and from which there are fine views of town, lake, and mountains.

Palais du Peyrou (Avenue du Peyrou) embodies Rococo Neuchâtel. It's a splendidly facaded eighteenth-century town palace set behind a topiary garden-cum-mini-café, that went up in the 1760s to the designs of a Bern-born, Paris-trained architect, for a local bigwig who befriended and published Jean Jacques Rousseau, and bequeathed his not-inconsiderable cache of Rousseau's printed works to the city. Superbly embellished state rooms which, though not actually open to the public, are worth a peek, if you can manage it. And while you make the effort, go out back to the small but worthwhile *Musée Cantonal d'Archéologie*—in the courtyard, and with exhibits spanning 50,000 years of regional archeology, even including a partial skeleton of a neighborhood Neanderthal gent, not to mention ancient bronzes and pottery, and a startlingly beautiful bust of a young Roman empress.

Musée d'Art et d'Histoire (Quai Léopold-Robert, near the lake) occupies spacious, high-ceilinged quarters. There are, to be sure, such painters of note as the early twentieth century's Ferdinand Hodler and Cuno Amiet in the fine-arts section, most of which is devoted to Swiss artists less well known to foreigners, like the last century's Albert Anker and Léopold Robert. But there is considerably older work, too: a Renaissance-era *Couronnement de la Vierge*—the Virgin Mary being crowned—is the standout. And there are charming portraits of eighteenth-century Neuchâtel gentry. Move, then, to the decorative arts/history galleries—a mix of furniture and silver, pottery and costumes, locally made clocks and watches, with the best saved for last: a trio of automated eighteenth-century puppets, the lot of them programmed at the time of construction—two centuries before computers were invented. They are still going strong. If you're in town the first Sunday of any month, pop in (at 2:00 P.M., 3:00 P.M., or 4:00 P.M.) and watch one of them write (to order), listen to the second make music (on command), and observe the third create drawings.

Vue des Alpes is the romantic, and at the same time dramatically accurate, name of the mountain pass less than half an hour's drive north of town, which cuts through the Juras, the while affording vistas, when the weather cooperates (the altitude is just over 4,200 feet) of such legendary peaks as the Jungfrau and Mont Blanc. And there's a restaurant.

SETTLING IN
City Hôtel (Place Piaget; Phone 25-54-12) has the virtues of a core-of-town situation, cordial ownership-management, and close to 30 fairly comfortable rooms, not to mention a pair of restaurants (one later counseled, the other Chinese) and a cozy bar. *Moderate.*

Beaulac Hôtel (Quai Léopold-Robert; Phone 25-88-22) is a graceless contemporary box, with likewise graceless accommodations (there are 50-plus rooms) and, in my experience, chilly reception-concierge staff. The cheaper of its two side-by-side restaurants serves competent bistro fare, but the principal attribute of the Beaulac is location: lakefront (there's a café-terrace) and adjacent to the harbor. Ambassador Swiss/Best Western. *Moderate.*

Touring au Lac Hôtel (Place Numa-Droze; Phone 25-55-01) is unpretentious albeit with an on-the-harbor situation that lures budget travelers; half a hundred adequate rooms, restaurant, and buzzy lakeview café. *Moderate.*

Eurotel (15 Avenue de la Gare; Phone 21-21-21): Were it down the hill, closer to the center, Eurotel would lead my Neuchâtel group because it's the best-equipped, with 110 mod-look rooms, welcoming lobby, and, not unimportant, this, welcoming staff. Its restaurant is later recommended. *Moderate.*

DAILY BREAD
Au Vieux Vapeur (Au Port—which is to say, moored in the harbor; Phone 24-34-00) is accurately labeled. This is an elderly lake steamer converted to service, in its twilight years, as a floating (and permanently moored) restaurant whose specialty—not illogically—is fresh-caught lake fish—filet of perch *Meunière,* most especially—to the accompaniment of a Neuchâtel white wine. The look is agreeably but not excessively nautical, and service is a pleasure. *First Class.*

Maison des Halles (Place des Halles; Phone 24-31-31) is an upstairs-downstairs proposition, with the setting a towered and turreted sixteenth-century building that is a proud Neuchâtel landmark. The street-level brasserie-café is indicated for coffee at an outdoor table, or the *plat du jour* at midday. The up-a-flight restaurant, attractively aged, serves fare that runs a gamut from, say, seafood-accented pasta through roast duckling and on to a groaning sweets trolley. Café: *Moderate;* Restaurant: *First Class.*

Restaurant Français (City Hôtel, Place Piaget; Phone 25-54-12)
makes a specialty of *entrecôte* steaks served with the house's
own sauce and a minimountain of *pommes frites*. But you may
opt for nicely prepared lake fish, grilled veal steak, or whiskey-
sauced roast chicken. Massive and magnificent sundaes are the
dessert specialty. *First Class.*

Brasserie du Théâtre (Place de la Poste; Phone 24-63-97)
serves lunch in fine weather at outdoor tables on the square it
fronts. Steaks, salads, snacks, to be sure, but best bet is the *plat
du jour. Moderate.*

Buffet de la Gare (in the railway station, Avenue de la Gare;
Phone 25-48-53) serves a prix-fixe menu which, in my experi-
ence, is recommendable principally for its modest cost.
Moderate/First Class.

Wodey-Suchard (5 Rue du Trésor)—the second word of
whose name relates to the onetime Neuchâtel location of the
Suchard chocolate factory—is quite the smartest *salon de thé*
in town. Order a cup of chocolate with your pastry. (A box of
Wodey-Suchard's pricey chocolates is a delicious Neuchâtel
souvenir.) *Moderate.*

SOUND OF MUSIC
Théâtre Municipal (Rue de l'Hôtel de Ville)—imposingly
neoclassic—is the venue for opera, ballet, and other entertainments. Office du Tourisme (below) has schedules.

Temple du Bas/Salle de Musique (Rue du Seyon) is an imaginatively converted church now seeing service as a concert hall.
Orchestre de Chambre de Neuchâtel is one of a number presenting programs.

Printemps Musical de Neuchâtel is an annual spring music
festival, with the Collégiale, Temple du Bas, nearby Château de
Bourdry, and other atmospheric locales as sites for programs by
local and visiting musical groups.

INCIDENTAL INTELLIGENCE ══════════════

The tourist office has schedules of steamer excursions on Lake Neuchâtel. *Further information:* Office du Tourisme, 7 Rue de la Place d'Armes, Neuchâtel.

16

St. Gallen

Appenzell and Liechtenstein

BACKGROUND BRIEFING

The Irish Connection in St. Gallen? The New World, to be sure. But Switzerland? Well, yes. And it goes back a long way: to the sixth century. Snail's pacelike communications of that era not-withstanding, word had trickled north to Ireland that not all of continental Europe was sufficiently God-fearing, by the standards, at least, of an austere monk, later sainted as Columban.

He took a dozen fellow clerics south. One of them head-quartered in a simple dwelling, or hermitage, at that point in Switzerland's northeast corner that evolved, first as a Benedictine monastery, later as the surrounding lay settlement that came to be named for the pioneer settler, eventually canonized—for his missionary accomplishment—as St. Gallen.

St. Gallen's successors at the monastery that grew from his hermitage were considerably more worldly than he. The Bene-dictine abbots became temporal rulers of an extensive region that included Appenzell (below) and in the thirteenth century were dubbed full-fledged princes of the Holy Roman Empire, of which St. Gallen was, by then, a Free Imperial City.

But the citizenry became restless under harsh arbitrary rule, and in the fourteenth century rebelled against the ruling prince-abbot, to join forces with the Swiss Confederation. Turmoil, a

consequence of the Reformation, followed for some time thereafter. Still, it was not until the early eighteenth century that the
prince-abbots lost political power, and St. Gallen—long since a
prosperous trading and mercantile center, befitting its situation
on the frontier of both Austria and Germany—became the seat
of a Swiss canton bearing its name.

More recently, St. Gallen has amassed considerable
wealth as textile manufacturing hub of the Confederation
(the embroidered Swiss hankies you take home as gifts are,
no doubt, of St. Gallen origin). And with its affluence came
cultural distinction.

What St. Gallen lacks, though, is recognition. Most of us don't
even know how to spell it (it's *Sankt Gallen*) in German, *St. Gall*
in French, both *St. Gallen* and *St. Gall* in English) with the saint's
name (*Gallus* in Latin) pronounced GAHlen or GAWlen, as you
prefer. Call it what you will, this lively city—population about
70,000, comparable to that of much better known Lucerne—
warrants acquaintance.

ON SCENE
Lay of the Land: I am partial to cities where the Bahnhof is
conveniently central; such is the case in this delightfully
walkable town. The train station on *Bahnhofplatz* is a next-door
neighbor of the skillfully designed, futuristic *Rathaus*, or Town
Hall. *Kornhausstrasse*, just opposite, leads south a couple of
blocks to *St. Leonhardstrasse*, perpendicular with it, and a means
of quick access to *Multergasse*, the main shopping street and an
interesting means of access, via Marktgasse and Spitalgasse, to
easterly *Museumstrasse*, site not only of major museums but of
both the opera house and concert hall. The very same
Marktgasse is, as well, in the core of St. Gallen's lovely *Alt Stadt*,
or Old Town. Earmark some time for strolls past the oriel windows and wrought-iron signs of lovely baroque—and even
older—houses on such streets as *Spisergasse*, *Schmiedgasse*, and
Galusstrasse. Which leave St. Gallen's major monuments, the
onetime chapel of the monastery (now the cathedral) and that
monastery's extraordinary library; they're just south of
Multergasse and easily reached by north-south *Webergasse* and
Gallusplatz, edging them on the west.

Kathedrale (a.k.a. *Stiftskirche,* Gallusplatz): The abbots of St. Gallen's Benedictine monastery were still temporal rulers—and, quite obviously, not without wherewithal—when the cathedral was built between 1755 and 1767, as the monks' chapel. It is the outstanding example in Switzerland of the light and lilting *genre*—actually more Rococo than Baroque—that became a commonplace of the landscape, urban as well as rural, in not-far-distant Bavaria. Set off by a pair of felicitous towers, each surmounted by a gilded cross and each with a clock, the cathedral begins with proportion in its favor; it's high and wide and massive. Look up from the nave, noting exuberantly frescoed ceilings. Glance to either side of the nave at pale green capitals of columns delineating it. Pause beneath the immense cupola, at the nave's far end, to take in the mural—theme is the Holy Trinity—surfacing it. You've reached, at this point, the gilt-decorated wrought-iron grill setting off a ravishingly beautiful high altar. It's flanked by black pillars, beneath sculpted angels with a quartet of minichapels in the foreground, and an angel-topped Baroque organ to either side. And—before it—carved-wood, gilt-embellished stalls of what has to be one of the most beautiful of Baroque choirs. The pulpit is no less so. Nor, for that matter, are confessionals lining side walls; those for women on one side, men on the other. They are all original, as indeed are the cathedral's elaborate, carved-wood pews.

Stiftsbibliothek, the Abbey Library (Gallusplatz): It is apparent not only from this monastery library but from others (that of Melk Abbey in neighboring Austria is a fine example) that Benedictine monks had great respect for learning. This repository of a hundred thousand volumes has as its special treasures some 200 hand-illuminated manuscripts, amassed during the Middle Ages long before the present quarters were built in 1758 by a prince-abbot rather memorably named Coelestin II Gugger von Staudach. The difficulty in concentrating on the library's permanent exhibits—illustrating the history of the abbey and its prince-abbots—lies in the lavishness of the environment. Not for nothing is this room considered the single most beautiful Rococo interior in Switzerland. The original parquet floor—its designs encircle a series of four central stars—remains; you pad about in slippers provided for the purpose, as you look the room over. Twenty types of wood were employed in the floor's design and in the creation of two levels of bookcases. Each case is flanked by pilasters of *faux-marbre* topped by Corinthian capitals that surface the four walls, with the pattern of the books' dark leather spines enlivened at strategic points by niches in which *putti*—tiny sculpted angels—repose. Each of the four ceiling frescoes, painted by Josef Wannenmacher from the Bavarian city of Ulm, depicts an Early Christian ecumenical council; they are framed in pink and white stucco, itself masterful and the work of a pair of German brothers, Matthias and Johann Gigl.

Historisches Museum (50 Museumstrasse): The History Museum's felicitous neoclassic facade gives you no clue as to its exhibits. But don't hesitate; this museum is an all-Swiss sleeper. Most spectacular are rooms from regional houses dating back centuries, moved *in toto*. When I say *in toto*, I mean that their original walls, ceilings, and even floors, came with them. They're mostly sixteenth century—bedrooms, dining rooms, reception rooms—but some are older. Furnishings and accessories are as nothing compared to the inlaid wood-patterned walls, beamed ceilings, designs of the floors. As you move along, you find much else to admire—polychrome medieval sculpture, stained glass, armor, toys, and a near-limitless collection of the immense, magnificently detailed wooden cupboards—*schranks*—in which affluent Baroque families stored worldly possessions.

Kunstmuseum (62 Museumstrasse), occupying still another classic-style Museumstrasse structure, pays appreciable attention to painters of the region, over a span of centuries. But it would not do to call it parochial. By that I mean you'll recognize such seventeenth-century Dutchmen as Van Goyen and Van Ostade, such later Swiss as Hodler and Giacommetti. And Frenchmen from several epochs—pre-Impressionists like Daubigny, Corot, and Courbet, Impressionists including Renoir and Pissarro; later masters like Le Corbusier. Have a look.

Textilmuseum (2 Vadianstrasse): My problem with museums celebrating the inherent art and/or artisanship in fields like textiles and wallpaper is that, more often than not, they appear—to me at least—as showcases in shops. There are exceptions, to be sure; Lyon's Musée Historique des Tissus is one such. But St. Gallen's Textilmuseum, despite priceless embroidery, laces, and silks—the lot of proud local origin—is not among them. You may feel otherwise.

Appenzell: The pretty little girl in a dirndl holding her mother's hand might well be the heroine of the Swiss children's classic, *Heidi*. And could that attractive blonde woman climbing a hill in the Alp-backed countryside be a stand-in for still another heroine—from neighboring Austria—in Hollywood's *The Sound of Music*? The approach, via a Toonerville Trolley–type of narrow-gauge train from northerly St. Gallen, through hamlets tucked into steep valleys, is made to order for photographers.

In Appenzell village, you're convinced that stage-set carpenters, masons, and facade-painters have only just preceded you. This little town, based on *Hauptstrasse* slicing through it, just has to be a film set. Houses surfaced in primary colors are embellished with friezes and frescoes and medallions based on traditional mountain motifs. Gables are steep. Store signs are of gilded wrought iron. Squares are fountain-centered, shops shaded by arcades. If you've hit the day right, country folk are all about, the women in traditional dark dress covered by long white aprons, beneath headdresses that are almost nunlike; the men no less quaintly garbed. It's agreeable to simply walk about. But you want to zero in on a trio of specifics: *Pfarrkirche St. Mauritius*, which began as a Romanesque church, is essentially Baroque with a joyous interior highlighted by frescoes embedded in gilt frames on a pink-stucco ceiling, and a lavishly gilded high altar surrounded on either side by a pair of only slightly lower, equally lovely altars. Smaller *Kreuz Kappelle* is of the same eighteenth-century era, albeit with 1960s glass in its windows. And *Heimatmuseum Appenzell*, quartered in a seventeenth-century house, is a mix of exquisitely paneled rooms, polychrome sculpture retained form medieval centuries, lace and pewter, furniture from village parlors of yore, implements that recall long-ago Appenzell farms and kitchens.

Crafts shops—the specialty is wood carving—are in good supply; so, for that matter, are hotels and restaurants (below), should you choose to headquarter here, the while making forays into the countryside, with a stop, perhaps, at a dairy so that you may watch Appenzell cheese being made, and at *Urnäsch*, a village whose lure is a charming folk museum. Unless your visit is height of summer, you'll see grazing herds of Appenzell's distinctive milk producers—cows known as Brown Swiss—at every turn. And if your stay in Appenzell village includes a Wednesday, the clusters of gents chattering away in cafés and on street corners will be area farmers. For as long as anyone in the village remembers, that midweek day is when they leave their wives (still, incidentally, without the vote in local elections) at home, the better to update themselves on regional gossip.

Principality of Liechtenstein, (in German, *Fürstentum Liechtenstein*) is Europe's Curiosity Country—an anachronistic but ever so solvent principality with a size about that of the District of Columbia (some 60 square miles), neither rail nor air access, a population of some 26,000 (only the males of which are allowed to vote for the 15-member *Landtag*, or Parliament), and a reigning prince who keeps his castle closed to the public but allows visitors to inspect samplings of his paintings; of the private collections, his is reputedly second only in global importance to that of Britain's Royal Family.

There is little doubt but that Liechtenstein's diminutive size has aided in the retention of its sovereignty. It was created in the early eighteenth century, when the Holy Roman Empire welcomed it as a fief created by the welding of the County of Vaduz and the Barony of Schellburg, both of which had been acquired from previous owners by a rich Austrian family, name of Liechtenstein.

The French invaded during the Napoleonic era, after which Liechtenstein joined the Germanic Confederation. In 1866 that entity was dissolved and Liechtenstein was on its very own, albeit linked to Austria in an economic union that lasted until after

World War I, when Switzerland took over in such areas as currency, customs, and foreign affairs.

The number of reigning princes has been relatively few, thanks to the excessively lengthy period that one ruler—Johann II—remained on the throne—from 1858 to 1929. That's seventy-one years, a near-record; it's only three years less than Louis XIV's seventy-four years, but it easily beats Victoria, whose reign lasted sixty-four years. The current ruler, Franz Josef II, assumed the throne in 1938 and—though not abdicating—bestowed considerable authority on his son, Hans Adam, in 1984. Though the princely castle, with a fairyland setting—it straddles its own eminence high above the village of Vaduz, the capital—is *geschlossen,* or closed, to the public, there are a trio of museums.

The significant one—*Liechtensteinische Kunstsammlungen*—contains works from the prince's art collection, on a rotating basis. By that I mean there's no guarantee as to which paintings you'll see. The display will be nothing like as representative as the exhibition of paintings, firearms, porcelain, and even an eighteenth-century golden carriage, which the prince sent over for temporary viewing at New York's Metropolitan Museum of Art in 1986. But chances are good that you'll see works by Rubens (there are a hundred-plus in the collection), by such Germans as Cranach, by such Dutchmen as Salomon Ruysdael, by such Flemings as Teniers, possibly even by such Italians as Piero di Cosimo.

Still another museum, *Liechtensteinisches Landesmuseum,* in a refurbished onetime Vaduz inn, is a historical survey—at its most absorbing in the case of medieval and Renaissance art and artifacts, but with its span prehistoric and Roman remnants through later pistols and postage stamps, these last in the specially designated *Briefmarkenmuseum,* in the art museum building (above). Passport P.S.: Ask at the tourist office (below) or your hotel, where you may have a Liechtenstein visa rubber-stamped into your passport. It will occupy a full page but will be nothing more than a souvenir, there being no immigration formalities arriving from or returning to Switzerland.

SETTLING IN

Einstein Hotel (2 Berneggstrasse: Phone 20-00-33) is, hands down, St. Gallen's No. 1, centrally situated behind the neoclassic facade of a onetime embroidery factory. Those of the 65 modern rooms and suites I have inspected are noteworthy for the lovely fabrics shading windows and covering beds—especially woven by the hotel's owners, who are textile manufacturers. There's a honey of a rooftop restaurant (later reviewed) and—off the bright, light lobby—a paneled bar-lounge with evening entertainment. Manager Jürg Studer is on scene, day through late evening, making sure that his creditable staff pleases guests. It does indeed. *First Class.*

Im Portner Hotel (112 Bankgasse; Phone 22-97-44) occupies a pair of charming Old Town buildings; the more recently refurbished—Pförtnerhof, it is called—has the more attractive of the 28 rooms and suites, modishly contemporary. And both the intimate bar and the restaurant (among the town's leaders) appeal. Friendly. *First Class.*

Walhalla Hotel (Bahnhofplatz; Phone 22-29-22)—just opposite the strikingly contemporary Rathaus—is itself contemporary, with agreeable public spaces that include a reliable restaurant, busy bar and brasserie-café (with tables in the square when weather is mild), and 52 rooms, half of them singles, half doubles, the lot clean-lined and compact. Ambassador Swiss/ Best Western. *First Class.*

Metropol Hotel (Bahnhofplatz; Phone 23-35-35) has two pluses: an opposite-the-train-station location and a perfectly delightful reception staff. Those of the rooms I have occupied or inspected—there are three dozen, almost half of which are singles—tend to be small and minimally attractive. And because the restaurant reuses tablecloths at breakfast, even when they're soiled, I was not interested in returning for dinner. Ambassador Swiss/Best Western. *First Class.*

Dom Hotel (22 Webergasse; Phone 23-20-44) is a hop and a skip from the shops of Multergasse and neat as a pin with baths attached to most—but not all—of its 40 rooms. Breakfast only. *Moderate.*

Appenzell Hotel (Appenzell; Phone 87-42-11) is typically Appenzell without, with a gaily decorated frame facade, but with agreeable late twentieth-century touches (like excellent marble baths) in its sixteen rooms—all of them fairly good-size doubles. The well-regarded restaurant moves to the garden in summer. Very nice indeed. *Moderate.*

Säntis Hotel (Appenzell; Phone 87-26-44) is Classy Rustic, on Landsgemeindeplatz, center of the Appenzell action (if that it may be called), with a pair of restaurants (one of which is evaluated on a later page), bar-lounge, and 33 rooms, some more elaborate than others. These include a group whose bathroom doors—rather oddly—are of transparent glass, thereby not affording occupants privacy. *Moderate.*

Löwen Hotel (Appenzell; Phone 87-14-02): I like the typically Appenzell accents in the Löwen. The premium rooms—nine out of two dozen—feature beautifully embroidered linen on beds, are decorated with a sense of style, and are equipped with fine baths. Not that the other accommodations are unattractive; they're nice too. Restaurant, bar. *Moderate.*

Krone Hotel (Appenzell; Phone 87-13-21) is a well-located budget house adjacent to the fresco-facaded Rathaus, or Town Hall, with 15 rooms—not all with baths—and a restaurant. *Moderate.*

Park Hotel Sonnenhof (Vaduz, Liechtenstein; Phone 2-11-92) is partially called after the parklike garden it occupies, on a hill backing the principality's capital. The name of the Sonnenhof game is space: more than half of the 30 rooms are balconied junior suites with curtain-separated lounge and sleeping areas. The indoor pool, glass-walled and giving onto the garden, has a sundeck. The restaurant is deservedly popular, and the hotel is managed by hospitable Emil Real, whose brother operates the principal competition (below). *First Class.*

Real Hotel (Vaduz, Liechtenstein; Phone 2-22-22) fronts Städtle, Vaduz's principal thoroughfare, and is the bailiwick of Félix Real, brother of the Sonnenhof's Emil (above). Although this house is known more for its restaurant (below) than its rooms, there are a dozen-plus of the latter. Functional and comfortable. *Moderate.*

DAILY BREAD
Stadtkeller (17 Spisergasse; Phone 22-00-88) has winning looks—white linen, orange candles, and silver place plates on tables, with walls cavelike, waitresses in spiffy black and white. Owner-chef Köbi Nett's cuisine is classic enough to be tasty, contemporary enough so as not to be over rich. There are a pair of prix-fixe menus. Ordering the lesser-priced, a meal might comprise smoked salmon teamed with dill-sauced asparagus, a turbot-sole platter accompanied by tarragon-scented morilles, roast shoulder of lamb in a port sauce partnered with a garnish of *gratin Dauphinois,* and a cooling dessert: house-made mango sherbet buried beneath two sauces, one red (strawberry), the other green (kiwi). Herr Nett makes the rounds of every table, and his staff is A-1. In my experience, Stadtkeller is one of Switzerland's best restaurants. (And it is but one of four restaurants in the Stadtkeller complex; the other three are more casual and less costly.) *Luxury.*

Schökli (17 Zeughausgasse; Phone 22-12-56) looks to be a twin-turreted medieval castle. Its quarters are a five-floor oriel-windowed, sixteenth-century townhouse, with appropriately atmospheric dining rooms on several of those floors, an especially good value prix-fixe lunch menu that changes daily (grilled ham steak, French fries, mixed salad—for example), and a more elaborate à la carte at dinner, with the range a white wine-based *risotto* or onion soup through *paupiettes* of sole or filet mignon, with a wide and rich dessert choice. *First Class/Luxury.*

Neubad (6 Bankgasse; Phone 22-86-83) is a cozy Altstadt environment—paneled walls, mullioned windows—where, with pleasure, you might tuck into a meal with Burgundy-style snails or *gulasch* soup as an opener, Italian-style veal *piccata* or Gallic-style *entrecôte* as entrées, with the delicious house-made *spätzli* counseled as a starch. Lovely service. *First Class.*

Galletto (62 St. Jakobstrasse; Phone 25-03-03) is the genuine Italian article, from the moment of opening with say, antipasto (to which you help yourself from a trolley), ravioli, spaghetti *carbonara, penne alla zingara,* or *lasagne verde* among pasta options; veal *scallopine, saltimbocca,* or *osso buco* among entrées, with Galleto's extra-rich *zabaione* as a sweet. Italian wines. *First Class.*

Roof Restaurant (Einstein Hotel; Phone 20-00-03) combines beamed ceilings and coarsely stuccoed walls with blond furnishings, contemporarily styled. Entrée specialties include good-quality roast beef, but there are fish, poultry, and other meat options. Under no circumstances skip a sweet. The hazelnut parfait doused with apricot sauce is one such. Prix-fixe lunch menus are good buys. Nice. *First Class.*

Bahnhof Buffet (Bahnhofplatz): Pop in, any time of day or evening, for a satisfying meal or snack. *Moderate.*

Roggwiller (Multergasse) is as smart-looking (brass chandeliers and sconces illuminate its tables) as it is good eating and tasting. This is the No. 1 konditerei; good pastry and coffee. *Moderate.*

Säntis Hotel Restaurant (Appenzell; Phone 87-87-22) is a quietly but agreeably decorated second-floor space, where the three-course lunch menu tempts. Chicken salad or cold roast beef with *rémoulade* sauce are typical starters; authentic Italian *saltimbocca* or roast lamb are among entrées; have Appenzell's celebrated cheese or a frozen sweet to conclude. Everything is tasty. *First Class.*

Appenzell Hotel Café-Restaurant (Appenzell; Phone 87-42-11): The changed-daily prix-fixe is herein counseled. It might run to vegetable soup, mushroom-sauced veal steak with noodles and grilled tomatoes, and the house's celebrated—and wickedly rich and gooey—*coupe Romanoff.* Attractive. *Moderate.*

Bärli (Appenzell; Phone 87-58-94) is indicated if, like me, you favor fresh-caught trout, prepared *meunière* style; Bärli's comes from local streams, May through August only. *Moderate.*

Laimbacher (Appenzell; Phone 87-17-14) is Appenzell's leading konditerei. Go for morning coffee or afternoon tea, not skipping the pastry. Casual lunches, too. *Moderate.*

Real Hotel Restaurant (Vaduz, Liechtenstein; Phone 2-22-22): It's called Au Premier because it's up a flight. Boss-host Félix Real is bound to be on hand to greet you, in advance of a meal that might be built around such specialties as thyme-seasoned lamb chops or leek-accented sweetbreads, with truffle-flecked noodles made on premises, as the favored opener, and chocolate soufflé to conclude. *First Class.*

Torkel (Vaduz, Liechtenstein; Phone 2-44-10) is set in vineyards belonging to the reigning prince. It should go without saying that a bottle of princely wine should accompany a meal that might be based on, say, veal steak or roast chicken. Fun. *First Class.*

SOUND OF MUSIC
Stadttheater (Museumstrasse) is the strikingly contemporary opera house, with the wood-ceilinged auditorium gained by an immense, irregularly contoured foyer-cum-café. Ballet, musical comedy, too.

Tonhalle (Museumstrasse)—across Museumstrasse from Stadttheater (above) is a noteworthy example of turn-of-century Art Nouveau. It is St. Gallen's principal concert space.

SHOPPER'S ST. GALLEN
Globus, a branch of a national department-store chain, faces Broderbrunnen, the fountain signaling the start of Multergasse,

the main street, on which *ABM;* a budget-price department-store chain, is also situated. Other shops include *Steiner* (chocolates); *Bally* (shoes); *Siegl* (jewelry); *Hennes & Mauritz* (women's clothing); *Sportsonderreger* (men's and women's togs); *Bücherer* as well as *Engler* (watches). Multergasse's extension, Spisergasse, has such shops as *PKZ* (men's wear); *Pelz Looser* (furs, leather); *Walter Ulrich* (pottery, ceramics); and a diverting mix of small boutiques and cafés.

INCIDENTAL INTELLIGENCE

How about a one-day excursion that will take in four countries? Be the first on your block to visit Vaduz in Liechtenstein (above), Bregenz in Austria, and Lindau on Lake Constance in Germany (see *Germany at Its Best*), between breakfast and dinner. No. 4 is, of course, Switzerland's St. Gallen, where you are based; do it by rented car or by bus. *Further information:* Verkehrsverein, Bahnhofplatz, St. Gallen; Verkehrsverein, Landsgemeindeplatz, Appenzell; Liechtenstein National Tourist Office, 38 Städtle, Vaduz.

17

St. Moritz

Rhymes with Glitz

BACKGROUND BRIEFING

How well you like, or do not like, St. Moritz—the southeastern village that spawned Alpine winter tourism in the mid-nineteenth century, when an innkeeper imported a party of English visitors to populate the progenitor of today's Palace Hotel—might well relate to your status, financial and social. If you possess either a title—it need not be top-of-the-line *Debrett's* (deposed royals and minor princes are acceptable)—or inordinate wealth, chances are that you'll be content. If, alas, you're a commoner with neither a drop of noble blood nor a solitary movie credit, and only middle bracket with respect to bank account, you will be welcomed. But, conceivably, more as a customer—St. Moritz promotes aggressively to maintain its No. 1-in-visitors-rank among Swiss mountain resorts—than as a guest.

If things go beautifully for the favored few in St. Moritz, they do not always work that well for the rest of us, an extraordinary range of facilities notwithstanding. It was not, of course, always thus. A visit a dozen years or so back was a personal pleasure. More recently though, I have found attitudes bordering on arrogance and—as at no other Swiss point in my experience—taxi drivers who did not arrive when ordered and hesitate giving change due in payment for fare, restaurant waiters disagreeably reluctant to accept credit cards when their establishments are affiliated with card plans, even careless hotel maintenance. All of the foregoing would be understandable if St. Moritz had no stiff competition. But of course it does, as I indicate in Chapters 5, 7, 8, 9, and 19 of this volume.

St. Moritz gives the impression of never having quite gotten over its operation, between World Wars I and II, as a playground for the prominent. (The pecking order of social acceptability, even today, descends from the membership of a select coterie in a trio of ever-so-exalted private clubs.) Still, postwar democratization of international travel—mass tourism as manifested in the phenomenon of Club Med and limitless quantities of packages—has not been spurned.

On the contrary. Blue-chip clientele is dangled as a lure. "Most fascinating guests and celebrities from all over the world" are indicated among St. Moritz's prime attributes in a tourist office-published flyer—for what still another tourist office publication terms "the lesser [sic] well known guests" who, the same release goes on, not unpatronizingly "have one thing in common [with the resort's "famous" customers]: they cherish quality and style."

The quality is, in certain respects, present. The style—reflecting an at times obsessional preoccupation with titles and wealth—is not necessarily to everyone's liking. Consider this country's own citizens; less than a third of visitors are Swiss, according to statistics. (And the Swiss, virtually every one of whom above the age of, say, three, is a skilled skier, do indeed spend time in their mountain resorts.) Still, there is little question but that this marketing formula packs in foreigners—a quarter of a million a year in half a hundred hotels. Even though, again to quote a tourist office release, "the élite of St. Moritz remain among their own," they unwittingly draw crowds.

ON SCENE
Lay of the Land: Unless you've come for treatment at the health spa in the lower-down part of town called *St. Moritz Bad* (its ungainly high-rises do not complement its setting), you'll spend most of your time in and around the upper part—*St. Moritz Dorf,*

fronting Lake St. Moritz. The main shopping street, *Via Somplaz,* cuts through the hotel-flanked square called *Plazza de la Posta Veglia* (street designations are in the Romansch language, still spoken by a tiny minority of locals; the majority is German-speaking). Additional shops line central *Via Maistra, Via del Mulin,* and *Via Traunter Plazzas*—with the *Corviglia-Piz Nair funicular station* at the last-mentioned's northern tip. The solitary—and leaning—tower you see near the east end of Via Maistra is *Schieffer Turm,* sadly all that remains of the sixteenth-century village church, which villagers razed (instead of taking the trouble to restore) in the nineteenth century. The *Bahnhof* is at the southeast corner of town, at the end of *Via Grevas.*

Engadine Museum (Via del Bagn) is housed in a typically Engadine house of four substantial stories, built by the museum's talented founder, the late Richard Campbell, with the aid of a skilled team of architects, at the turn of the present century. It shelters an extraordinary collection gathered by Mr. Campbell, not only of Engadine artifacts—superb furniture and pewter, swords and costumes, pressed flowers and pipes, embroidery and framed family trees—but of complete rooms transferred *in toto* from houses in the area, at the time they were razed. Showplace room is a regional variation on the theme of exuberant Baroque—seventeenth century, with lavishly carved ceiling and walls, each of whose pilasters is a wood-sculpted masterwork. Take your time as you move about, not failing to note the Engadine features of the house itself, including oriel windows and sumptuous *sgraffito,* the name given to decorative patterns etched into the stone facade.

Segantini Museum (Via Somplex, west of the center and not far from the Engadine Museum [above]) is named for a minor Italian-born artist who lived and painted in the neighborhood during the second half of the nineteenth century. About 40 of his works are on view.

Corviglia, Piz Nair, and other elevated points: Corviglia is the most popular of the mountain destinations for four valid reasons. First, accessibility; you go by funicular train from St.

Moritz Dorf—a scenic half-hour journey. Second is Corviglia itself—at an elevation of 8,168 feet, about 2,000 feet above town. Third is a restaurant (below) that's one of the best in the area. And fourth is the cable car—departing Corviglia for *Piz Nair* where, once arrived, you're at an altitude of 10,029 feet— some 4,000 feet above St. Moritz, with a café-restaurant-sundeck and views of surrounding mountains and lakes, given luck with the weather. You may, as well, take a cable car from *St. Moritz Bad* upward to the station at *Signal*, itself the site of a restaurant, from which you may continue to Corviglia. From St. Moritz's satellite village of *Suvretta*, directly west, there's a chairlift to restaurant-equipped *Randolins*. Somewhat farther west is the pretty village of *Sils-Maria*, whose low-traffic cable car links it with *Furtschellas*. Saved for last is the highest elevated point in the neighborhood, at some 10,400 feet: *Korvatsch*, reached by cable car from the village of *Silvaplana*, between St. Moritz and Sils. Its lures are summer skiing, a restaurant-sun terrace, and smashing panoramas.

SETTLING IN
Carlton Hotel (Phone 2-11-41) is located just far enough away from the core of the village—a five-minute walk along a scenic and elevated path—to afford a fine perspective of it, of Lake St. Moritz and of the mountains. This is a rambling nine-story house that opened in 1913. Lounges are high-ceilinged, some with paneled walls, with immense fireplaces and fine stuccoed ceilings. There's a trio of restaurants—I evaluate them in a later paragraph—convivial bar-cum-dancing, honey of an indoor pool, sauna, gym, tennis courts, even an ice-skating rink. Sunday evening buffets are a Carlton tradition, as are weekly classical music concerts, in tandem with dinner. Those of the 110 rooms and suites I have inspected are good-size, good-looking, and with good baths; most face the lake and the mountains. Distinguished Hotels/Robert F. Warner. *Luxury.*

Palace Hotel (Phone 2-11-01) was opened in the closing years of the last century—Princess May of Teck (who would become Queen Mary, consort of Britain's George V) led the inaugural ball—by Caspar Badrutt, son of Johannes Badrutt, the very same whose earlier hotel pioneered winter tourism in the Alps some decades earlier. Caspar's two grandsons are the guiding force of today's Palace, under whose single green-tiled tower—a heart-of-St. Moritz landmark—is a ten-story house sheltering 222 rooms (some of them mammoth and with correspondingly mammoth baths) and 38 elaborate suites. Public spaces—dark-paneled, with high coffered ceilings and doorways framed by mock-Gothic arches—are quite the most atmospheric in town, and even if you're staying elsewhere, you want to pop in for tea or a drink. One lounge has an enormous painting of the Virgin Mary that may—or may not—have been created by Raphael but is, nonetheless, known as the Raphael Madonna. The main restaurant and grill are smart, and a neighboring seventeenth-century house, Chesa Veglia—operated by the Palace and later evaluated—contains several restaurants. There are, as well, a disco (for hotel guests and *their* guests, but, alas, no outsiders), and a fitness facility that includes a spectacular indoor pool and an outdoor pool as well, gym, sauna, indoor golf, quartet of tennis courts (with a resident pro), squash court, and sun terrace. The Palace is, to understate, dressy. Except in the disco and casual K-Bar Café, gents are required to wear jacket and tie throughout the premises after 7:00 P.M. (with a *dark* suit or tuxedo required for dinner in the principal restaurants). Member, Leading Hotels of the World. *Luxury.*

Kulm Hotel (Phone 2-11-51): The big yellow-stucco complex at the top of the hill in the core of the village is a St. Moritz old timer. Lobby and lounges—beneath a high ceiling supported by Doric-style columns—sport deep leather chairs. The main dining room is crystal-chandelier-hung, in tones of ivory. There's a bar with dancing and a pair of additional eateries, one of which, Rôtisserie des Chevaliers, I accord space on a later page. The big indoor pool is glass-walled and looks out to the garden, edged by tennis courts and an ice-skating rink. And there are 200 rooms and suites of varying sizes and degrees of comfort. *Luxury.*

Suvretta House (a mile west of St. Moritz; Phone 2-11-21): A pair of mock-Norman towers center the massive, pitch-roofed

facade of this country hotel, on scene since 1912, and to understate, full-facility, with 224 distinctive suites and rooms,
well-operated restaurants, a lake out front that becomes an ice
rink in winter, pair of bowling alleys, tennis courts, indoor pool,
and gym. From casual conversations I've had with Swiss across
the Confederation, this seems to be their favorite St. Moritz
hotel. Caveat: no credit cards. *Luxury.*

Albana Hotel (Phone 3-31-21) is conveniently central, its decor
based on traditional Engadine motifs. Those of the 60 rooms I
have seen are agreeable and well-planned. There are both a restaurant and a rustic-look grill (about which I write on a later
page). *First Class.*

Neues Posthotel (Phone 2-21-21), which was *Neues* (new) in
1908, has a situation not all that different from that of the nearby Palace, overlooking Lake St. Moritz and the mountains, from
rear rooms, and the town from front accommodations—of
which there are 50 all told; those I have inspected are attractive
and with modern baths. There's a restaurant about which I write
in a later paragraph, and a fitness center. *First Class.*

Monopol Hotel (2-44-33) is centrally positioned with 50 rooms
(decor is Louis XV, Louis XVI, or Swiss rustic), rooftop sundeck
adjacent to an indoor swimming pool, and a pair of restaurants.
One specializes in *fondue* and *raclette,* the other—*Grischuna* by
name—features grilled specialties and has a bar with dancing in
conjunction. *First Class.*

Schweizerhof Hotel (Phone 2-21-71) is an elderly, centrally located house that has been gradually updated. I have inspected
both recently renovated (tiny) doubles and older (bigger twin)
rooms; there are 85 altogether, as well as several restaurants and
bars (one of which I evaluate on a later page). *First Class.*

Hauser Hotel (Phone 3-44-02): Behind its poured-concrete facade (and a restaurant/outdoor café operated by a different
management) are 55 modern rooms. Location is central. Breakfast only. *First Class.*

Belvedere Hotel (Phone 3-39-05) is a five-minute walk from the center, in the direction of St. Moritz Bad. This is a nicely updated house—decor of public spaces is attractive nineteenth-century—with just under 60 rooms; those in the rear have lake and mountain views. Breakfast only. *First Class.*

Steffani Hotel (Phone 2-21-01) is core-of-town, with 80 rooms, some of which have balconies, small lobby, pair of bars, and restaurants, in one of which is served quite the most unappetizing and meager buffet breakfast I have encountered in Switzerland. Service and maintenance—in my experience, at least—are uneven. Ambassador Swiss/Best Western. *First Class.*

Soldenella Hotel (phone 3-36-51) is centrally situated, with cozy public spaces (including a restaurant and bar) and 36 neat rooms, some mountain-view. *Moderate.*

Chesa sur l'En Hôtel (Phone 3-31-44) might fill the bill if you would be content in the countryside, on a hill overlooking St. Moritz Bad. Surrounded by its own big garden, the Chesa is at its best in public spaces; lounge and restaurant are decorated in intricate Engadine style. All 15 rooms have baths. *Moderate.*

DAILY BREAD
La Marmite (Corviglia; Phone 3-63-55) is a principal reason for the funicular ride (above) to Corviglia. Pick a sunny day, booking in advance if you fancy a meal in the à la carte restaurant (which I counsel); there's a cafeteria and snack bar, as well. Caliber of the cuisine surprises first-timers who expect the view (in and of itself fabulous) to surpass the fare. You might open with the house *pâté*, continuing with a deliciously sauced local fish, or a veal or beef entrée. Bear in mind that the dessert buffet is celebrated. *First Class.*

Chesa Veglia (2 Via Veglia: Phone 3-35-96) is a seventeenth-century farmhouse on a hill behind the Palace Hotel (above), which owns and operates it. The look is Spiffy Rustic; good-quality antiques are dotted about and the paneling—start at the exquisitely carved front door—is from venerable Engadine houses. There are three restaurants (not to mention an unexpected pair of bowling alleys). *Partrizierstuben*—with Swiss as well as foreign fare—is appropriate for lunch on a sunny day, when the terrace is open, but serves dinner (following tea dancing) as well. *Chadafo Grill* (for charcoal-broiled steaks) is dinner-only, and there's pasta as well as pizza in *Pizzeria Napoleone. First Class/Luxury.*

Tschine (Carlton Hotel; Phone 2-11-41) deceives with its Engadine ambience; it's actually a smart restaurant where the à la carte is French-accented. Start with smoked salmon or shrimp salad; continue with trout *meunière* and/or filet of veal. Desserts rate a card of their own: frozen mousse doused with Kirsch is a favorite, ditto *mousse au chocolat*. Dinner only. *Luxury.*

Rôtisserie des Chevaliers (Kulm Hotel; Phone 2-11-51) is romantically vaulted, its walls hung with crossed swords. This is the place to splurge on *foie gras frais*—poached fattened duck or goose liver—as an opener. The Rôtisserie does interesting things with seafood (shrimp, especially) and Dover sole, as well as veal. Sauced entrées are invariably delicious. *Luxury.*

Veltinerkeller (11 Via del Bagn, in St. Moritz Bad; Phone 3-40-09) is as good a reason as any for a Bad sortie, as reputed for well-priced prix-fixe menus (among the town's best values) as for delicious fare—salads, soups, hearty entrées such as roast goose (a specialty), and corking good desserts. *Moderate.*

Albana Hotel Grill Room (6 Via Maistra: Phone 3-21-21) is a mix of brick columns, beamed ceiling, and gold-hued linen. The prix-fixe menu, especially at lunch, is temptingly tabbed, and might run to shrimp cocktail, vegetable soup, roast chicken or an omelet. And waiters smile; the only such I have encountered in an in-town, midcategory restaurant. *First Class.*

Neues Posthotel Restaurant (3 Via dal Vout; Phone 2-21-21) has as its ace in the hole a wall of picture windows giving onto lake and mountains, making the prix-fixe lunch (which might embrace soup, mixed grill, and dessert) a scenic adventure—if you snag a good table. Dinner is pricier, fare is competent, staff unsmiling. *First Class.*

Acla (Schweizerhof Hotel, 54 Via del Bagn; Phone 2-21-71) is relatively costly à la carte at dinner; with satisfactory pastas and pork chops. But decor is undistinguished and service can be disagreeable. *First Class.*

Hauser Hotel Restaurant (7 Via Traunter Plazza; Phone 3-44-02) is called by the name of the hotel in which it is situated, even though managements are separate. The prix-fixe menu—*Wiener schnitzel* served with sautéed potatoes and an eggplant tomato mix, as an example—is tasty, but service can be grudging. Caveat: no credit cards. *Moderate/First Class.*

Hanselmann (8 Via Maestra; Phone 7-38-64): With an international reputation as the town's preeminent *konditorei*—on scene since 1894—it would not be at all surprising, given St. Moritz's proclivity for bad manners, if service at Hanselmann was offered on a take-it-or-leave-it basis. Such is not the case. You are seated promptly and, quick as a flash, one of the staff of mature waitresses, smile on her face, English at her command, is ready for your order. Go midmorning or midafternoon, and you had just better have the hot chocolate (it comes in two sizes) than which there is none better anywhere in the Confederation. Pastries are celebrated; the *nusstorte* especially. But you may, as well, go for lunch—the prix-fixe might be built around roast beef or a chop—or for a breakfast omelet. And I defy you to pass by the counter on the way out without purchasing a box of chocolate truffles. Excepting the costly candy: *Moderate/First Class.*

SHOPPER'S ST. MORITZ
Not surprisingly, shopping options are exhaustive in wealthy St. Moritz. The area around the Palace Hotel—again not surprisingly—is hardly for the budgeteer, with *Cartier,* the Italian-origin firm of *Ritzino* (for shetlands, cashmeres, and other sportswear); *Victor Golfarb* (furs); *Les Ambassadeurs* (watches, clothes); *La Serlas* (with jewelry from the Italian firm, *Bulgari*); *Casa Grande* (with Hermès duds and accessories);

and—at the opposite end of the gamut—*Merkur* (a branch of a food-shop chain) with wines for hotel-room aperitifs and, in my experience, surly service. Via Maistra has branches of the *Bücherer* and *Gübelin* watch chains; *Schening* (women's sportswear); *Feinkeller* (men's clothes); *Lamm* (cashmere); and *Edy Rominger* (Engadine crafts, including pottery, tapestries, rugs, and furniture). *Grischune Souvenir Shop* (in the Schweizerhof Hotel) has a good choice of Swiss Army knives. Via Somplaz's shops include *Wega* (books and gifts); *Ebreter & Cie* (handkerchiefs and embroidery); *Kriemler-Müller* (smart clothes); and *Geronimi* (delicatessen). *Galleria Caspar Badrutt* (near the Beledevere Hotel) is a shopping mall for pricey clothes and shoes, with such firms as *Gucci, Jill Sanders, Walter Steiger,* and *Yves St. Laurent,* while nearby *Misani* has big wine selections and a deli. Suvretta House Hotel shops include *Vivaia* (with Emilio Pucci couture); *Chez Casagrande* (Hermès); and *Ermenegildo Zegna,* an Italian men's clothing chain.

INCIDENTAL INTELLIGENCE

St. Moritz is on the route of the Glacier Express, which cuts through the Alps—this is one of the most beautiful of train rides—way westward to Zermatt. Travel time is seven and a half hours—the day long—and there's a cramped diner in which a full course (albeit undistinguished) lunch is cheerily served; you must have reserved seats for both train and restaurant car. And if you haven't traveled via Swiss Postal Bus, consider departing St. Moritz for Lugano (Chapter 13), to the south. *Further information:* Verkehrsbüro, Via Maistra, St. Moritz.

18

Schaffhausen

Stein am Rhein and the Rhine Falls

BACKGROUND BRIEFING

Turn to the front of this book and the map of Switzerland. Look at its northernmost bit of territory, a kind of arrowhead that juts north into Germany, with the Rhine River flowing through its widest point, and Lake Constance but a few miles to the east.

You'll observe, as you peruse the map, that Schaffhausen is this triangle's chief town, that the mighty Rhine Falls—the closest Europe comes to North America's Niagara, South America's Iguaçú, or Africa's Victoria Falls—is to its southwest, and that an enchanter of a Middle Ages village called Stein am Rhein lies to the east. Taken together, they constitute a Swiss scenic spectacular—too often bypassed—of special beauty.

It is to Schaffhausen's great credit that despite contemporary eminence as an industrial center—population hovers about 35,000—it stubbornly retains a Middle Ages ambience, proud of its founding as a monastery by Benedictine monks as long ago as the mid-eleventh century. By the thirteenth, secular citizens had expanded it into a substantial enough town to be dubbed a Free City of the Holy Roman Empire, governed by abbots doubling as temporal princes. The Vienna-based Habsburgs eventually succeeded the prince-abbots, staying on until the early decades of the fifteenth century, by which time

Schaffhausen's trade guilds had become powerful enough to take over the reins of government. In 1501, the thriving town joined the Swiss Confederation, in which today it remains important; Schaffhausen is capital of the canton to which it gave its name.

ON SCENE

Lay of the Land: Schaffhausen's *Rheinuferstrasse* borders the Rhine, from which the town works its way northward by means of a number of thoroughfares; *Klosterstrasse* is the most central. It leads to *Münsterplatz* and the complex embracing both the old cathedral, or *Münster,* and the adjacent onetime monastery, *Kloster Allerheiligen,* now the town's principal museum. *Vordergasse,* the main street—lined not only with shops but also landmark houses dating back centuries and beautifully decorated—runs east-west and leads to *Bachstrasse* and *Munot,* the town's great circle of a Renaissance fortress. Admire the fountain-centered squares, *Frohnwagplatz* and *Kirchofplatz.* Watch for venerable gates and towers like *Schwabentor, Obertor,* and *Diebesturm.* And note that the *Bahnhof* edges the town at its western flank, while the pier for passenger steamers to Stein am Rhein and Lake Constance is at the southeastern corner of the city.

Münster (Münsterplatz) is Schaffhausen's principal remaining link with its medieval founding. Though Protestant since the Reformation, it was built as an abbey church by Benedictines in the eleventh century, and remains somberly and splendidly Romanesque, its central nave flanked by original stone arches. The adjacent cloister evokes the complex's earlier centuries, when contemplative monks walked silently under elegantly scaled arcades.

Kloster Allerheiligen (Münsterplatz): The building that had for long served as the monks' monastery serves admirably today as Schaffhausen's museum of history and art. There are skippable galleries devoted to contemporary industry. What you want to zero in on are the sublimely beautiful illuminated manuscripts, weathered documents, and other memorabilia relating to the town's earlier eras, not to mention paintings—the lot of them Swiss and embracing a span of five centuries.

Haus zum Ritter (Vordergasse) is the showplace house on a street of showplace houses, with oriel windows and decorative frescoes. Hope that the sun will be shining, the better to bring out extraordinary details (protected in part by overhanging eaves) of a five-story facade painted four centuries ago by a talented local master named Tobias Stimmer.

Munot (Bachstraasse) is arguably the finest historic fortress in Switzerland, with a solitary tower piercing the Schaffhausen skyline and a brilliant circular keep believed to be based on architectural principles outlined by Germany's greatest Renaissance painter, Albrecht Dürer. It went up over the course of two mid-sixteenth century decades. A visit pays off with a fine view of the town, the Rhine, and surrounding countryside.

Rhine Falls (a.k.a. Rheinfall, located just below Neuhausen on Schaffhausen's southern flank) remain—unlike Niagara which comes immediately to mind—blessedly bucolic. This is nothing less than Europe's largest waterfall, tumbling from the Rhine River (500 feet wide at this point) from a height of 70 feet, over rocks extending 150 yards in width, and with a velocity of a thousand-plus tons per second. Best locale for a view? Hie yourself to *Schloss Laufen*, a venerable castle-cum-restaurant/café, from which you proceed to a series of observation platforms. Or, if you're adventurous, enter the foamy fray by means of a rented boat.

Büsingen and Diessenhofen are Rhine River villages just east of Schaffhausen. The former, on the river's north shore, is an oddball anomaly—surrounded by Swiss territory but technically on German soil, with the Swiss franc the legal currency; a post office which vends Swiss postage for mail to Swiss destinations, as well as German stamps (which must be paid for in deutsch marks, obtainable in exchange for Swiss coins), and a police force consisting of a solitary German constable. Diessenhofen, across the river, is distinguished by *St. Katharinenthal,* a dazzler of a Rococo church, flamboyant in shades of coral and pink, its facade surmounted by a host of trumpeting angels in glittering gold.

Stein am Rhein, fronting the river about halfway between Schaffhausen and the German town of Konstanz, is a delightful hour-and-three-quarters steamer ride from Schaffhausen, and approachable as well by surface. Hauptstrasse, the main street, parallels the river and terminates at *Rathausplatz,* the square taking the name of the *Rathaus,* or Town Hall, distinguished by its clock tower. It's one of a number of extraordinary structures—some Renaissance, some medieval—the lot of them exuberantly frescoed, sometimes partially half-timbered, each with its own wood-carved oriel window, and the lot constituting an al fresco art gallery unique in Switzerland. The Rathaus shelters a small but choice museum of local lore—armor and mail, halberds and crossbows, tapestries and stained glass. *Puppenmuseum* (136 Schwarzhorngasse) displays some 400 antique mechanical dolls, meticulously costumed. Concentrate then, on facades of such inns as *Zum Weissen Adler, Roter Ochsen,* and *Sonne* (below). Consider ascending the hill behind town for a view of the countryside from medieval *Burg Hohenklingen,* a fairytale castle whose *Moderate*-category restaurant is a good lunch bet, concluding at *St. Georg Kloster,* a Benedictine monastery that goes back nine hundred years, whose museum brims with carved-wood sculptures and fine frescoes.

Konstanz, on the German shore of Lake Constance (a.k.a. Bodensee), at a point where the Rhine flows into it, can be reached by riverboat from Schaffhausen, and is the subject of a chapter in *Germany at Its Best,* as are also the lake-bordering towns of *Lindau* and *Meersburg.*

SETTLING IN
Fischerzunft Hotel (8 Rheinquai, Schaffhausen; Phone 5-32-81) could not be more romantic: a rambling house of respectable age, with a Rhine-front location, small capacity (there are but half a dozen no-two-alike rooms) bar-lounge, and handsome

restaurant reputed enough to accord it separate space in a later paragraph. *First Class.*

Parkvilla Hotel (18 Parkstrasse, Schaffhausen; Phone 5-27-37), gray-stoned and turreted, is an updated turn-of-century house that's centrally situated, with 35 comfortable rooms, closed-weekends restaurant, and bar-lounge. Welcoming owner-management. *Moderate.*

Klosterhof Hotel (Stein am Rhein; Phone 42-42-42), despite its youth, blends into the traditional Stein am Rhein ambience. There are 68 smart rooms, a terraced restaurant as well as a less-pricey café, and a piano bar. Attractive. Ambassador Swiss/Best Western. *First Class.*

Rheinfeld Hotel (Stein am Rhein, Phone 41-21-44) is strategically situated near the trans-Rhine bridge. There are seven adequate rooms and a popular terrace restaurant, evaluated below. *Moderate.*

DAILY BREAD
Fischerzunft (8 Rheinquai, Schaffhausen; Phone 5-32-81), counseled above as an inn of no little charm, rates kudos as well as Schaffhausen's No. 1 restaurant. Cuisine bears the mark— or should one say the taste?—of owner/chef André Jaeger, who welcomes you with an *amuse-gueule* (a gratis pre-appetizer course of his own creation). Order then, if you are very hungry indeed, from the gargantuan Menu Gastronomique, or select from the à la carte, noting that Herr Jaeger does especially well by trout and lobster. French imports are among the cheeses, and house-made sherbets are exemplary. *Luxury.*

Theater (23 Herrenacker, Schaffhausen; Phone 5-05-58) is a conveniently located neighbor of the Stadt Theater. Grills—by which I mean steaks of beef, veal, and pork—are good bets, and prix-fixe menus are good-value. *Moderate/First Class.*

Gerberstube (8 Bachstrasse, Schaffhausen; Phone 5-21-55), name notwithstanding, has Italian fare as its specialty, with a range of pastas, including an exemplary ravioli. *First Class.*

Alte Rheinmühle (in Büsingen, the village just east of Schaffhausen; Phone 5-22-47) could not be more atmospheric, set as it is in a seventeenth-century mill, walls half-timbered, interior antiques-accented, setting Rhine-front. Super soups are among the starters, freshwater fish are among the entrées, and desserts are sumptuous. Worth the taxi ride from Schaffhausen, if you're without a car. *Luxury.*

Sonne (Rathausplatz, Stein am Rhein; Phone 41-21-38) is earlier brought to your attention as a fifteenth-century landmark house. But it is hardly less distinguished as a restaurant. Fine old paintings line white stucco walls beneath an aged beamed ceiling. There are several prix-fixe menus, but the name of the Sonne game is fish, be it from the Rhine, Lake Constance, or a nearby trout stream. Local game is featured, too. *First Class/Luxury.*

Rheinfeld (Stein am Rhein; Phone 41-21-44) is at once a small hotel (above) and a terraced-restaurant (location riverfront, near the bridge), with well-priced prix-fixe menus centered on the house's fish specialties. *Moderate.*

SOUND OF MUSIC
Stadttheater (Herrenacker) is Schaffhausen's classic-style opera house; the tourist office (below) will fill you in on dates of concerts and other entertainment.

Johanneskirche (Kirchhofplatz) is a venerable Schaffhausen church, celebrated for its acoustics and a once-every-three-ree-years *Bach Festival.*

INCIDENTAL INTELLIGENCE

Untersee und Rhein is the name of the steamship company whose boats ply the Rhine, in the neighborhood of

Schaffhausen; the tourist office (below) will give you a timetable. The Schaffhausen area is an easy one-day excursion out of Zürich (Chapter 20) with which it is linked by fast and frequent trains. *Further information:* Verkehrsverein Schaffhausen, 12 Vorstadt; Verkehrsverein Stein am Rhein, Hauptstrasse.

19

Zermatt

In the Shadow of the Matterhorn

BACKGROUND BRIEFING

It is, perhaps, a debatable premise. But I submit that the two European villages that most immediately trigger reactions at mention of their names are England's Stratford-upon-Avon, with which the association is of William Shakespeare, his plays, and his romance with Anne Hathaway. And Zermatt, the tiny town in southwestern Switzerland that nestles in a valley enclosed by a clutch of towering Alpine peaks, none higher or more formidable than the distinctively hooked 14,688-foot Matterhorn. Indeed, the Matterhorn itself is celebrated, because its initial mid-nineteenth century ascent remains to this day a drama-packed adventure at once sublime and tragic.

It could not have happened in a more tranquil hamlet. Until as relatively recently as the eighteenth century, isolated Zermatt had had no experience of foreigners. The earliest to arrive—geologists and botanists—stayed in villagers' homes. The first hotel, subsequently rebuilt and still operating as the Monte Rosa, opened in 1838; it consisted of three beds in a private house. Only in 1852 did the village see its first proper hotel, the predecessor of the still operating hostelry called after the French-language designation for the Matterhorn— Mont Cervin.

In 1877, by which time Zermatters had long since shed their eighteenth-century antipathy toward strangers, the village government went into the hotel business as owner of the Zermatterhof, a luxury hostelry that remains under municipal ownership. By that time Zermatt was on the map. Alpinism had become a respectable profession in the neighborhood. Area peaks like the Kleine Matterhorn, Breithorn, and Monte Rosa had been ascended. What remained to be conquered was the toughest and tallest of the lot, the Matterhorn.

That came about in 1865. The date—July 14—is as easily remembered in this region of Switzerland as it is in France where it's Bastille Day—the No. 1 holiday. What happened on July 14, 1865, is that a multinational climbing party—comprised of Englishmen Edward Whymper, Lord Alfred Douglas, the Reverend Charles Hudson (who had made the first ascent of Monte Rosa a decade earlier), and an inexperienced 19-year-old student, Douglas Hadow, guide Marcel Croz from Chamonix in France, and Zermatt guides Peter Taugwalder and his son Peter, Jr.—reached the summit, having started the day before at 1:40 in the afternoon; they were jubilant at their historic achievement.

But the descent was a disaster. Young Hadow slipped, setting off a house-of-cards reaction. He knocked over the guide Croz in front of him, who in turn caused Hudson and Douglas to stumble. In so doing they parted the rope that had joined the foursome and they plunged to their deaths some 4,000 feet down the Matterhorn's north wall, despite efforts by Whymper and the Taugwalders, father and son, to save them.

Withal, the Matterhorn's bittersweet ascent established Zermatt as a center not only of what had come to be called Alpinism—the climbing of mountains—but of skiing and ancillary winter sports. This came about as a consequence of the opening, in 1899, of the remarkable railway (Europe's highest in the open air as distinct from tunnels) that, in the course of a spectacular 45-minute journey, links 5,315-foot Zermatt with 10,272-foot Gornergrat.

The wonder of Zermatt is that, global celebrity notwithstanding, it remains unpretentious, unassuming, and, despite a whopping 6,600-bed visitor capacity, refreshingly devoid of preoccupation with titled and showbiz clientele that typifies St.

Moritz (Chapter 17), the only Swiss mountain resort whose annual visitor count is in excess of Zermatt's (though not by much.
Davos [Chapter 5] is No. 3, in case you're wondering.)

To call Zermatt plain as an old shoe would be inaccurate. It
has a pair of luxury hotels, its fair share of first-class hostelries,
and some good moderate-category houses, not to mention a fair
proportion of above-average restaurants. There are, as well, a
pair of ice rinks, indoor swimming pool and tennis courts,
squash courts, a winter-summer ski school with a faculty of 175,
35 mountain railways, and ski lifts whose total length is just
under 40 miles. And from Gornergrat, less than an hour from
your Zermatt hotel, you may observe 29 of the 38 Swiss peaks
whose altitude is in excess of 12,000 feet.

ON SCENE
Lay of the Land: Access, first. Zermatt, to its credit, bans motor
vehicles. How lovely, you say. It's fun to be in a village where the
only vehicles are horse-drawn. No problem, of course, if you arrive by train, on the line from Visp and Brig to the north. But if
you're driving, you must park your car at a nearby point. Täsch,
three miles distant, with a big parking lot and shuttle service to
Zermatt, is the closest, but there are parking lots also in Visp,
Stalden, St. Niklaus, and Randa. Upon arrival, transfer to a
horse-drawn taxi (the sleighs, in winter, are a treat) which will
take you to your hotel; bigger hotels have their own transport
and meet trains. Life in Zermatt revolves around *Bahnhofstrasse*,
a north-south thoroughfare and the only street that locals bother calling by name. Hotels, restaurants, cafés, and shops rarely
identify their location by street address; if they're in the village
but not on Bahnhofstrasse—at whose northern end lie both
main railway and Gornergrat railway stations, as well as the
tourist office—simply ask along the way for directions.

By train to Gornergrat and beyond to Stockhorn: The Swiss
tell you, as you move about their country, that the view from
Gornergrat (10,272 feet) of the Matterhorn and its satellite
peaks, with Zermatt way below, is the best in the Alps. And I
suspect they're correct. Get off the train from Zermatt, on the
way up, at *Riffelberg*, if you like, for the perspective from that

point (about 7,500 feet) and with a restaurant-café-sundeck. Or plan the journey so that you arrive at Gornergrat in time for lunch-cum-panoramas at its restaurant. After lunch, continue to ascend—now by cable car—via a stop at Hohtälli (10,790 feet) —to Stockhorn (11,240 feet).

Visits to other peaks: As if the rail line to Gornergrat (above) is not engineering marvel enough, there is still another of consequence—an *underground* funicular that takes you in short order from Zermatt upward to *Sunnega*, where the lure is a restaurant-café-terrace-flanked lake, at an altitude of 7,500 feet. But don't stop there; rather, continue to climb, by means of a cable car which stops first at *Blauherd* (8,500 feet and restaurant-equipped), continuing to its terminus, *Unter Rothorn*, at 10,200 feet. Still another breathtakingly beautiful excursion is to *Schwarzee*, an Alpine body of water that translates as Black Lake. You go via cable car, with an intermediate stop at *Furri* (with a restaurant). The lake is splendidly sited at the base of the Matterhorn. Plan your day so as to arrive for a lakeside lunch, continuing afterward via another cable car, that goes by way of *Furgg*, to *Trockener Steg* (9,700 feet and an alternate lunch stop). It is from Trockener Steg that you will proceed—on Europe's highest altitude cableway—to *Kleine Matterhorn*, the so-called Little Matterhorn, at a not so "little" altitude of 12,533 feet. Pray for clear weather on this, highest up of the excursion destinations, with quite the most fabulous of vistas.

Alpine Museum: Museums in small Swiss mountain towns can surprise with their excellence; Davos's Kirchener Museum (Chapter 5) and St. Moritz's Engadine Museum (Chapter 17), are two such. Zermatt's Alpine Museum, just off Bahnhofstrasse, is a third, in a building whose architecture is typical of the area, especially built to house its contents in 1958. Take your time as you amble about two floors of exhibits. Most absorbing are those relating to initial conquest of the Matterhorn in 1865 (an entire room is filled with mementoes of that climb) and of other area peaks. There are period rooms— including a bedroom and a kitchen from a seventeenth-century house in the neighborhood, champion skiers' equipment, mellow prints of Alpine flowers, even stuffed eagles. You'll learn a lot.

Englischekirche (a.k.a. St. Peter's Church and west of Bahnhofstrasse) testifies to the English presence in Zermatt for well over a century; it went up in 1870. Services, not surprisingly, are in English on Sunday mornings—just about the only time the *kirche* is *geöffnet*.

SETTLING IN

Mont Cervin Hotel (Phone 66-11-21) is the successor of the original Mont Cervin, which was opened in 1852 as Zermatt's first proper hotel, by Alexander and Katherine Seiler, whose great-grandchildren operate it along with three other village hotels. Located on Bahnhofstrasse, the Mont Cervin is Zermatt's smartest. A spacious lobby, traditional but with engaging contemporary touches, sets the pace for a house embracing 114 rooms (those I have inspected are handsome, good-sized, and with excellent baths) and 27 suites (some of them clean-lined duplexes with two baths). The dressy main restaurant is supplemented by a pair of casual eateries, one that specializes in Swiss favorites. There's dancing in the evening and a smasher of a swimming pool-sauna-solarium-gym complex. The pool gives onto an immense lawn, dotted with chaise longues in summer. Member, Leading Hotels of the World. *Luxury*.

Zermatterhof Hotel (Phone 66-11-01) is the lovely Bahnhofstrasse house which, in its original form, was founded by Zermatt village elders well over a century ago, and still is village-owned. You walk through the garden—at its best in summer when guests loll about in deck chairs—to reach the lobby, high-ceilinged and crystal-chandeliered. Those of the 80 rooms and suites I have inspected are quietly tasteful, generously proportioned, and thoughtfully equipped. There's a pair of restaurants (one of which is later evaluated), convivial bar, honey of an indoor pool, and fitness center. And the staff is gracious. *Luxury*.

Monte Rosa Hotel (Phone 67-19-22)—another historic Seiler house on Bahnhofstrasse, heart of town. Its windows are all red shuttered, and its lobby is a mix of distinctively decorated lounges (one pine-paneled; another beamed; another red, white, and blue). There are 55 rooms and a quartet of suites, the lot engagingly traditional, some with balconies. The bar is charming and there's a pair of restaurants, one renowned for *fondue* and *raclette*. And guests have privileges at the Mont Cervin's indoor pool. Member, Leading Hotels of the World. *First Class.*

Pollux Hotel (Phone 67-19-46): The beauty part of the Pollux is that, despite its central situation on Bahnhofstrasse, it has a delightful intimate quality. There are just 35 rooms and suites. Twins can be small, but junior suites—with dark leather seating to contrast with brown-and-beige plaid bedspreads—are capacious. And I like the public spaces—lobby-lounge, Restaurant Français (later reviewed), casual café, bar with dancing. *First Class.*

Schweizerhof Hotel (Phone 66-11-55) is smack amidst the Zermatt action, its ground floor fronted by Bahnhofstrasse shops, the pattern of its facade's dark wood balconies unprepossessing. But things are better once you're inside. The lobby is light, bright, and has a fireplace. And the mix of restaurants is diverting; there are both a bar-lounge and a disco, as well as an indoor pool/fitness center. The 75 rooms and suites are Modified Chalet in style, and of varying sizes. *First Class.*

Alex Hotel (Phone 67-17-26)—at the end of a little alley off Bahnhofstrasse—is one of a kind. Proprietor Alex Perren, tenth generation of a Zermatt family, enjoys chatting up his guests and designed the interiors in collaboration with his attractive wife, Gisela. The 45 rooms and suites are no-two-alike (those in the newer wing are fitted with bronze doors). Restaurants (one of which is evaluated in a later paragraph), bar-lounge, jumbo kidney-shaped indoor pool, and gym are bold and color-drenched. There's an indoor tennis court and the lawn out front is agreeable for summer sunning. *Note:* Alex also operates the neighboring *Alex's Schlosshotel Tenne* (pricier, smaller, newer) with its own restaurant, and swimming, tennis, fitness center, and squash privileges for guests at the parent hotel. Both are *First Class.*

Walliserhof Hotel (Phone 67-11-74) has the virtues of a Bahnhofstrasse location and a charming staff, but its rooms are the smallest of any I have observed in a Swiss first class hotel. There are 40 all told (some, of course, larger than others), as well as a café and restaurant, in which breakfast is a pleasure. Ambassador Swiss/Best Western. *First Class.*

Gornergrat Hotel (Phone 67-10-27) is a near neighbor of the railway station, on Bahnhofplatz. It's neat as a pin, with an attractive restaurant, busy bar, and 40 functional rooms. *Moderate.*

Derby Hotel (Phone 67-24-55) is, to be sure, no frills. I bring it to your attention only because it is central—on Bahnhofstrasse—and because all of its rooms have bath; and some, little balconies. Breakfast only. *Moderate.*

Excelsior Hotel (Phone 67-30-17) is an engaging small house that's an easy walk from Bahnhofstrasse with a dozen rooms— some smallish—as well as a pair of bars and a restaurant worthy of review on a subsequent page. Friendly. *Moderate.*

Julen Hotel (Phone 67-24-81) is an attractive 30-room house that pleases, with a lobby-lounge that's a felicitous mix of rustic and contemporary. There are two restaurants (one casual), as many bars, and a sauna/solarium. Every room has a balcony and Bahnhofstrasse is within walking distance. *Moderate.*

Butterfly Hotel (Phone 67-37-21) is the first hotel in my experience—anywhere—to be so named. But why not? It's fairly central—walking distance of Bahnhofstrasse—with 28 functional rooms, restaurant, and bar. *Moderate.*

Bristol Hotel (Phone 67-14-75) comes off very nicely in its public spaces, with an inviting lobby, pair of good-looking restaurants, and bars. There are three dozen neat rooms with balconies, and Bahnhofstrasse is within walking distance. *Moderate.*

DAILY BREAD
Alex Grill (Alex Hotel; Phone 67-17-26): You are impressed with the antique wood panels and posts, and the contemporary stained-glass mural that covers a solid wall. Tables are set in pale blue linen, with light from the candles of the same hue illuminating them at dinner. The carefully composed à la carte is conveniently trilingual (German, French, English). But the day's prix-fixe menu is hardly to be overlooked. You might open with a slice of melon buried under fresh shrimps, continue with a lovely leek soup, move along then to *oeufs Florentine* (poached eggs on a bed of spinach), then select the makings of a salad from a trolley wheeled to your table. As an entrée, how about the French classic, *gigot d'agneau à la fleur de thym* (thyme-scented roast lamb) carved tableside and served in tandem with the potato masterwork, *gratin Dauphinois?* Close either with a sweet—peach Melba is tasty—or cheeses from a platter. Top-notch service. In my experience, one of Switzerland's best restaurants. *Luxury.*

Seilerhaus (Phone 66-11-21), though actually part of a modest hotel whose name it takes, has its own Bahnhofstrasse entrance and a warm-weather terrace giving onto the street. Within, it is a happy mix of flagstone, timber, and glass; this last in enormous picture windows. The tuxedoed mâitre d'hôtel extends a cordial welcome, and you order either the pricey prix-fixe menu embracing half a dozen courses, or opt for à la carte, perhaps opening with a hearty vegetable soup, followed by expertly grilled lamb chops, deliciously garnished. Desserts arrive on a trolley; cakes are especially lavish. A delicious experience. *First Class/Luxury.*

Restaurant Gornergrat (Phone 67-22-19): Plan your rail excursion to Zermatt's most celebrated peak (above) around lunch here, selecting either the good-value menu or—if the day is nippy—a soup-bratwurst-*rösti* repast. Sundeck. (Consider also a meal at *Restaurant Schwarzee* (Phone 67-22-63) in the course of still another excursion [above]. And bear in mind that there are some 30 eateries gracing Zermatt area mountains. You will not go hungry.) *Moderate/First Class.*

Rotisserie (Zermatterhof Hotel; Phone 66-11-01) is stylishly rustic—dark wood panels surface three walls, copper hood covers the rotisserie—open to view—of the fourth. Beef and lamb ordered from the à la carte are celebrated here. But the prix-fixe menu, embracing perhaps a mushroom omelet, the day's soup, a green salad, veal *médaillons* served with French fries, and cheese or dessert—are tasty, too. Delightful service. *Luxury.*

Arvenstube (Pollux Hotel; Phone 67-19-46): You're seated at a pine table set with green linen, framed by pine ceiling and pine walls. Order from an extensive à la carte. *Entrecôte*—the beef is of good quality—served with sauce Béarnaise and, *gratin Dauphinois* is a standby special, and with good reason. *First Class.*

La Ferme (Excelsior Hotel; Phone 67-30-17) is bright and cheerful. Fresh flowers are everywhere, and fare is bracing. Order from the good-value menu, starting with consommé topped by a poached egg, or asparagus dressed with hollandaise. Select grilled lamb or pork chops from among the garnished entrées that are followed by salad and a choice of desserts, *Coupe Danemark* (a super sundae) usually among them. Friendly. *First Class.*

Vieux Valais (Phone 67-20-31), unassuming but welcoming, is a sensible choice for an Italian meal, with pizza (in half a dozen guises) as reliable as pasta. *Moderate/First Class.*

Viktoria (Phone 69-38-71) is a near-the-Bahnhof eatery whose claim to Zermatt fame is imported-from-the-U.S. steaks. Order sirloin with a baked potato. *First Class.*

Bahnhof Buffet's (Phone 67-33-45) prix-fixe menu is a good buy. But so are such à la carte specialties as—of all things—Spain's national dish, *paella*. And Italian-style scampi, too. *Moderate/First Class.*

Hörnli is one of a number of good konditorei in central Zermatt. This Bahnhofstrasse establishment has its bakery at street level and its café up a flight. Go for pastry (*strudel*, blanketed in vanilla sauce, is excellent) and coffee, or for a casual lunch with pasta (ravioli, especially) invariably available. *Moderate.*

SHOPPER'S ZERMATT

Shopping is a snap in little Zermatt; it's concentrated on central Bahnhofstrasse, where options include *Langenthaal* as well as *Sturzenegger* (embroidery and linens); *Stäuble* as well as *Le Must de Cartier* and *Bücherer* (watches and jewelry); *Metzgerei* (mouthwatering fancy groceries); *Merkur* (a national chain, with wine, chocolates, and groceries), *Wega* (gifts and doodads, with a big English-language book department in its basement); *Ski & Sport Shop* (duds and equipment); *Natasha* (smart men's and women's clothes, including skiwear), *Zur Arche*, a first-rate source of handicrafts and handknits); *Elsa's* (children's clothes); and *Zellner* (delicious chocolates and pastries.).

INCIDENTAL INTELLIGENCE ═══════════

Zermatt is western terminus for the Glacier Express, a fabulous reserved-seat rail adventure that runs daily and links the eastern Alps around St. Moritz with the western Alps; travel time is about seven and a half hours and there's a restaurant aboard that's more congenial than delicious. Zermatt's Skischule is one of Switzerland's best sources of ski instruction, both summer and winter. The tourist office publishes a weekly-events calendar in three languages. *Further information:* Verkehrsbüro, Bahnhofplatz, Zermatt.

20

Zürich
Switzerland's Metropolis

BACKGROUND BRIEFING

Credit the Swiss as city planners and site-selectors. Nary an urban center in the Confederation is ill-situated. Geneva (Chapter 6) is backed by no less celebrated a peak than Mont Blanc, and fronted by the inland sea of a lake that takes its name. Bern's (Chapter 3) core is a peninsula surrounded by the loop of a river, with the brilliant Bernese Alps behind it. Lucerne (Chapter 12) has its namesake lake as a playground, and a generous clutch of peaks encircling it. Lugano (Chapter 13) is blessed not only with mountains due north but a trio of lakes—one edging it, others immediately east and west.

But, you are bound to say, those towns are all considerably smaller than Zürich, Switzerland's metropolis. Surely a city its size—just under 400,000, a veritable megalopolis by Swiss standards—cannot be pristinely pretty and perkily populous at one and the same time. But it is, indeed. A snowy range frames it from the rear, with one river, the Sihl, bisecting its west flank, and another—the not-too-wide Limmat—gently winding through its agreeably low-slung core into Zürichsee, the municipality's very own twenty-five-mile-long lake.

This proclivity toward and concern for esthetics is understandable when one considers the elevated site where early ancestors of the present Zürichers established themselves. As long ago as the second decade before the first Christian century, an outpost was constructed by the Romans on a felicitously sited point that sloped to the shore of the Limmat River. It became the nucleus of the Altstadt, or Old Town of Zürich. Ruins of the Romans' handiwork—their original customs house and a later castle—still are to be seen on this eminence, for long called Lindenhof, and now, as it was when Romans first settled in, a lovely point to position oneself to gain Zürich perspective.

Romans stayed on well into the early Christian era, departing only in the early fifth century. Post-Roman Zürich knew a succession of pagan Allemanni, piously Christian and expansionist Franks, and the Germanic Swabians, hardly stay-at-homes themselves. In the tenth century, increasingly mercantile Zürich became a proper city, and an imperial palace dominated the Lindenhof. Within a century the twin-towered Grossmünster, or cathedral, still a Zürich landmark, had gone up.

The line of nobles that had ruled the town for the Holy Roman Emperors expired in the early thirteenth century, and so, in 1218, Zürich became a Free Imperial City, the while seeing its merchants become more prosperous and its artisan guilds—those of textile weavers especially—more powerful. Within a hundred years wealthy Zürich joined the Swiss Confederation.

But it's sixteenth-century Zürich that was especially momentous. The year 1519 is a landmark; it was then that Swiss-born Ulrich Zwingli, ordained as a Catholic priest, by then vicar of Zürich's Grossmünster, began to preach against the granting of indulgences and obligatory celibacy for the Catholic clergy. Predating Jean Calvin in Geneva (Chapter 6), he had begun the Protestant Reformation in Switzerland.

Within half a decade, as a consequence of Zwingli's *Theses*, priests were allowed to marry and images as delineated in frescoes, paintings, and stained glass no longer decorated churches. Convents and monasteries were disbanded, order of worship was revised, Zwingli himself made public what had been a secret marriage, and his doctrine spread to other parts of Switzerland, carried forward after his death (in 1531) by his successor in Zürich, Heinrich Bullinger, and thereafter by Calvin.

If it was never again to be the scene of anything as decisive and far-reaching as the Reformation, post-Zwingli Zürich was hardly placid. It was the site of two wars in the eighteenth century. In the nineteenth, it set about achieving the dominance it has retained in higher education (the University of Zürich is Switzerland's largest, its Polytechnic Institute globally respected), banking (Zürich's is No. 1 in a nation of banks), and culture.

What Geneva is to French-speaking Suisse Romande, Zürich embodies for German-speaking Swiss. It's their intellectual hub, as dynamic in realms of opera, music, and theater as it is skilled in international finance. But there is still another dimension of Zürich. Severities of the Zwingli-inspired Reformation of earlier centuries notwithstanding, this is a lighthearted city with a sense of humor and an appreciation of the good life; less elegant, perhaps, than Gallic-accented Geneva, but neither less sophisticated nor less fun.

ON SCENE

Lay of the Land: It is not at all a bad idea to begin where the Romans (above) of early *Turicum* began—at *Lindenhof,* the park with remains of their early customs house and fourth-century fortress, as well as of the later imperial palace. You'll have a fine view of town, lake, and mountains. Proceed, then, to the most famous of Swiss main streets. Many central thoroughfares are named for railway stations flanking them, but none is more celebrated than Zürich's *Bahnhofstrasse.* It runs north (from the lavish beaux-arts facade of the *Hauptbahnhof,* with the mock-medieval towers of *Schweizerisches Landesmuseum*—the Swiss National Museum—directly to its rear), past the smartest shops in town, and *Paradeplatz*—the busy tramcar terminus—to *Bürkliplatz,* on the shore of *Zürichsee,* with *Quaibrücke,* a bridge due east that leads across the Limmat to *Bellevueplatz* and the East Bank. *Général Guisan Quai* parallels the lake, in a westerly direction, with the *Tonhalle* (principal concert venue/ *Kongresshaus*) complex nearby.

Across the relatively narrow river—you're never far from one of seven core-of-town bridges—*Limmatquai* is at once shop-lined and the site of such monuments as the *Rathaus,* or City Hall; *Wasserkirche,* a neighboring church; and, going inland, the

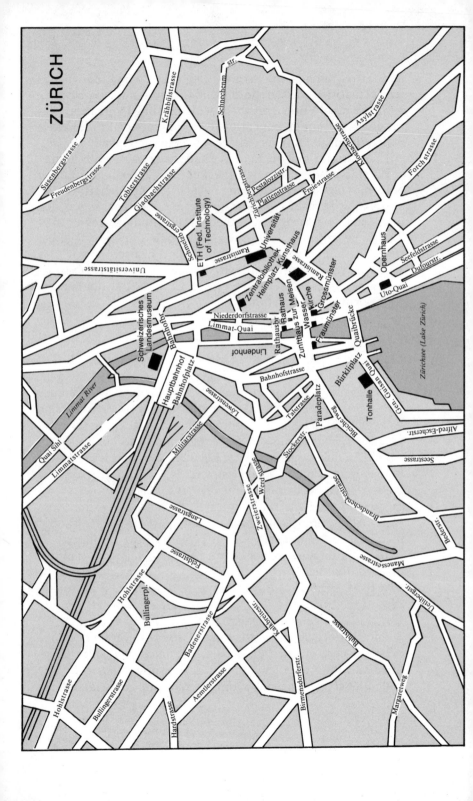

twin-towered *Grossmünster,* or cathedral; *Kunsthaus,* the art museum; and *Opernhaus.* A nice walk on this bank would take you east and uphill from Limmatquai, via *Mühlegasse* to *Zentralbibliothek,* the main public library with churchlike spires and exhibits of its treasures, and farther east, along *Schienhutgasse,* to the adjacent complex of the so-called *ETH* (the domed Federal Institute of Technology or Polytechnic) and the tall-towered *Universität.*

Which leads to three words of counsel with respect to streets close to the riverbank, on either of its sides: don't neglect them. That includes the quarter on the East Bank in the shadow of the Grossmünster—*Münstergasse, Marketgasse, Mühlegasse, Niederdorfstrasse*—and narrow streets leading from everbustling *Limmatquai.* They're lined with fine old houses, contemporarily sheltering cafés, boutiques, and restaurants. And the West Bank streets just beyond *Rathausbrücke*—most central of the bridges—in and about *Weinplatz,* including *Storchengasse, Strehlgasse,* and *Schwannengasse*—make delightful strolling territory.

Grossmünster (Grossmünsterplatz) rates priority in the pecking order of explorable destinations, primarily because history was made within—Zwingli, preaching from its pulpit, brought about the Swiss Reformation—and because the identical Gothic towers that define its facade are standout Zürich landmarks. The Romansque cloister to the side, originally early thirteenth century, is beautifully arcaded. The also-Romanesque north portal with an exquisitely carved tympanun—the overhead portion—retains an original and intricate frieze on either of its sides. And the busy play of columns supporting vaults in the crypt is noteworthy. But the essentially Romanesque interior is handicapped by infelicitous proportions and virtually unrelieved severity. Such cathedrals as those in Basel, Bern, Lausanne, St. Gallen, and yes, even the Geneva cathedral in which austere Jean Calvin preached, are certainly, in this appraiser's view, more esthetically exciting.

Kunsthaus (Heimplatz): You may wonder, as you enter the formidable gray stone pile sheltering Zürich's art museum, what

manner of treasure the bourgeois citizens of this rich, albeit republican, city have amassed without the benefit of centuries of
royal patronage—the kind, say, of the art-loving Habsburg emperors, as displayed in the Kunsthistorisches Museum in
Vienna, not far to the east. Well, you need not worry. The
Kunsthaus, with two high-ceilinged floors of galleries, succeeds
superbly well with what it undertakes. Its collection is not a
wide-ranging survey. Renaissance Italians are in short supply, a
tiny Fra Angelico and a pair of Tiepolo saints the stellar exceptions. And you must not expect Spaniards or eighteenth-century
English portraitists. But compensations are extraordinary.
Sculpture, for example: Rodin and Matisse, Maillol and Calder,
Arp and Brancusi, Switzerland's Alberto Giacometti and America's George Segal. Early Swiss religious work—a striking series
of fourteenth-century crucifixions, equally early interpretations
of the Annunciation, Nativity, and Adoration of the Kings are
no less absorbing than portraits of medieval Swiss burghers, by
talented if uncelebrated masters. Go on then to Baroque
paintings—a Rubens of Spain's Philip IV, Van Dyck's *Triumph of
Bacchus*, Rembrandt's *St. Simon*, a dapper Hals gent in the black
and white of the period, a bucolic village of the kind that
Hobbema made his trademark, an ethereal Van Ruysdael landscape. The nineteenth-century French—Géricault, Corot,
Daumier—preceding the Impressionists—come on strong in
preparation for Monets (my count is eight), Cézannes (I note
half a dozen), quite as many by Van Gogh, as well as Manet and
Renoir, Pissarro and Degas. There are sprinklings of Rousseau,
Utrillo, Roualt, Bonnard, and Vuillard. German Expressionists?
You find Max Liebermann, Lovis Corinth, what I term the "K"
trio (Kandinsky, Kokoschka, Kirchner), and my favorite of the
group, ever-exuberant August Macke. Late Greats—Léger and
Gris, Mondrian and Magritte, Chagall (who designed the
stained glass of a Zürich church [below]), and of course, Picasso.
The New York school's Morris Louis and Mark Rothko bring
pleasure, too. As, indeed, do such Swiss as Johan Fussli (eighteenth century), Arnold Böcklin (nineteenth century), the
inscrutable albeit absorbing Paul Klee, and in my view the greatest of the lot—he lived well into this century—Ferdinand
Hodler. Café.

Schweizerisches Landesmuseum (Museumstrasse, just behind the Hauptbahnhof): Four cities bid for the Swiss National Museum after Parliament legislated its creation in 1890. Needless to say, Zürich won, and the architect it selected to design the museum's quarters, Gustav Gull, evoked, with great success, a rambling medieval castle, towered and turreted. His building's two high-ceilinged floors contain some eighty galleries. Herr Gull's goal was quite obviously ambience rather than ease in getting about. You'll walk apparently interminable distances and you'll no doubt get lost. But you'll have a good time. The most dazzling space—the Gothic-vaulted Armory—is massed with suits of mail and weapons, with Ferdinand Hodler murals of historic Swiss battles on its walls. But there's so much more— jewellike treasures such as a celestial globe crafted in 1596 and a set of exquisitely gilded drinking vessels of the same period, miniature paintings and great frescoes, embroidery and silver, stained glass from long-razed churches, pewter and costumes, porcelain and pottery, displays which reconstruct phases of Swiss history, Roman Legions onward. And I save best for last: a series of period rooms—with original walls, ceilings, floors, windows, furnishings, and accessories, paneled Renaissance reception room through to a parlor from the height of the Belle Époque. Plan to make a return visit; you discover new exhibits each time.

Wohnmuseum (20 Bärengasse) is a pair of joined seventeenth-century houses whose interiors have been reconstructed to shelter a series of 30 rooms, by the Swiss National Museum (above), whose idea has been to portray domestic life in Zürich for the near two-century span beginning in the Late Renaissance/Baroque period (1650) through to the Biedermeier era terminating about 1840. No room is without interest, but some—Renaissance living-dining room with a great porcelain stove, seventeenth-century kitchen, Rococo ballroom, kids' playroom, gentleman's study—are standouts.

Zunfthaus zur Meissen (20 Münsterhof, with the entrance on the Fraumünster side): Draws here are twofold. First is the riverfront building itself, an extraordinarily beautiful Rococo mansion—with a series of porticos set against steeply pitched roofs supported by a series of pilasters, in the classical style—that is surely the handsomest of the city's guildhalls. Wisely, the Swiss National Museum selected this eighteenth-century landmark as the setting for its collection of eighteenth-century porcelain. The emphasis is on Zürich's own, but there are pieces from foreign points, including Strasbourg and Meissen. Exhibits and setting blend beautifully.

Fraumünster (Fraumünsterstrasse) would be just another much-restored Gothic church were it not for the remarkable stained glass in its windows, by Marc Chagall, executed in 1970 and 1978. Those with more familiar themes—*Virgin and Child, Crucifixion, Lamb of God*—are perhaps the most immediately moving. But take your time moving about; notice as well the additional window by Augusto Giacometti (*The Heavenly Paradise*, 1947) in the ruined cloister. An attendant at the postcard stall happily answers questions.

Rietberg Museum (15 Gablerstrasse—a taxi or tram ride from the center) is a historic house (mid-nineteenth century neoclassic with a statue of Wagner in the garden, commemorating his visits) with a superlative collection of non-European art—Chinese Buddhas and jades, Japanese calligraphy and pottery, rare Benin bronzes and other works from Africa, including masks—of a caliber seldom come upon in Switzerland.

Stiftung Sammlung Bührle (172 Zollikerstrasse, a tram or taxi ride from the center) traditionally keeps such absurdly limited hours (Tuesday and Friday afternoons and a six-hour stretch starting at 2:00 P.M., but only on the first Friday of each month) that I hesitate calling it to your attention. Still, within its walls is a superlative cache of French painting, with the nineteenth century—pre-Impressionists like Corot, Courbet, and Delacroix; Impressionists including Cézanne, Degas, Gauguin, Manet, Renoir, and Van Gogh—especially strong, and with earlier and later work, as well. Go if you can.

Rathaus (Limmatquai at Rathausbrücke) is a Zürich architectural treasure. With its well-detailed Renaissance lines it could be a ducal palace rather than the City Hall. You pass by the Rathaus often. On at least one occasion, pause to admire its facade's busts of historical figures, both Zürich and ancient. Go inside, then, to the banquet room, lavishly Baroque (the building went up in the late seventeenth century even though the exterior looks to be earlier) with frescoed walls and stuccoed ceilings.

Wasserkirche (Limmatquai, and entered through *Helmhaus*, the building to which it is attached) is curious waterside Gothic, much restored over the centuries but still with superb proportions and vaults, not to mention strikingly modern stained glass by Giacometti and also-contemporary tapestries. Pop in as you pass by.

Am Römerholz (95 Haldenstrasse, in the city of Winterthur, a half-hour train ride northeast of Zürich): Oskar Reinhart, a wealthy native of Winterthur who died in 1965, bequeathed not only his paintings—Old Masters and works by later French masters—but the house in which they repose, to the Swiss Confederation, to be operated as a museum. This is one of the outstanding originally private collections. Impressionists—represented by Manet (a floral still life), Toulouse-Lautrec (the Moulin Rouge clown, Cha-U-Kao), Van Gogh (*Summer Evening near Arles*) among many—are perhaps the most exciting paintings. Consider also canvases by Cranach and Holbein among the Germans; Rubens and Bruegel among the Flemings; El Greco and Goya from Spain; Poussin, Chardin, Delacroix, Daumier, Ingres, Bonnard, and Picasso among the non-Impressionist French. But that's not all the art in Winterthur. The same Dr. Reinhart gave still another collection, known as the *Oskar Reinhart Foundation* (6 Stadthausstrasse) to the municipality. It, too, operates as a museum with its emphasis on Swiss, Austrian, and German artists of the eighteenth, nineteenth, and twentieth centuries. Highlights for me are paintings by Ferdinand Hodler (1853–1918), but you'll come across Romanticists like Friedrich, realists like Albert Anker and Arnold Böcklin, and more recent Swiss work by Cuno Amiet and

Giovanni Giacometti. *Schloss Sülfingen*, an essentially eighteenth-century castle, exuberantly decorated, is now a restaurant and makes for an atmospheric lunch stop; it's a taxi ride from the center.

SETTLING IN

Baur au Lac Hotel (1 Talstrasse; Phone 221-16-50) is proof positive that a hotel can have it both ways. By that I mean a location so central that you may walk everywhere *and* so bucolic that you've a garden, flanking Zürichsee, at the front door. This is a hotel with the patina of age, as well. The chap whose name it takes—an Austrian immigrant called Johann Baur—came to Zürich as a baker's apprentice in 1830. By 1838 he had opened his first hotel, the nearby Savoy Baur en Ville (below) and in 1844, he shrewdly purchased a plot of lakefront property, and built the Baur au Lac. Wings were added over the decades and by 1890 the hotel assumed the appearance it maintains so impeccably today. General Manager Michel Rey is never far from wherever the center of the action may be—a gala civic dinner or *your* arrival at reception. Public spaces—especially the spacious, dark-paneled lounge massed with bouquets of flowers—are welcoming, and include a bar, a disco, and a trio of restaurants: Le Français with tables illuminated at dinner by oversized silver candlesticks; Pavilion (in the garden, with picture windows on the lake and tables on the lawn in summer), and the paneled Grill Room (evaluated on a later page). There are 170 rooms, good-value minimum-rate singles through to lakeview suites. Many are variations on the theme of Louis XVI; others are more contemporary; each is distinctive with respect to color scheme, textiles, size, and exposure. This is one of Switzerland's best-operated hotels. Member, Leading Hotels of the World. *Luxury.*

Savoy Hotel Baur en Ville (a.k.a. The Savoy, Poststrasse 12; Phone 211-53-60): You will have read in the paragraph above about this hotel's establishment by the very same Johann Baur who later opened the Baur du Lac. Common antecedents notwithstanding, the two are not related today. This house—Zürichers call it The Savoy—though entered on Poststrasse, overlooks both Paradeplatz and Bahnhofstrasse. Its monumental facade is among the more superior in Zürich. The high-ceilinged lobby is smartly contemporary, as are the Grill (a marriage of warm-toned wood accents with beige and brown textiles) and Café Baur, with tables spilling onto vibrant Paradeplatz. Solo travelers might be pleased to learn that 78 of the 112 rooms are singles. There are eight suites (those I have inspected, with terraces giving onto the square, are a pleasure); so are the doubles I have seen. Which brings us to service. Congenial owner-manager Manfred Hörger and his staff are quite obviously pros who enjoy their work and their guests' company. *Luxury.*

Dolder Grand Hotel (65 Kurhausstrasse; Phone 251-62-31); How about headquartering in a corker of a grand hotel, smack atop a mountain overlooking Zürich, its lake, and the mountains beyond? And with a funicular linking you to the center, ten minutes distant? There's a nine-hole golf course next door, tennis, minigolf, an outdoor pool and (in winter) an ice hockey rink out back. Long and low-slung—its facade is punctuated with a trio of pinnaclelike towers—the Dolder shelters a half-moon-shaped restaurant that moves to a terrace-cum-panoramas in warm weather (I review it on a later page), a series of lovely lounges (one of which is the bar), and 200 no-two-alike rooms and suites; I need not tell you that you want to specify one that overlooks the city. Happiness in Zürich is a Dolder room-service breakfast served on your balcony, Zürich spread out beneath you. Member, Leading Hotels of the World. *Luxury.*

Eden au Lac Hotel (45 Utoquai; Phone 47-94-04): You like the Eden even before the doorman takes your bags from the taxi, what with its classic-style facade, an on-high portico supported by caryatids and fronting a tower, itself topped by a tiny cupola. It should go without saying that none of the 54 rooms and suites in this handsomely updated nineteenth-century house are identical. Aim for a front one; they're balconied and offer panoramas of the lake out front, and the city to the west, with Bahnhofstrasse a ten-to fifteen-minute walk. The Eden's forte is its intimate quality and a staff (including many veterans) that is at once skilled and smiling. The bar is congenial and the restaurant so good that I accord it space in a later paragraph. Distinguished Hotels/Robert F. Warner. *Luxury.*

Atlantis Sheraton Hotel (234 Döltschiweg; Phone 463-00-00) is a likable contemporary house, with a pair of restaurants (one gala, the other casual), a bar that offers evening dancing, and a honey of a picture-windowed indoor pool-sauna leading from the humming lobby. There are just 200 rooms and suites, many with deep leather-upholstered club chairs, the lot with fine baths. General Manager Peter Gantenbein, whom I first met when he was with the Brussels Hilton, oversees a dedicated staff, not only in the hotel proper, but in a guesthouse annex across the road, which has 62 terraced rooms. Location is just enough away from the center that you want a car. *Luxury.*

Zürich Hotel (42 Neumühlequai; Phone 361-63-63) has the dubious distinction of being central Zürich's only skyscraper. I say "central" because you're but a quarter-hour's walk from Bahnhofstrasse. Clean-lined contemporary, the Zürich has 210 functional rooms of varying sizes, ten suites, piano bar, and a pair of restaurants. Groups are a specialty. *Luxury.*

Schweizerhof Hotel (Bahnhofstrasse; Phone 211-86-40) is a long-on-scene favorite that closed down for a fairish period a half-decade or so back, to completely refurbish, melding today's look with yesterday's—and successfully. A restaurant, ivory-paneled, and a softly lighted bar with dark leather chairs surrounding tables, lead from the lobby. There are 115 rooms and suites of varying sizes and situations; those I have inspected—in warm pastels with floral pattern spreads and draperies—are charming. And location is just opposite the station. *First Class.*

St. Gotthard Hotel (87 Bahnhofstrasse; Phone 211-55-00) is a Bahnhofstrasse leader, with gracious public spaces, excellent mix of restaurants: Steakhouse (later evaluated), Café St. Gotthard (with tables spilling into the street) and Bouillabaisse (for seafood), bar, disco, and 140 rooms and suites; those I have inspected—comfortably traditional style—are delightful. *First Class.*

Central Hotel (1 Central; Phone 251-55-55) is accurately titled. It's a near neighbor of the Hauptbanhof, with a nineteenth-century facade and an interior—the look is wicker furniture and potted plants against buff-colored walls and nubby textiles—that is distinctly late twentieth-century. Those of the hundred rooms and suites I have inspected are thoughtfully equipped with such U.S.-inspired amenities as hair driers and disposable slippers and, upon occasion, circular beds, not to mention ice-cube machines on every floor, praise be. There are two good restaurants and an amusing bar called Casablanca, with blown-up stills of Bogey and Ingrid, from the movie of that name, plastering the walls. Friendly. *First Class.*

Carlton Elite Hotel (41 Bahnhofstrasse, but entered on Nüschelerstrasse; Phone 211-65-60) is nicely situated, nicely furnished, and equipped with 50 rooms and suites (some are snazzy duplexes), two restaurants (one later reviewed), and a café-bar. Animated. *First Class.*

Glarnischhof Hotel (30 Claridenstrasse; Phone 202-47-47), because of its location a block inland from Bahnhofstrasse and the river, tends to be overlooked. It shouldn't be. Location is central, public spaces are quietly attractive, there are 70 well-equipped rooms (some of them good size), as well as a reliable restaurant, informal café, and relaxing bar. Ambassador Swiss/Best Western. *First Class.*

Glockenhof Hotel (11 Sihlstrasse; Phone 211-56-50) is well situated, just off Bahnhofstrasse in the direction of the station. The bright lobby, furnished with oversized leather chairs, is inviting; no less so are the pair of memorably titled restaurants, Glogge Stube (No. 1) and casual Glogge Egge, which moves to the pretty garden in summer. Rooms—35 all told—are neat-as-a-pin modern. Ambassador Swiss/Best Western. *First Class.*

Zum Storchen Hotel (Weinplatz; Phone 211-55-10) has had so much going for it for such a long time—its roots go back half a millenium and its situation is on a venerable Altstadt square, riverfront—that it's a pity its interior (creditable restaurant excepted) is now severely contemporary, virtually devoid of embellishment, and that, moreover, its 77 rooms (at least those I have either inhabited or inspected) are small, with little more than functionalism to recommend them. Still, there is no denying either the charm or convenience of the location. If you do stay, insist that when you ask the concierge for a taxi to the station, you mean a proper, meter-equipped taxi, rather than (as has been the case with me) a hotel limo with the meter hidden in the glove compartment, to be used only if you insist. *First Class.*

Ammann Hotel (4 Kirchgasse; Phone 252-74-39) is unpretentious and small (there are just under 20 rooms), but neat and delightfully situated—heart of the Altstadt, a hop and skip from the Grossmünster. Restaurant, café. *First Class.*

Züricher Hof Hotel (21 Zahringerstrasse; Phone 47-10-40) is a pleasant 30-room house; some accommodations are traditional, some modern. Walliser Keller, the restaurant, is popular with Zürichers and guests alike, and location is central. Ambassador Swiss/Best Western. *First Class.*

Europe Hotel (4 Dufourstrasse; Phone 47-10-30) has a lovely old-fashioned air, with an antiques-accented lounge, and 30 rooms and suites, elaborately Louis XV or Louis XVI, and with well-equipped baths. This is what the Swiss call an *alkohol-frei* hotel; only coffee, tea, and pastries are served in the lounge. There is no bar, and minibars in bedrooms are stocked only with soft drinks. But of course you may bring your own. Location is a quarter-hour walk from Bahnhofstrasse, near the opera. Breakfast only. *First Class.*

Tiefenau Hotel (8 Steinwiesstrasse; Phone 251-82-46) is a fair-sized schlep, make no mistake, from Bahnhofstrasse. But if you've a car, you might enjoy this good-looking Louis XV-style house, built in 1835 and converted to hotel use in the early

1980s, with eighteenth-century antiques as accents. Those of the 35 rooms and suites I have inspected are charming; ditto the restaurant. *First Class.*

Chesa Rustica Hotel (70 Limmatquai; Phone 251-92-91) may be just the ticket, if you seek a budget-priced house with a bit of flavor, and a central situation. Chesa Rustica has 20 pleasantly furnished rooms (aim for one on the river), amicable administration, and a pair of restaurants—high-ceilinged *Schiff,* with brass chandeliers and ladderback chairs, and rustic *Cave,* where *fondue* is the specialty. *Moderate.*

Florhof Hotel (4 Florhofgasse; Phone 47-44-70)—though not central (Bahnhofstrasse is a 20-minute walk)—is special. This originally sixteenth-century structure was thoroughly refurbished in the mid-1970s to emerge as a 33-room hotel. Furnishings are mostly contemporary and undistinguished, but bits and pieces from older days—ceiling stucco work, a great rococo porcelain stove—still are to be encountered. Restaurant. *Moderate.*

City Hotel (34 Löwenstrasse; Phone 211-20-55) is on a street parallel with Bahnhofstrasse, not far from the station. Some of the 40 spotless rooms are bigger than others, but count on all of them to be well equipped. Small restaurant and bar. Nice. *Moderate.*

Simplon Hotel (16 Schürzengasse; Phone 211-61-11) is a near neighbor of the Hauptbahnhof, opposite the Gotthard Hotel (above). Most—but not all—of the 75 rooms have baths, and there's a bar-café wherein light meals are served, as well as a disco. *Moderate.*

Montana Hotel (39 Konradstrasse; Phone 42-69-00): You're behind the Hauptbahnhof at the Montana, but only a hop and a skip. There's a restaurant and bar, and 60 neat rooms. *Moderate.*

Hilton International Zürich Hotel (Flughafen, Zürich; Phone 810-31-31) would be near the top of my Zürich hotels grouping,

were it central. This airport hotel is an elongated pavilion with
300 contemporary rooms, all with super U.S.-style baths.
(*Danke*, New York-based Hilton International!), lively bar-
lounge, indoor pool, coffee shop with authentic U.S.-style
hamburgers, Sutter's Grill—a ranker of a restaurant, at once
posh and delicious, meeting rooms for business travelers flying
in from various points to converge for conferences, and, in my
experience, super service. *Luxury.*

DAILY BREAD

SMART RESTAURANTS

Agnes Amberg (5 Hottingerstrasse; Phone 251-26-26): Named
for its proprietor-chef, who also operates a cooking school, this
is a perfect square of a space and a veritable symphony in green,
what with the palest of green walls, apple-green taffeta swags
framing windows, and grass-green porcelain on the dozen tables. Fare is a happy marriage of France's often sparse *nouvelle*
and the hearty fare of Switzerland. The four-course prix-fixe,
for example, might embrace a delicate mousse of scallops *im
grünen nest* (with a garnish, not surprisingly, of greens);
artischockenschaumsuppe—a frothy artichoke-based potage;
lamm curry mit gemüsen—the *gemüsen* being a fresh vegetable
garnish, and—for dessert—*früchtegratin*, a meld of grapes and
apple slices blanketed by meringue, with a dollop of raspberry
sorbet for tang. Service is skilled and smiling. In my experience
one of Switzerland's best restaurants. *Luxury.*

Kronenhalle (4 Rämistrasse; Phone 251-02-56) is a beloved
Zürich institution, long on scene, congenial (its bar is as popular
as its restaurant), and with an extraordinary collection of modern paintings lining walls. There is no catalog of the art, more's
the pity, but my notes indicate works by Bonnard, Chagall,
Giovanni Giacommetti, Klee, Matisse, Miró, Picasso, Renoir,
Rouault, and Signac, and I suspect I've missed some. But I suspect, also, that you would like to know about the food. It's
delicious. The à la carte is relatively limited but with good things
to eat. You might open with the house's own ravioli or the dried

beef called *bündnerfleisch*. Rosemary-scented roast chicken and veal *médaillons* are two favored entrées. And chocolate mousse is indicated to conclude. Pleasant service. Near the opera. *First Class.*

Chez Max (53 Seestrasse, bordering Zürichsee, in the suburb of Zollikon, a quarter-hour's drive or taxi ride from town; Phone 391-88-77): Ideally, you want to make this outing on a sunny day, when you may lunch under an umbrella on Max's terrace. But indoors is nice, too. Brown linen napkins, similar in tone to the draperies, complement beige tablecloths. The prix-fixe menus at lunch are sound value, and might include a *foie gras terrine* or frog's leg soup to begin, with veal or lamb entrées, substantially garnished. Dinner is pricier. But at either meal, the dessert to order is the hot *soufflé*, flavored with Poire William *eau-de-vie. Luxury.*

Grill Room (Baur au Lac Hotel, 1 Talstrasse; Phone 221-16-50): A tuxedoed captain shows you to your table, and you are as interested in the room—mock-Renaissance ceiling, Art Nouveau arches framing windows, tables dressed in gray linen centered by silk-shaded lamps and yellow flowers—as in your fellow lunchers. The chaps at the next table open with dry martinis, served with twists. The nearby pair of ladies in hats sip white wine as an aperitif between bits and pieces of Zürich gossip. A quartet of Yuppie Yanks quaff beer as they await sustenance. The four-course lunch might commence with a beef salad vinaigrette, continue with the day's *potage*, in preparation for the entrée, a platter combining *goujons* (deep-fried fingers of sole) with crayfish. From the *chariot de desserts*, wheeled to table, you do well to select a pastry; *tarte aux fraises* with *crème fraîche* spooned over the glazed strawberries by the waiter—is, to understate—a winner. And a veritable platoon of service staff takes excellent care of you. *Luxury.*

La Rotonde (Dolder Grand Hotel, 65 Kurhausstrasse; Phone 251-63-21): Take your choice of the crescent-shaped restaurant proper, or the similarly contoured terrace with Zürich and its lake way below. The lunchtime prix-fixe menu is a pleasure, with half a dozen choices for both opening and entrée courses. I like to begin by having a little of this and a little of that—by which I mean a little of everything—from the hors d'oeuvres spread offered from a *voiture* wheeled to table. Escalope of veal is a delicious main dish, and it is so difficult to select desserts from the trolley that the waiter, sensing your conflict, insists that you have samplings of two or three. Why not? Super service. *Luxury.*

Restaurant Français (Eden au Lac Hotel; 45 Utoquai; Phone 47-94-04) is an intimate room, with widely separated tables, exquisitely set, beneath a series of crystal chandeliers. You do well to order from the prix-fixe, starting with consommé, double-laced with sherry, or brochette of grilled scampi, moving along to seafood thermidor or filet of beef accompanied by a superb sauce Béarnaise, concluding with a choice of cheeses, fruit from a giant silver bowl, or the day's special desserts. Hospitable staff. *Luxury.*

Savoy Grill (Savoy Baur en Ville Hotel, 12 Poststrasse; Phone 211-53-60) is a choice composite—tall white tapers, bowls of red roses, wood-paneled walls, high-backed chairs, captains and their crews in black and white. The extensive à la carte tempts. Smoked Irish salmon is a favored opener, with lobster *bisque* no less satisfying. Fish are a Savoy specialty—filet of sole particularly. Veal steak in a rosemary-infused cream sauce is a winner, too. And—to quote the hardly modest menu—*les Entremets sont au bénéfice d'une carte privilégiée.* By which management is telling you that desserts rate their own card. If you haven't ordered the chocolate soufflé well enough in advance, settle for a rich cake or pastry. Friendly. *Luxury.*

St. Gotthard Hotel Restaurants (87 Bahnhofstrasse; Phone 211-55-00): Hungry Zürichers gravitate to the St. Gotthard for any number of reasons. One is the beef in its *Steakhouse;* second is lobster and oysters, in the *Hummer Bar.* And a third is the *tagesmenu*—well-priced and invariablly delicious *plats du jour* preceded by the day's soup and followed by the day's sweet—in *Café St. Gotthard.* Everything I have sampled here is tasty, and service is first rate. *Moderate* (the Café) through *Luxury* (the Hummer Bar).

GUILDHALLS AND BEERHALLS

Zunfthaus zur Waag (8 Münsterhof; Phone 211-07-30): Sensibly—and appropriately—seeing service (for the most part, at least) as restaurants, the centuries-old structures, built by wealthy guilds as their headquarters, are a not-insignificant dimension of Zürich's architecture and its history. Best way to experience them is to lunch or dine. Zunfthaus (Guildhall) zur Waag, dominating the handsome square called Münsterhof, heart of town, is for me the smartest, tastiest, and most intimate: a charming upstairs space in the originally eighteenth-century, steeply gabled, onetime seat of the city's inspectors of weights and measures. Bright and light, its windows are framed by white tiebacks, its tables centered by flowers and flanked by early nineteenth-century chairs. Zur Waag's swift-moving and amicable waitresses serve well-priced prix-fixe menus built around veal and pork specialties—sometimes casseroles—accompanied by tartly dressed salads, preceded by subtly seasoned soups, with rich desserts to conclude. Candlelit dinners. *First Class.*

Zunfthaus zur Safran (54 Limmatquai; Phone 47-47-22)—the spice merchants and apothecaries' guildhall—has fourteenth-century roots, but the present complex is essentially Baroque, at least within, where the up-one-flight *Safranstube* (the former assembly chamber) is as much visitable for its carved-wood ceiling and paneled walls as for its fare. There are two prix-fixe menus. The cheaper might open with a chicken *terrine*, continue with both fish and meat courses (*grenadine de veau*—a veal specialty—is delicious) and conclude with cheese or dessert. Ask for a table by the picture windows that give onto the river. *First Class.* (And note that there's a convenient ground-floor café that is *Moderate.*)

Haus zum Rüden (42 Limmatquai; Phone 47-05-90)—a Baroque rebuilding of a much older house—has been headquarters of the *Gesellschaft zur Constaffel*, originally an élitist society of noblemen, since the fourteenth century. The-up-a-flight restaurant, its so-called *Gotischen Stube*, or Gothic Room, is distinguished by a 33-foot wood-beamed, barrel-vaulted ceiling. There are several prix-fixe menus, with fare, in my experience, an unexceptional blend of traditional Swiss with contemporary. (The so-called Business Lunch might consist of a chicken liver pâté, and a garnished veal steak, with dessert not included, although the pricier Menu du Jour is more generous.) Service in my experience can be patronizing toward foreigners. *First Class.*

Bierhalle Kropf (16 In Gassen; Phone 221-18-05) is conveniently central—just off Paradeplatz—and though nothing like as monumentally proportioned as Zeughauskeller (below), with a politer, more professional staff and, in my experience, considerably tastier food. There are plats du jour, bargain-tabbed for lunchers only, and more costly dinner specials. You might open with vegetable soup, preparatory to tackling a delicious *entrecôte* accompanied by crispy French fries and a fresh vegetable. Or order à la carte, concentrating on one of an inordinate selection of sausages, expertly grilled and presented in tandem with potato salad, or as good a plate of *rösti* potatoes as you'll encounter. *First Class.*

Zeughauskeller (28 Bahnhofstrasse; Phone 211-26-90)—a onetime armory dating all the way back to 1487—looks better than it tastes, what with its massive proportions and a fabulous painted ceiling. The concept of stick-to-the-ribs favorites at popular prices is indisputably commendable and, if you order the simplest things—*bündnerfleisch* (air-dried beef) as an appetizer, veal steaks or grilled sausages as entrées, opting for French fries or a green salad rather than *rösti* (the poorest such I have had in Switzerland), you'll be okay. But don't expect cordial service; waiters are stone-visaged and not especially speedy. *Moderate/ First Class.*

Augustiner (25 Augustinergasse; Phone 211-72-10): This invariably busy, always humming, agreeably congenial oldtimer does well by the likes of bouillon in which a pair of liver dumplings float—as an opener; filet of wild boar accompanied by *spätzli*, as an entrée, with complex ice cream concoctions to conclude. *Moderate.*

ITALIAN

Cantinetta Bindinella (7 In Gassen; Phone 221-25-44) is an utter charmer; stylishly Art Deco, candlelit at dinner, with authentic Italian fare presented in good-value prix-fixe menus. Commence with prosciutto and melon, the house's superlative ravioli, or a pasta. Veal piccata or veal scallopine would be fine entrées. And there's an ample choice of Italian wines. *First Class.*

Orsini (3 Waagasse; Phone 211-47-00): Open the wrought-iron gate and peer through the courtyard to the nineteenth-century house sheltering Orsini—with brown leather chairs around smartly set tables, under atmospherically beamed ceilings. If, like me, you're a nut for *stracciatella*—Italy's answer to the eggdrop soup of China—open with it at Orsini, opting for any number of pastas and following with *fegato alla Veneziana*, calf's liver Venetian-style, or super Florentine beefsteak. Italian wines. *First Class.*

Santa Lucia (7 Waagasse at Paradeplatz; Phone 211-65-25) is indicated for an unpretentious albeit satisfying Italian lunch. Position yourself at a table either on the main floor or the basement; the former is more fun as the kitchen is open to view. *Antipasto misto* is a good appetizer, but so are the day's soups. You may, of course, open with pasta, but it makes a good midday entrée, *fettucini al pesto* most particularly. *Moderate.*

GOOD VALUE

Eating at the Hauptbahnhof (Bahnhofplatz): You may get lost in this cavernous, ever-frenetic railway station—surely it is Switzerland's busiest—albeit never for long. But you won't go hungry, what with nine venues for sustenance, the lot of them sharing a management. My favorite—I like the high, mock-Renaissance arches supporting its coffered ceiling, and the fascinating mixed-bag clientele—is the *Brasserie*, with standbys like the minced creamed veal that is a Zürich specialty, as well as sausages and *rösti*, and good-value prix-fixe menus. Other options include the self-service *Cafeteria*, *Bistro de la Gare*, and—priciest of the lot—*Au Premier*, whose name designates its location—up a flight from street level, with roast beef brought to table on a silver wagon its *pièce de résistance*. Au Premier is *First Class*; the others, *Moderate*.

Mövenpick Feldschlössen (81 Bahnhofstrasse; Phone 211-50-34) is one of several Zürich outposts of the national Mövenpick chain. Have a beer (there are ten sizes of glasses!), coffee, a snack on the terrace. Or go upstairs for a proper meal, concluding with sweets from the fabulous dessert buffet. *Moderate/First Class*.

Bündnerstube (Carlton Elite Hotel); 41 Bahnhofstrasse; Phone 211-65-60): You want to be a party of two or more for this ever-so-Swiss restaurant's primary specialty: *fondue Bourguignonne*, in which you dunk cubes of beef in boiling oil with one long fork, transferring it to another fork after you've cooked it to the doneness you prefer; a choice of dipping sauces lies to the side. *Geschnitzeltes*—minced veal in cream sauce—is excellent here, too. Fun. *First Class*.

Turm (19 Oberezäune; Phone 69-52-00) occupies a mellow Altstadt house. It's Spanish-owned, so that you'll find *gazpacho* among the soups, and upon occasion, *paella* as an entrée. But the primary draw is an extraordinarily generous and delicious dinner-only buffet. *First Class*.

Le Pavillon (Fifth floor, Globus department store, Bahnhofstrasse): With the appearance of a garden—white trellises and hanging plants—this is a convenient stopping point for a casual lunch or brief respite in the course of shopping, with the range sandwiches and omelets through milkshakes (do try *Schokolade*

Eisfrappé) or, if you prefer, a Scotch and soda. Everything, save imported spirits, is *Moderate*.

CAFÉS

Schober (4 Napfgasse; Phone 251-80-60) calls itself the *"älteste Konditorei von Zürich, seit 1834."* If you haven't taken it in, in the course of that span of years, now is the time. It occupies charming and unabashedly old-fashioned quarters extending over three levels of an Altstadt house. Go only to look at its extraordinary displays of cakes and candies (I doubt you will be able to resist making a purchase), or, better yet, for lunch or coffee and pastries (the *guglhupf* is celebrated) in its *salon de thé. Moderate/First Class.*

Grand Café (Limmatquai, near Rathausbrücke): It's an outdoor table you want here—order a cold drink, coffee, or a snack—to take in not only the ambulatory traffic, but the river and the city, on its opposite shore. *Moderate.*

Sprüngli (Paradeplatz; Phone 221-17-22) is globally renowned, as much for chocolates (see Shopper's Zürich, below) as pastries. But it is, as well, a street-level café whose tables spill onto the sidewalk in warm weather) and an up-a-flight restaurant, with a counter that's convenient for solitary lunchers, as well, of course, as tables, as popular with Zürichers as visitors, with the lure reasonably tabbed prix-fixe menus, invariably concluding with pastry. As an eatery (if not as a candy shop or bakery): *Moderate.*

SOUND OF MUSIC
Opernhaus (Sechseläutenplatz): Zürich's opera house is a Belle Époque treasure that opened in 1891 with a performance of Wagner's *Lohengrin,* when the "grand" in grand opera was taken very seriously indeed. It is nothing if not formidable from without—fronted by a colonnaded portico, itself supporting a colonnade surmounted by Corinthian capitals and beneath a rooftop balustrade flanked by sculptures, with a domelike tower bringing up the rear. The gilded four-level auditorium is no less

flamboyant. You want to take in a performance of the resident company (the range is *La Traviata* through *Tristan und Isolde*, with Broadway classics like *A Chorus Line* presented as well) along with classics and contemporary works danced by the *Zürich Ballet*.

Tonhalle (Général Guisan Quai), though a part of the pre-World War II Kongresshaus complex, dates to the early 1890s, and is a splendid space—high-ceilinged, hung with magnificent chandeliers, with an immense stage backed by the massive pipes of its organ—for concerts of Zürich's celebrated Tonhalle Orchester. Chamber music and other programs are presented in the building's No. 2 hall, *Kleiner Tonhallesaal*, and at other venues, as well, the *Grossmünster* and *Wasserkirche* among them.

Schauspielhaus (Rämistrasse) is the principal theater, with plays presented in German; *Theater am Neumarkt* (Neumarkt) and *Kammertheater Stok* (Hirschenbragen) are two others.

Pop concerts and other entertainments take place in the *Kongresshaus* (entered on Gotthardstrasse).

SHOPPER'S ZÜRICH
Department stores are clustered on—and just off of—the Hauptbahnhof end of Bahnhofstrasse, and just off that street, on Löwenstrasse. *Globus*—No. 1—has an excellent basement supermarket, a big chocolate shop on Main, with women's clothing up a flight and menswear on the second floor, as well as in the Herren Globus shop in an adjacent building. *Jelmoli*, Globus's major competitor, is somewhat less trendy, but with some excellent departments, including English-language books, luggage, and worth-knowing-about money exchange and optical repair (all on Main), and wine and food in the basement. *Migros City*, an outlet of the national Migros chain, occupies six levels; its house-brand boxed chocolates—excellent value, these—are sold on Main (with chocolate truffles the standouts). The basement is a huge supermarket. Women's clothes are on Two, and there are a pair of restaurants on Four. Zürich is unsurpassed among Swiss cities with respect to handicrafts, with

furniture, wood carvings, linens, pewter, embroidery, handkerchiefs, toys, and dolls. *Schweizer Heimatwerk's* main shop is at Rudolf Brunbrücke, with other locations (and smaller selections) at 2 Bahnhofstrasse (near the Baur au Lac Hotel) and 14 Rennweg. *Watches* are perhaps more abundant only in Geneva. Zürich sources include *Les Ambassadeurs* (64 Bahnhofstrasse) with its own-make models good buys, but Audemars Piguet, Omega, and other brands as well, along with costly women's clothing and jewelry; *Beyer* (31 Bahnhofstrasse), besides its own label watches, vends Patek Philippe and Rolex. *Bücherer* (50 Bahnhofstrasse) is, in my experience, the most ineptly operated link of this usually crackerjack chain; four sales floors. *Les Must de Cartier*—very expensive in Switzerland as everywhere—is at 47 Bahnhofstrasse; *Gübelin* (36 Bahnhofstrasse) is part of a Switzerland-wide chain, and costly. *Meister* (28 Bahnhofstrasse) is a long-on-scene and well-respected Zürich house; ditto *Türler* (Paradeplatz). *St. James's Gallery* (5 Rämistrasse) is a source of antique watches and clocks. *Barth* (94 Bahnhofstrasse) makes a specialty of gold and diamonds. *Seguin-Dorman* (69 Bahnhofstrasse) sells Baccarat crystal, Christofle silver flatware, Meissen, and other porcelain; *Ditting* (35 Rennweg) and *Rosenthal Studio-Haus* (47 Bahnhofstrasse) are two other sources of porcelain and crystal. *Chocolate* is as ubiquitous as watches. *Globus* department store (Bahnhofstrasse) has big selections of name brands. *Teuscher* vends its luscious chocolates in a very small and very costly shop on Storchengasse, as well as at a special Globus counter (and at U.S. branches, as well). *Sprüngli* (Bahnhofstrasse) is at once a café-restaurant (above) and a celebrated source of costly chocolates; it has a branch shop (sans café) in the Hauptbahnhof. And *Migros City* department store, just off Bahnhofstrasse, sells its boxed house-brand chocolates at considerable savings over famous makes. This is a modishly dressed city: *Grieder* (30 Bahnhofstrasse) is quite the toniest of shops for women's and men's designer fashions; Bahnhofstrasse clothing shops include St. Laurent, Charles Jourdan, Bally, Hermès, Bruno Magli, and Walter Gross. Still others are *Beatrice Dreher* (14 In Gassen), with Chloë, Krizia, Oscar de la Rente, and Anne Klein the stars; *Oscar Rom* (12 Seefeldstrasse) with Ungaro among its labels; *Salvatore Ferragamo* (8

Bliecherweg); *Gianni Versace* for both men and women, at 23 Storchengasse; *Valentino* (12 Münsterhof) (for both men's and women's clothing); *Loden-Frey* (Werdmühlplatz) (loden-cloth coats for both men and women); and *Herrenmode Excelsior* (56 Löwenstrasse) with name brands for gents, Burberry through Zimmerli (the expensive Swiss underwear that is the world's snazziest). That leaves such shops as *Souleiado* (Provençal printed cottons by the meter and made into placemats, and the like, at 5 Strehlgasse); *A. C. Bang* (1 Bahnhofstrasse), a branch of the Danish fur house; *Niedermann-Picnic* (46 Bahnhofstrasse), a fancy grocery; *Leder-Locher* (18 Münsterhof) for leather; *Librairie Payot* (9 Bahnhofstrasse)— a link of a Switzerland-wide book chain, with an English-language section; *Teddy's* (34 Limmatquai), Swiss Army knives; *Sotheby's* (20 Bleicherweg) and *Galerie Koller* (8 Rämistrasse), Zürich branches of international auction houses.

INCIDENTAL INTELLIGENCE

Zürich's intercontinental airport, due northeast of the city, is state of the art and linked with the Hauptbahnhof on Bahnhofplatz, heart of the city, by comfortable trains; they depart as often as quarter-hourly and take but ten minutes. Access to them is by means of a succession of three air terminal escalators; if your baggage is heavy, take along a collapsible luggage carrier, as I do. With it, there's no need for a porter, despite the multi-escalator journey to and from the train. Note, too, that once through customs at the airport you may check your bags from a well-marked Arrivals Hall desk to *any* railway station in Switzerland, for a nominal charge. The other direction? From a hundred-plus train terminals throughout the Confederation, you may check your baggage via Zürich or Geneva airports, through to your flight destination, again for a nominal charge. *Zürich News*, the free, well-edited weekly What's-On bulletin, is available from hotel concierges. The tourist office (below) can give you schedules for Zürichsee boat cruises. *Further information:* Verkehrsbüro, 15 Bahnhofplatz (just outside the Hauptbahnhof), Zürich; Verkehrsbüro, Bahnhofplatz, Winterthur.

Acknowledgments

Credit first, where it is due: The idea for this book was that of Helmut Klee, currently deputy director of the Swiss National Tourist Office, based at headquarters in Zürich, suggested while he was heading SNTO's office in New York—with imagination and flair. I am most indebted to him and want to extend appreciation, as well, to his successor in New York, Chris Zoebeli, and—most especially—to Erika Faisst, press officer of SNTO in New York and a veritable encyclopedia of matters Swiss, who has been of help in innumerable ways from the commencement of the project, always cordially and expertly, and never without a disarming Swiss smile. Appreciation, too, to Erika's neighbor-colleagues at Manhattan's Swiss Center—Wolfgang Schnekenburger, Swissair's public relations director for North America, and his associate, Maura Raphael. My gratitude, as well, to the team at the Foreign Press section at SNTO in Zürich—Urs Eberhard, Corinne Berger, and Susan Raeder—with whom I worked in the course of the extensive—and endlessly absorbing—trans-Switzerland research trip which preceded this book's writing.

I am grateful, too, for the expertise and enthusiasm of the Big Three at National Textbook/Passport Books—S. William Pattis, Leonard I. Fiddle, and Mark R. Pattis; to Senior Editor Michael Ross, ever patient, sympathetic, and skilled; to Louise Fisher, who typed the final manuscript; to my agent, Anita Diamant and her associates, Robin Rue and Al Madocs; and—alphabetically—to the following friends and colleagues in Switzerland and on this side of the Atlantic, as well, for their personal kindness and professional cooperation:

Kurt Alchenberger, Esther Alder, Ralph Alder, Mireille Alioth, Marguerite Allen, Miri Bachner, Pierre-Alain Bardellini, Ruth Baumann, Gianni Biggi, Emanuel Berger, Luigi Bonalumi,

Marlyse Bosshard, Gwen Braendly, Pierre L. Bravin, Walter Bruderer, Paolo Brunetti, Willy Buholzer, Urs Bührer, Ernst Cadalbert, Scott Calder, Christiane Campia, Elisa C. Cohen, Eduardo Crivelli, Karon N. Cullen, André Dähler, Falko Daxer, Claudia Derungs, Antoinette Dormond, Christoph Donatsch, Max Drechsler, Ruth Dudler, Erwin Ehrsam, Jean-Pierre Fath, Eugenio Foglia, Cynthia Fontayne, Georges Fraschina, Michael Furler.

Also Joseph A. Giacoponello, Nina Maria Gorrissen, Philippe Grandjean, Andreas J. Gredig, Jenny Grosclaude, Urs Gsell, Benjamin Güller, Linda Gwinn, J. Häberli, André W. Hauri, Ruth Hoffmann, Markus Holdener, Manfred J. Hörger, Rolf Jäggi, Carola Jokisch, Sylvia Kartaschoff, Virginia Kelly, Max Keller, Peter C. Kerkhof, Silva Kovacs, Elizabeth Kretz, Helmut Kuen, Peter Laube, Jean-Pierre Lanz, Aniello Lauro, J. F. Lichtenstern, Lia Mann, Enrique Marlés, Werner Muench, Yvonne Müller.

Also Inès Osterwald, Norbert Perren-Julen, Amadé Perrig, Urs Petermann, Anne Pfister, Dirk J. Post, Patricia Puracchio, Willy Raess, Felix Rainholter, Jürg R. Reinshagen, Michel Rey, Thierry Sax, Bob Schaeffer, Elisabeth Schläppi, Ernst Schoch, Morris Silver, Fabio Sorgesa, Jürg Studer, Brigitte Stutzmann, Claudio Tame, Georges Taxe, Maurice R. L. Urech, Marie-Laure Vatran, Reto Von Tscharner, Wolfgang Wettstein, Rolf Widler, and Mauro Zoppi.

R.S.K.

Index

ABOUT THE AUTHOR

Robert S. Kane's initial writing stint was as editor of the (Boy Scout) *Troop Two Bugle* in his native Albany, New York. After graduation from Syracuse University's journalism school, he did graduate work at England's Southampton University, first making notes as he explored in the course of field trips through the Hampshire countryside. Back in the United States, he worked successively for the *Great Bend* (Kansas) *Daily Tribune, Staten Island Advance, New York Herald Tribune,* and *New York World-Telegram & Sun* before becoming travel editor first of *Playbill,* later of *Cue* and *50 Plus* magazines; he writes regularly for *Travel & Leisure* and leading American and Canadian newspapers, and frequently discusses travel on TV and radio talk shows. *Africa A to Z* was the progenitor of his acclaimed 14-volume A to Z series, which in turn led to creation of the current World at Its Best Travel Guides. A past president of both the Society of American Travel Writers and the New York Travel Writers' Association, Kane makes his home on the Upper East Side of Manhattan.